O9-ABF-666

CREATE YOUR OWN
STAGE EFFECTS
Gill Davies

CREATE YOUR OWN
STAGE EFFECTS
Gill Davies

Back Stage Books
an imprint of Watson-Guptill Publications
New York

First published 1999 by
Back Stage Books, an imprint of
Watson Guptill Publications
BPI Communications
1515 Broadway
New York
NY 10036
USA

ISBN 0-8230-8811-1

Published simultaneously in the UK by
A & C Black (Publishers) Limited
35 Bedford Row
London WC1R 4JH

ISBN 0-7136-5050-8

© Playne Books Limited

CIP catalogue records for this book are
available from the British Library and the
Library of Congress.

All rights reserved. No part of this publication
may be reproduced or used in any form or by
any means - photographic,electronic or
mechanical, including photocopying,
recording, taping or information storage and
retrieval systems - without the written
permission of the publisher.

Create Your Own Stage Effects
was conceived, edited and designed by
Playne Books Limited
Chapel House
Trefin, Haverfordwest
Pembrokeshire SA62 5AU
United Kingdom

Editor
Janice Douglas

Technical editor
Tony Curtis

Designers and illustrators
Jonathan Douglas
Craig John
David Playne
Freya Pratt

Typeset by Playne Books Limited
in Glypha

Printed in China

Contents

Contents

Contents

How to use this book

Following on the other highly successful titles in the *Create Your Own* stage series, this latest title aims to help theatre companies, schools, colleges, amateur groups and interested individuals to explore a wide range of special effects and to learn how to use these smoothly, effectively, and safely.

While many books concentrate on a particular technical aspect, the aim here is to cover many different kinds of special effects that can be used across the various disciplines – and so, drawing on the relevant information in each field, discovers a variety of technical know-how – whether lighting, sound, scenic effects, costume, fast changes, transformations, projection, make-up, properties, pyrotechnics, weather effects, fire, smoke and water! Some special projects are analyzed in detail – as well as the various historical settings.

So whether you want to change Cinderella's rags into a ballgown, fly an astronaut up to the ceiling or make Banquo's ghost appear at the dinner party, this book will tell you how!

Highly illustrated with clear step-by-step instructions, *Create Your Own Stage Effects* will help readers to discover the – generally elusive – answers to all their questions about how to create special effects. And because a wide range of possibilities are explained, they should be able to give a professional lift to their productions without going over budget.

Because the book is divided up into chapters that cover the various disciplines, it is assumed that these chapters may be read independently by the particular backstage personnel concerned. To this end, some of the general guidelines on organization may be repeated in these chapters, but throughout the book it is stressed that one of the most vital elements in creating successful special effects is close cooperation between these various departments. So they may do well to read each other's chapters, while any director or producer will certainly benefit from a general overview of this fascinating subject.

Special Effects covers a vast range of techniques and, while providing lots of information on practical know-how, the intention in this book is to inspire and help those involved in theatre to realise just how much can be achieved. It is hoped that readers will also explore the wealth of other books that specialize on a particular technical aspect – in more detail than can possibly be covered in a book of this wide scope. We should, of course, recommend the other titles in this *Create Your Own* series!

Hazard symbols indicate where the situation is potentially dangerous and caution is required.

In particular, using pyrotechnics and 'flying' people are highly specialized fields and involve hazardous activities. While the book describes some of the techniques, it is vital to seek professional advice and management of these effects.

While every care has been taken to verify facts and methods described in this book, neither the publisher nor the author can accept liability for any loss or damage, however caused.

Introduction

If stage effects are ill-managed or go wrong, the results can be disastrous. The audience will snigger, have hysterics or feel very uncomfortable. Special effects need to be done well to work well!

However, it is certainly worth taking up the challenge, for, when handled efficiently, special effects will give a professional edge to any stage production. If the technical aspects are running smoothly, the audience can relax and enjoy live theatre at its best. In fact, they may be scarcely aware of the straightforward sound and lighting effects, when these are working efficiently, but will be conscious that, overall, the show and atmosphere felt right. At the same time, some of the more spectacular effects can impress, astound and add enormous and memorable impact to dramatic effect.

The aim of this book is to explain in simple terms how even the smallest company with a limited budget can create the most effective special effects and so give every production

that extra polish – one which gives a boost to both audience enjoyment and pride in performance.

It has proved difficult at times to decide just what constitutes a special effect. A sound effect, for example, may be deemed to be part of the conventional theatre experience and not really 'special' at all. However, it is an additional element, requiring technical expertise, that not only 'seeds' the production with greater realism but which can be great fun to explore further. If there is an opportunity to simulate a thunderstorm or a steam train arriving, for instance, then the sound effect certainly becomes a special one.

In the same way, lighting may be merely a matter of 'on' or 'off' but has the capacity to take the production and audiences into many exciting experiences, with light curtains, gauze transformations and starlit skies – to name just a few. Make-up can have its moments too with 'specials' – such as wounds and bleeding,

false noses, perspiration and tattoos. In fact, all the theatre technical 'departments' are covered for each has its special moments to contribute.

Many of the effects – sets, properties, costumes, make-up and so on – will often involve fast changes so there are suggestions on how to smooth the passage of these and achieve a really quick 'turn-around'. Whatever the effect, the play needs to maintain pace. If it takes too long to change the set or costumes, the audience will lose concentration and interest, becoming restless in the process.

Team spirit is all important. The technical know-how is vital but will not work in isolation. The aim is that everyone works together to achieve the best effects possible. And has a great time doing so!

Gill Davies

Getting organized

Planning and organization

Whether putting on a stage production is a fresh venture for a new group or whether this is yet another play in a long line of plays for a long-established group, it is equally important to be well organized. The organizers of every aspect of the production will need to plan ahead properly and to make sure that they have everything necessary in good time to stage a successful show – the right paperwork, the right people primed and ready to help, and the right equipment.

If staging a production that involves special effects, this is especially important. These exciting stage effects may seem to an audience to happen like magic but are in fact the result of a lot of thinking, preparation and hard work. Moreover, special effects generally cross the boundaries of many of the different theatre 'departments' and often involve a combination of sound, lighting and scenery, for example.

So excellent communication and coordination across the various production aspects are vital, with good stage management, as well as a clear view in the eye of the director – and thence all those others involved – of the overall effect that is required. This will not happen without a well organized structure as the backbone of the production.

Plan ahead

Who does what?

An essential ingredient of a good production is that the technical aspects run smoothly. If this is to happen, always ensure that:

A storm at sea

Sound
Wind noises
Creaking timbers
Rolls of thunder
Slapping water
Final crash onto rocks

Lighting
Projection of storm clouds
Lightning
Ripple water effect

Costumes
Quick change into bedraggled,
torn, soaking clothes

Make-up
Wet hair plastered down
Jim needs wound on arm

Sets
Agitate the ships' timbers
Set falling mast in action
Fly ropes

Properties
Broken timber
Raft
Life belts

**Stage manager and
pyrotechnics**
Smoke machine to spray mist as
ship sinks
Wind machine

Cast off stage
Shouts and screams
Yelled orders

A special effect will often involve many people and several technical teams. Imagine, for example, what might be needed for a storm at sea/shipwreck scene.

---

1 Every part of the special effect is clearly allocated, that somebody is responsible for its functioning properly at the right moment and that . . .

2 This 'somebody' is fully aware of this allocation of responsibility.

If the special effect crosses the boundaries of more than one department, ensure that the various personnel work it out between them and also coordinate over any changes that crop up during rehearsal.

Make sure the stage manager is aware of all the special effects, their requirements and their cueing.

Planning the technical effects in a production

Whether the effect that has to be produced is a transformation from pumpkin to Cinderella's coach, an explosion in a factory, an electrical storm, a starlit sky, a train thundering past or a ghost floating across the stage, there is a consistent straightforward plan that should be followed by every member of the backstage team responsible for creating these effects.

1 Read and understand the play, its setting and style.

2 Highlight the special effects in the text and then make a list of these.

3 Analyze the particular effect in its particular situation: place and time and style of play.

4 Discuss ideas for creating the effects with the director/producer and any other stage departments that might be concerned in the creation of a successful effect.

5 Do any necessary further research on the exact effect needed and the means to achieve this.

6 Highlight the special effects in the cue sheet: discuss the requirements and overlapping areas of responsibility with other members of the backstage team. Then make a timetable showing exactly who does what when.

7 Check that existing equipment is adequate and in working order.

8 Attend rehearsals and incorporate any changes into the cue plot.

9 Organize the renting or manufacture of any equipment needed.

10 Prepare the special effect equipment in good time. Try to allow plenty of time to practise with it in rehearsals.

11 Check the safety of all the equipment.

12 Supervise special effects at dress and technical rehearsals. Check that everything works well and looks and sounds as planned – and that everyone else involved is happy with the results too.

13 Make any adjustments.

14 Oversee effects throughout all the performances.

15 After show, remove, return or store equipment as required.

16 Keep a note of any particularly effective special effect and, if it is likely to be used again, record how this effect was achieved so that it can be repeated in future without dupli-

---

SPECIAL EFFECTS
NOTES FOR FUTURE REFERENCE

*ALADDIN
JANUARY 1999*

*GENIE'S
APPEARANCE*
PYROTECHNICS
SMOKE MACHINE
FLASH POWDER
GREEN UP LIGHTING (GEL 39)

MAKE-UP
PALE FOUNDATION WITH GREEN
HIGHLIGHTS AND STRONG OLIVE
SHADOWS

SOUND
LAUNCHING ROCKET EFFECT
(NO 12 ON CD NO 3)

CAVE
SET
BLACK TABS AT REAR
USE HANGING STAR CURTAIN GALAXY
EFFECT BUT WITH BRIGHT FOIL FOR
JEWELS
CHRISTMAS TREE BALLS SET
INTO BOULDERS MADE FROM
EXPANDED POLYSTYRENE
COVERED IN PAPIER MACHÉ.

SOUND
TINKLING ICICLES (NO 7 ON CD 5)

---

cating all this initial research and experimentation.

Each backstage department will need to plan like this, to mark up a script very carefully, making cue sheets that give a clear indication of what has to happen when.

An established theatre group will probably have a committee and a pre-determined system to deal with all the official 'red tape' but for special effects that are by their very nature 'different' the procedure may be a new one. The particular requirements of, say, using explosives or a stroboscopic light will need to be investigated and understood, so it is wise to find out if there are any specific safety or 'official' problems well in advance.

Check out the venue

Make sure not only that the dates of the performance themselves are booked but that any essential rehearsal and set-erection time is also organized as well as the time to clear up afterwards.

Find out if there are any specific restrictions the venue committee imposes or aspects of the production that they might be unhappy about. For example, if flying the fairy means opening the ceiling space, is this permissible? Will you be allowed to paint the back wall of the stage for that sunset sky lighting effect? Is the hall going to be free when hired equipment arrives? Do you need to organize someone to be there to receive the equipment?

Copyright and license to perform

In order to protect the work of hardworking authors and music composers – and also to protect the professional theatre from direct competition from any local amateur groups performing the same play at the same time as a professional presentation, permission to perform a particular play at a particular time and

Health and safety regulations

place is necessary. A fee for each performance will be levied according to the audience capacity and a royalty will be due to the author through the publisher or supplier. Check the play script and the suppliers' notes for further information and also to find out if separate clearance is needed for a musical score.

Entertainment license

Performing for a paying audience requires an entertainment license. Do check if there are any particular requirements to be met, such as the correct numbers of audience in a specific seating plan.

There will, in any case, be a limit on the audience capacity, which is restricted according to the size of hall concerned. Usually, a seating plan will have to be submitted to the local authorities. Aisles must be a stated width and exit signs clearly visible, with emergency batteries to keep them glowing if there is a power failure. These should be standard fittings in a commonly used hall.

However, a special effect might require a special light, a follow spot, a screen for projection at the side of the stage, or you might be dreaming of fireworks in the finale – not something the fire officer would approve!

Make sure that your plans are compatible with an acceptable seating plan, that they will not block any aisles or exits and that they are not contrary to any of the rules, as fireworks undoubtedly are!

It will be far worse to have to change or to drop the effects during the week of the play's performance – and flouting the regulations might jeopardize the entire production.

Technical rehearsals

These are vital. It is essential to allow a generous portion of time, for even relatively simple tasks can take a long while to set up, adjust, and hone to perfection.

All too often, restless actors who have put in many hours at a dress rehearsal may, justifiably, resent having to drum their heels while a special effect or technical hitch is sorted. Never try to combine the dress rehearsals with the technical set-up and run-through. It is doomed to failure. Tiredness and irritability will lead to compromise rather than full exploitation of the equipment. It is much better if all the lighting, sound and special effects have been run through and worked out before the actors are involved.

Then, when the special effects are first combined with a full rehearsal, the basics are already ironed out. There are bound to be some adjustments, of course, but tempers will be far less frayed than if everything has been left to the very last minute.

So . . . make sure when the rehearsals are planned that plenty of time is allocated for technical rehearsal. If there are lots of special effects, you will need every available minute.

Health and safety regulations

Insurance and public liability

In any public hall, insurance and public liability should be covered already, but it is a wise precaution to ensure that the policies are up to date and provide sufficient coverage for both the audience and the group – for rehearsals and performances.

Fire regulations

These can be quite strict when there are large numbers of people gathered together – and fire officials are empowered to stop a show mid-performance if they feel the necessary precautions have not been taken. It is absolutely vital to make sure you are aware of the requirements and are following them.

For example, all the scenery and drapes must be properly fireproofed. Flammable material should not be stored below the stage.

Fire extinguishers should be sufficient, well placed and in good working order.

Generally, a fire prevention officer will call around and check the venue prior to the performance and will advise on any specific requirements.

Pyrotechnics, especially, will have to comply with safety regulations, but special effects rental companies can advise on this. Storing explosives will require a license and the fire and/or police department may need to be contacted for permission to use the pyrotechnics.

Guns

You may need a special license to use a gun – even a starting pistol. Check this with the appropriate authorities and ask the advice of whoever is loaning the gun to you.

Electricity

Check that the electrical current supply is adequate to deal with all the lighting equipment that will be used. Special effects and exciting lighting effects may stretch your resources beyond the levels of safety. Your local Electricity Board (or Electrical Control Board) will provide an additional supply if necessary.

Food and drink

If there is any intention of selling alcohol to the audience, a license will be needed. A local public house (tavern) may be able to organize this for you. Alternatively, permission must be sought through the local authorities. The official granting of licenses takes place at well-spaced intervals and only so many are permitted for any one group in any one year, so this will need to be planned well in advance.

Once you are familiar with the rules and regulations and the order of events necessary in your particular area, this will all become routine procedure for future productions.

In the interests of hygiene, the preparation of food for public consumption is subject to all sorts of rules and regulations and the group needs to be aware of these.

Equipment

Checking that everything works

It is essential when dealing with any mechanical equipment to keep it in good working order. Few amateur companies will be staging shows throughout the year. Generally, there will be breaks in between and any equipment left idle is likely to be temperamental. On the other hand, if you are in a semi-professional theatre group staging continuous productions, then the equipment will be subject to a lot more wear and tear – while brand new equipment may well have 'teething problems'. So, whatever

the circumstances, good maintenance is vital. Moreover, faulty electrical equipment is dangerous. It can result in an electric shock and may be a fire hazard too.

There should be a properly planned system of testing and inspection – and a record kept of this.

1 Check that every piece of equipment needed is there, that it has not been lent out elsewhere or put away somewhere elusive.

2 Make sure everything is working properly – early on.

Rewireable fuse

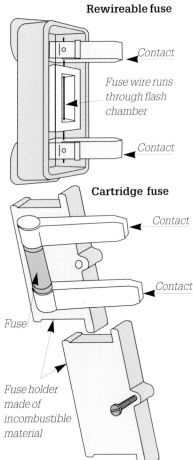

Contact

Fuse wire runs through flash chamber

Contact

Cartridge fuse

Contact

Contact

Fuse

Fuse holder made of incombustible material

3 Check that all the batteries are functioning.

4 Make a careful visual inspection of all the plugs, connectors, cables and casings.

5 Check that the correct fuses are in place – with the right rating for the appliance or appliance/cable.

6 Check that all the lighting fixtures and bulbs are working.

7 Mark the outside of the equipment with the date so you will know when it was last checked.

8 Order any new equipment or replacement parts in good time.

In the same way, the flats and scenery should be given the once-over. In particular, any safety chains or support mechanisms must be in good order.

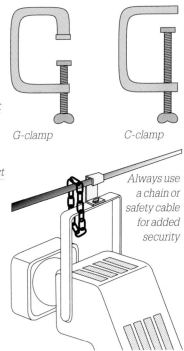

G-clamp   *C-clamp*

Always use a chain or safety cable for added security

Basic essentials and sound equipment

Setting up

Fired with enthusiasm for a new project, you'll be tempted to buy all the appropriate 'gear', the exciting new kit that is in all the stage equipment catalogues. Before spending any money, however, it is vital to assess exactly what is really essential and precisely how much the company can afford. If you are starting from scratch, much will depend on this budget and there will not be money in the 'kitty' from previous production profits to boost the cash-flow.

1 A big enough stage. A temporary extension may be needed. Special effects often involve a gauze curtain or a cyclorama, and if the depth of the stage is minimal these can be very restricted.

If the performance is to be in the round, then the body of the hall might be used, rather than a stage. In this case, do ensure that the seating arrangement will allow all the audience to see what is happening.

2 Sufficient entrances and exits for a free flow of actors.

Invest in good quality speakers

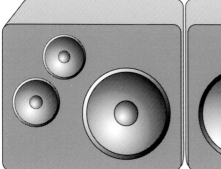

3 Changing rooms. The actors will need somewhere to change, even if only a curtained-off area.

Sound equipment

Sound is an essential ingredient of any production. The equipment to create good sound in a large space is expensive but if the group cannot afford a big outlay, it can be accumulated gradually.

Whatever the play, besides sound effects during the performance, music will be needed before and after the show, and during the intermission.

On-the-spot sound effects created mechanically, rather than recorded sounds, work very well, so it may not be necessary to record any at all for a first production. However, in due course, the professional edge will be given to a show where an expert sound person or team provide all the right sounds on cue – whether mechanical or recorded. It is good to demand high standards from the word go and develop a caring, enthusiastic sound department who enjoy their contribution and will concentrate on the job in hand. This is not a task to give to someone who is unen-

A basic sound kit can be purchased as a package. Kits vary in price according to the amount and standards of equipment, but will probably cost several thousand pounds or dollars. A typical portable sound kit would consist of:

1
a 12-way mixer

2
an amplifier &
one pair of speakers plus stands

3
a cassette deck

4
a compact disc player

5
a wheeled flight case for ease of transportation

6
microphones and stands might be added to this, and you also need:

7
all the cable, plugs and necessary electrical fitments.

For recording in a studio you will also need to add to the above:

8
a reel-to-reel tape recorder

9
and all the editing tools
(see page 35).

thused (and certainly not as compensation for being overlooked in the casting).

If you can afford it, a stereo digital recording system will provide an ideal system that is light to carry around, provides good digital sound quality and is simple to use.

Sound effect tapes or CDs

Although these can be borrowed from libraries, they are relatively inexpensive and it can save a lot of time to have a few 'in house'. You will also need a good selection of music for pre- and post-performance. As with the play scripts, copyrights may need to be cleared and permission granted to use the music chosen.

The tape recorder and sound system

A reel-to-reel tape recorder is able to record sounds, store them and then reproduce the sounds and play them back again. The sounds are stored on a tape that moves across the magnetic recording head. This tape is capable of being magnetized – and it is the variations in the magnetic field across the gap in the head, as the tape moves across it, that reproduce the various sounds we hear.

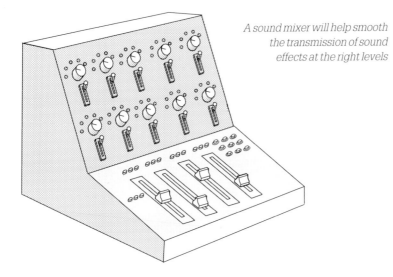

A sound mixer will help smooth the transmission of sound effects at the right levels

Multi-track

A multi-track replay system allows the different components of a more complex sound effect to be mixed on the spot and adjusted instantly to suit what is happening on stage.

Cartridge machines

A NAB (National Association of Broadcasters, USA) cartridge player has a beautifully quiet, immediate start. It has a continuous loop of tape, is compact and makes random selection of sound effects or music a simple matter. Hence cartridge players are gaining in popularity but are more expensive to purchase than a reel-to-reel. Digital cartridge players are also becoming available now.

Compact disc players

Although ideal for home entertainment, these can be quite complicated to operate smoothly during performances. They can be very useful, however, for providing the background music – and compact discs will certainly provide a good source of sound effects for re-recording onto the main sound tape.

Mixer

A mixer enables sounds to be played at the chosen level and through the chosen loudspeaker or speakers.

For more detailed information on sound techniques and using this equipment, see pages 25-38.

A multi-track system allows sound effects to be mixed on the spot

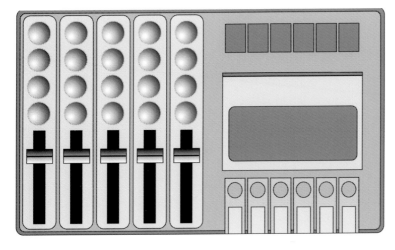

Lighting equipment

Lighting equipment

The play needs to be seen. If resources are limited, it is possible to light a stage with only six lights, provided these are angled properly. A few spots with different gels set out front or behind ground rows will be very useful for special effects.

The basic kit

When starting from scratch, if the budget is already stretched, it may be better to rent lighting equipment. If the decision is taken to purchase a kit, this can be done over several productions and combined with rented equipment until a full complement is built up. Try to acquire the following:

1

Four 500 watt Fresnel spotlights

2

Two 500 watt zoom profiles

3

One three-way dimming pack with an integrated controller

4

One 10-metre (30 feet) control cable

5

One tripod lighting stand

6

A six-lantern suspension bar

In addition, it is a good idea to purchase a safety plug which will detect any earth leakage and make the kit safe to use.

You will also need all the appropriate cable, plugs and bulbs, barn doors and safety chains.

Obviously, the more lighting equipment you buy, the greater the flexibility of the kit and the more advanced the lighting special effects can be.

Both the lighting and the sound team may, if there is no purpose-built depot, need to beg, borrow, rent or buy scaffolding to build a tower or some other secure temporary structure to provide a convenient depot with a good overall view of the acting area.

Types of lighting units

Profile spot

This gives a high density beam of a fixed size and is very good for lighting specific objects or areas. The beam can be focused to be either hard- or soft-edged. The narrower the beam angle, the greater the intensity of light. Metal patterned plates, called gobos, can be fitted onto a profile spot to create the outline of a shape such as a star shape or a more random pattern like dappled leaves.

Fresnel spot

Originally designed by Monsieur Fresnel for use in lighthouses, the Fresnel lens creates a good general smooth wash of light for overall illumination. A Fresnel has no gate but the shape of the beam can be controlled to some extent by the different ways in which the 'barndoors' at the front can be angled. But there is always some light spill.

If you wish to light adjacent areas with no hard edges, then the softer edges of a Fresnel beam will disguise the 'seams'.

Pebble convex

These are similar to Fresnels but the back of this lens is convex and stippled so the beam is diffused and semi-hard-edged. There is no flare.

Floods

A flood (or reflector floodlight) is a simple unit which gives a flat, even wash of light over a wide area. The flood can be masked but otherwise there is no real way of altering the shape of the light. Floods are good for lighting large areas, such as a cyclorama or backdrop, or to flood the stage with light. Several may be fixed on a batten and suspended above the stage or used on the stage floor as floats or footlights.

Pars

These make an intense oval-shaped beam, rather like an old-fashioned car headlight. They are ideal for a strong bright beam, such as might be needed for sunlight through a window or dramatic key light. The oval shape can be rotated to be used either as a portrait or a landscape oval.

The dimmer and control panel

Together these comprise the nerve centre of the lighting control system. Without a dimmer, lights are either on or off and smooth changes are impossible. Fading different lights in and out is part and parcel of any special lighting effect.

Gentle dimming will also help to increase the life of the lamps. The control board is used in conjunction with the dimmer to control all the lights and fading effects.

Fresnel spots are the most versatile lights and can provide small concentrated spots of light – or flood a large area.

A profile spot works well from a distant location and allows you to use gobos

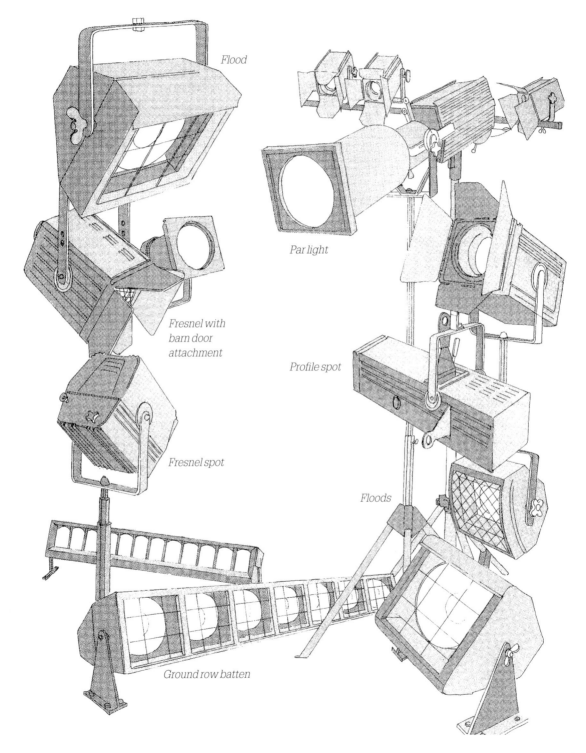

Flood

Par light

Fresnel with barn door attachment

Profile spot

Fresnel spot

Floods

Ground row batten

Sets and properties

Sets and properties

Sets

Sets can be very primitive and still work well. Groups who perform in festivals have to design mobile sets that can be erected quickly; they soon discover what is essential. Dialogue and costumes may convey time and place but sets will enhance this, even if only with differently lit (or differently coloured) tabs or drapes. One essential is to make sure that the actors waiting to enter can be screened from audience view.

Needs vary, play by play. To begin with, a variety of steps or risers are most useful. Set securely around the perimeter of a stage, they allow for a good choice of entrances. Placed on stage, they make a mix of levels. Raised platforms and trucked units add to the versatility. Good quality curtains, drapes, tabs, drops, gauze, canvas – and the means to hang and manoeuvre these – are vital for plays with many scene changes and special effects, while simple boxed sets require versatile, sturdy flats and fixings, windows and doors.

Properties

What is needed will always depend on the particular play. There are no 'golden rules' over what should be bought or made when setting up, for every play will be different. However, whatever the production, the essentials will be good organization, a notepad, tape to mark up the position of properties on the stage floor and price lists from the local party or magic shop which may be very useful as a source of tricks or fun props for special effects.

If pantomimes or pageants are performed annually, invest in making some good strong cut-out trees, a throne, a log or tree-stump seat, milestones, signposts, strings of sausages, clouds and cauldrons. These will be used time and time again.

For conventional plays, sets of china and cutlery will be in demand always, and suitable furniture owned by cooperative friends and neighbours should be earmarked

Tools of all kinds, scissors, Stanley knives, box cutters, and so on need to be accrued and looked after.

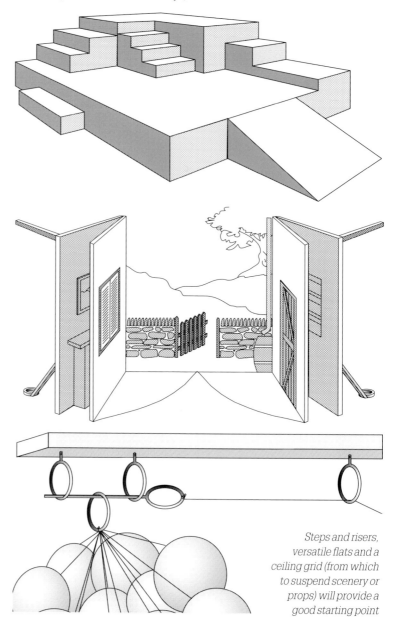

Steps and risers, versatile flats and a ceiling grid (from which to suspend scenery or props) will provide a good starting point

Make-up kit

Compared to lighting and sound equipment, a good make-up kit is relatively inexpensive but can make a vast difference: it helps the actors feel far more confident about their roles.

However, do not be tempted to rush out and buy a huge range of colours and specialized items that may not be used in the foreseeable future. Choose just those colours needed for the ongoing production and then build up the stock as the varying needs of the plays require.

It is better, initially, to buy just the basic foundations, powders, eye colours, pencils and mascara. Use any spare cash to invest in an excellent set of brushes that, taken care of, will last a long time.

Buy special effect make-up as and when needed. Wigs and hairpieces,

You will also need the following:

1
make-up remover

2
cold cream

3
powder puffs

4
sponges

5
cotton balls and cotton buds (swabs)

6
gum and adhesives

7
hair grips and pins.

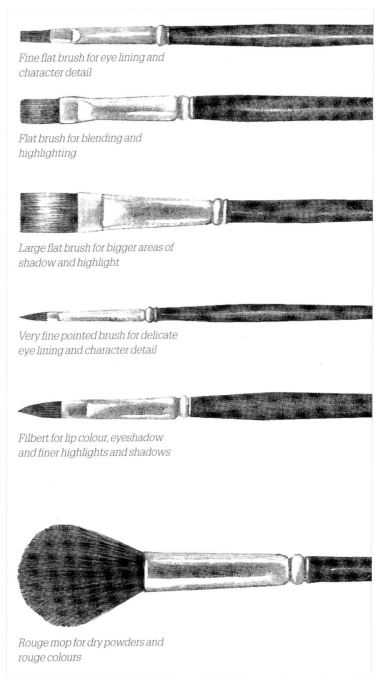

Fine flat brush for eye lining and character detail

Flat brush for blending and highlighting

Large flat brush for bigger areas of shadow and highlight

Very fine pointed brush for delicate eye lining and character detail

Filbert for lip colour, eyeshadow and finer highlights and shadows

Rouge mop for dry powders and rouge colours

artificial hair for beards and moustaches, false eyelashes, stage blood, nose putty, false fingernails and the like will all be accumulated as play follows play and makes its own particular demands.

Make-up kit

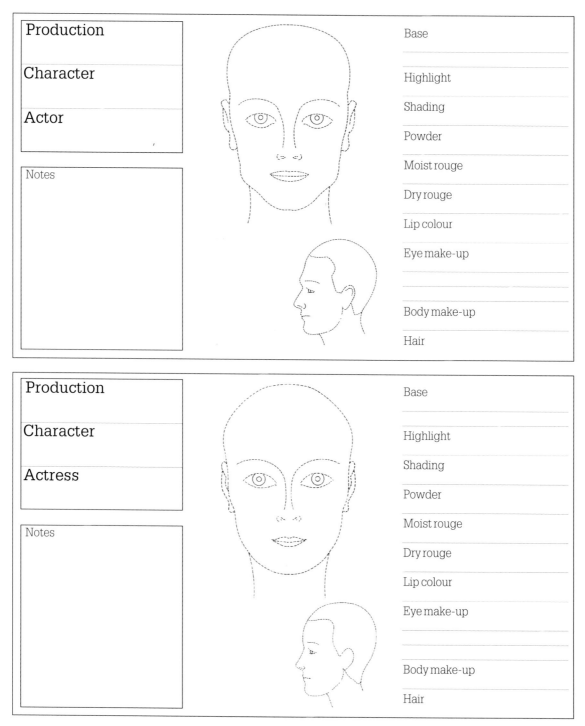

Production		Base
Character		Highlight
Actor		Shading
		Powder
Notes		Moist rouge
		Dry rouge
		Lip colour
		Eye make-up
		Body make-up
		Hair

Production		Base
Character		Highlight
Actress		Shading
		Powder
Notes		Moist rouge
		Dry rouge
		Lip colour
		Eye make-up
		Body make-up
		Hair

Plan and record each character's make-up on a chart

Costumer's gear

Costumer's gear

Specific costume requirements will be dictated by the play but meanwhile, ask for and collect as many donated costumes as you can. Outgrown or unwanted men's suits are often relegated to the local drama group. Scour jumble or rummage sales for curtains, drapes, sheets or bedspreads that can be converted into clothes. White ladies' blouses, and long skirts will be used time and again. Generously sized white men's shirts will be useful for converting into Regency style or pirates' shirts.

Keep a checklist and ensure that stocks are always adequate for the next production and any extras or alterations are costed into the budget.

Organize clearly labelled boxes – and jars – to store all the smaller odds and ends like buttons, jewellery and lace.

The creation of costumes often falls into the lap of an experienced seamstress who already has the essential equipment, but here is a list of requirements:

1
A reliable sewing machine

2
Iron and ironing board

3
Notebook: make notes on particular requirements of the play and keep a permanent record of the measurements of regular members of the cast

4
A hat block

5
Measuring tape

6
Pins, safety pins, needles, threads

7
Scissors and pinking shears

8
Chalk and soft pencils

9
Paper for making patterns

10
Tapes, braid, bindings, buckram ribbon and stiffening fabric

11
Fastenings: Press studs; hooks and eyes, buttons, zippers, Velcro

12
Elastic

13
Dyes, paints and sprays

14
Adhesives

15
Stapling machine

16
String and cord

17
Milliners' wire

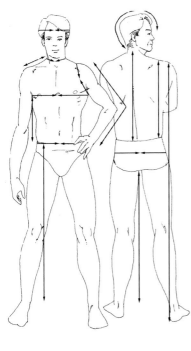

Keep clear records of all the actors' measurements

a	Circumference of head	h	Waist
b	Neck to shoulder	i	Waist to ankle
c	Neck (collar size)	j	Forehead to nape
d	Armholes	k	Backnape to waist
e	Chest/bust	l	Centre of shoulder to waist
f	Underarm to waist	m	Shoulder to ground
g	Outer arm–shoulder to wrist (with arm bent)	n	Hip circumference
		o	Inside leg

Pyrotechnics

Investing in the future

A dictionary defines pyrotechnics as the controlled use of fire in chemistry, metallurgy and gunnery – and/or fireworks. However, in theatrical terminology, it generally means bangs, flashes and smoke – which can be a great addition to the special effects department.

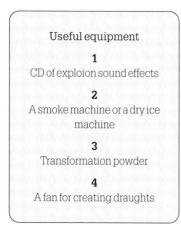

Useful equipment

1

CD of exploion sound effects

2

A smoke machine or a dry ice machine

3

Transformation powder

4

A fan for creating draughts

These items should be in the hands of an expert – not an inexperienced amateur who has no knowledge or practical experience of the chemistry and physics involved. However, if you do have the right expertise on tap and the manufacturers' instructions are followed faithfully, pyrotechnics will add greatly to the impact and fun of a production.

Investing in the future

What should a group, school or society invest in if there are extra monies in the kitty? This is always a difficult decision as each department will have its own priorities. The lighting team will beg for a better dimmer or a new spotlight, while the sound team might hanker after a more sophisti-cated loudspeaker system. The stage manager and set-building team will beg for new drills and wood-working tools. Set designers long for new stage blocks, steps and bridges, a trapdoor or swivelling flats. And the musical director may complain, 'That old piano just has to go!', believing that a new piano or keyboard should be considered the strongest contender for any available cash.

The decision may be dictated by the immediate needs of the next production: 'This forthcoming music hall desperately needs a stroboscopic light for the silent-movie routine.' or, 'We simply cannot stage this play without a cyclorama.'

Often it is the most dominant person with the strongest will who makes his or her demands most vociferously and so wins through. Therefore it helps if those with the spending power, whether committee, producers or whatever, have a clear balanced idea of the company's most vital needs.

Much depends on the type of production the company generally presents. If the group regularly does musicals, for example, a colour wheel or a smoke (fog) machine will be invaluable. If the society often goes 'on tour' or enters festivals, then lightweight versatile mobile scenery will be a great asset.

Meanwhile, here are a few thoughts on general purchases that will be cross-departmental:

1 A decent set of strong, safe ladders is always a good investment and will be used by everyone.

2 Good lighting and mirrors will be appreciated in the dressing room.

3 Storage needs to be considered too, as any new equipment has to be kept safe and dry between productions. The more money and time that is spent building up a stock of equipment, the more important it is to ensure that storage is adequate and that proper cover is provided by an insurance policy.

4 Books: a small library of reference books on the many aspects of theatre production will be a useful source of information and inspiration.

Strong, safe stepladders are a good buy and will reduce the risk of accidents

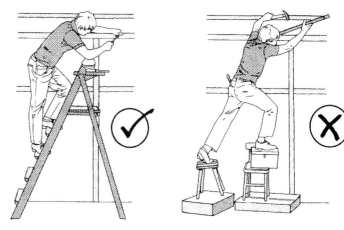

Secure dry storage for props, costumes and other kit will prove an excellent investment. Otherwise, suspend broom poles between stepladders to hang clothes or use refuse sacks.

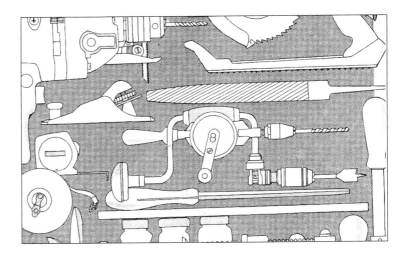

5 Tools and creative kit: Members are often loathe to bring along their own gear as it can be too easily 'borrowed' and forgotten or lost. Moreover, it can be useful to keep a set of carpentry tools, paint brushes, buckets, and the like – so that any empty-handed volunteers who turn up to help on set-building weekends have the means to do so.

6 A communications network: it can be enormously useful to establish a means of immediate contact between the various departments and the stage manager. During a performance the various personnel may be scattered throughout the auditorium and backstage. Integrated cues for various special effects can be better controlled if people can talk to each other directly.

A baby-alarm system will provide front to back stage contact but a more sophisticated telephone or radio contact system will be a huge bonus. A television monitor backstage will allow those waiting for a cue to see and hear what is happening. Perfect timing can make all the difference to a special effect and will be easier with a networked system.

Special effects pointers

When establishing a new group, buying or organizing equipment, or planning any production – bear in mind that to achieve magical special effects you will need the following:

1
Imagination

2
Expertise in a variety of technical skills

3
Lots of rehearsal

4
Determination to get it right

5
Clear communication between the various contributors

6
Good committed teamwork

7
Patience and a sense of humour

Sound

Sound is a complicated effect. There is much to be understood about sound techniques and several very helpful books already cover this highly technical subject in great detail.

The purpose here in one brief chapter is to explore what can be achieved by an enthusiastic sound team to add to the effectiveness of a production. It is assumed that the technicians concerned already understand the mathematical and electronic principles and so can handle sound equipment safely.

So this section has been written to be assimilated by any member of the production team who – without delving waist-deep into information on oscillation, harmonics and 'amplifier output impedance' – wants to know more about how to make sound work

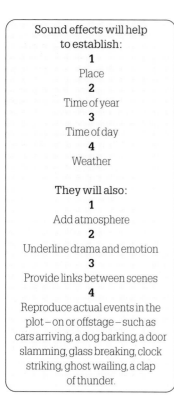

Sound effects will help
to establish:
1
Place
2
Time of year
3
Time of day
4
Weather

They will also:
1
Add atmosphere
2
Underline drama and emotion
3
Provide links between scenes
4
Reproduce actual events in the plot – on or offstage – such as cars arriving, a dog barking, a door slamming, glass breaking, clock striking, ghost wailing, a clap of thunder.

for the team and the production and so attain the right special effects with the help of those experts who do understand all these terms and what they imply!

What is sound for?

In any production it is essential first and foremost to hear the play, the dialogue, the plot.

Additional sound effects over and above the actors' voices are used to establish time and place and add atmosphere. In no way should they ever intrude or interrupt unless this is part of the plot, such as a bomb exploding or a gun shot.

Good background sound effects will scarcely be noticed if they are handled appropriately.

Think sound

Sound is one of the five senses but can be easily overlooked when everyone is concentrating on the acting and visual elements of a production.

Moreover, sound and lighting effects are not generally introduced in the earliest stages of rehearsal, and in some instances, where rehearsals take place in another venue, may not arrive in their entirety until a few days before the live performance.

Planning them, however, should be part and parcel of the production right from the first reading of the script.

There are some instances where the need for a sound is obvious, stated in the play as an essential element – like a bang or explosion – but be imaginative. Such sounds may add to the effectiveness of other scenes too – in, say, a play set during wartime when

the sound of explosions will underline what is going on. Bangs will add to a magic effect such as the arrival of a genie or give extra emphasis and reality to a humorous farce scene – for example, the bang or explosion heralding the appearance of someone staggering on stage blackened by smoke and in disarray.

There are plenty of these explosion sounds available on pre-recorded compact discs and cassettes and a variety of explosive effects can also be achieved by blowing gently into a microphone. If you have professional expertise to handle pyrotechnics, there is no real substitute for a 'bomb' which is in effect a firework set off in a safe tank. See page 126 in the Pyrotechnics chapter.

As another example of how sounds will work for you, think about the way in which eerie sounds can add enormously to the tension of a scene.

Eerie sounds

An echo microphone can produce a very effective voice for a ghost or a giant.

Wails, whoops and cackles can all be pre-recorded, or performed live.

Wind noises can add a lot of atmosphere to an eerie scene, whether howling or gusting through trees.

Whispers, footsteps and creaking noises may be appropriate too or a loud heartbeat.

All in all, whatever the play, or setting, sound is a vital part of it.

Do not overlook the use of silence. This can be a very effective dramatic tool!

Sources

Using sound to the full

It can be a very useful exercise to listen to some radio plays or productions to seek inspiration. Here there is no visual distraction: the sound is everything so it is exploited to the full.

Other than that, close your eyes occasionally during a film or television drama and concentrate on the sound and music. How much does it tell you about what is going on? Music, especially, is very emotive and the same scene played against a different mood of music can change in interpretation to quite a startling degree. A jolly tinkling tune can even mutate the scene from one that is highly charged with drama to a comic routine.

CDs and cassettes

There is a huge variety of pre-recorded sound effects available on compact disc (CD) or tape. These can be bought for permanent ownership by the group or borrowed from libraries who stock a general selection of commercial recordings. If there is a special sound or theatre library in your area, make sure you go armed with all the information on your exact needs. Ideally try to obtain a detailed list of what the library has to offer first so that you do not make a wasted journey

if the particular sound you are seeking is not available.

Most of the CDs of general recorded sounds will comprise birdsong, traffic noise, bells, aircraft, the odd scream or two, dogs barking, footsteps, fairground sounds, telephones, music, waves crashing, farmyard sounds, trains and so on.

Other more specialized tapes might concentrate on traffic, war, animal noises and the like.

The major problem with these recordings is that the effect is generally very short, over almost before you have appreciated which particular sound effect this is – so you may need to re-record and edit the effect several times to create a sound effect that is of any useful length. You may do this by making a loop tape.

A loop tape

A continuous 'loop tape' can be made by splicing the beginning of a sound onto the end. Place this loop onto a tape machine, making sure the necessary tension is maintained for it to run smoothly while you play it back for as long a time as necessary, and record it onto a second tape machine.

Even quite a long loop can sound repetitive and short ones certainly will. However, with a little experimen-

tation – such as playing some sounds backwards or playing two identical loops at the same time but out of synchronization – the rhythm can be broken up and made much more interesting and natural.

Recording your own effects

It can be a fun challenge to record your own sound effects and then package together a suitable sound track for a production.

Indoor sounds like clocks ticking or the radio news are not too problematic to record at home or in a studio.

It is also possible, of course, to go 'on location' to record bells chiming, traffic roaring by, birds singing and so on, but it can be very difficult to avoid extraneous noise and attain the precise effect required.

This can be fun and your optimism may be rewarded, but in general it is often easier to simulate some of these sounds as suggested in *On the spot sound effects* on pages 28-29 and then record these for your own use. For example, thunder can be simulated by breathing softly onto a microphone or water lapping by swishing water against the side of a plastic bucket.

Anyone who has seen those fascinating clips of how radio programmes are recorded will have the general idea. It is amazing what the human voice itself can simulate, apart from all those tricks with paper, wood and water.

Having done all this for several productions, you will gradually build up a useful library of sounds for future use. Keep a record of all the sounds in some logical order and note clearly where all these can be found before you pack everything away and forget!

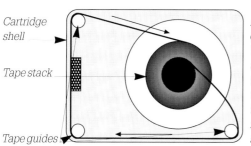

Cartridge shell

Tape stack

Tape guides

A plan view of a NAB cartridge or looped tape
The tape is pulled from the centre of the reel, passing the playback, and then wound on the outside of the spool. Lengths can range from ten seconds to seven minutes

Planning ahead

ENSURE ECHO MICROPHONES PLUGGED IN
  ▶ *FADE OUT 'HOUSE' MUSIC WHEN S.M. SIGNALS*

Scene 1 Mission Control *CUE SOUND EFFECT 1*
(COUNT-DOWN VOICES, EXPLOSION, AND ROCKET TAKE-OFF)

House Lights fade fast so audience is plunged into a black-out. Curtains remain closed.

Mission Control personnel, in formal poses, all around auditorium, speak in loud thunderous voices.

1 10, 9, 8, 7, 6, 5, 4, 3, 2, 1, ZERO!

Loud explosion and 'take-off' sounds. Brilliant light flashes. Smoke swirls.

Voices
We have lift-off, we have lift-off
And it looks like a good one
Mission Cinderella is on her way; Spaceship Sentaprize is looking good, Sir.
Mission Control wishes to inform The Showman that launch is successful.

The Showman Calling Mission Control. This is the Showman. Congratulations!

Voices   Thank you, sir.
Cinderella is in outer space, Cinderella is in space.
And she's looking good.

Mission Control personnel on stage relax. Others break through from auditorium and join them. Shouts also come from the lighting gantry.   *REMEMBER TO SHOUT ! ★*

Well done!
Super job!
Sock it to them, Mission Cinderella.
Three cheers for Mission Control! Hip Hip Hooray!
★ Hip Hip Hooray!   *REMEMBER TO SHOUT ! ★*
Hip Hip Hooray!

Song: Bye Bye Cinders

CUE SOUND EFFECT 2 AT END OF SONG (COMPUTER NOISES)

Scene 2 The Spaceship

Curtains open to reveal interior of spaceship. All is silent. All is still. In frozen animation, are the Cinderella-Hardup family, encapsulated in 'cocoons'. Slowly wheels start whirring, computers buzz, lights flash on and off.

2 ▶ *The ship is waking. Messages flash across screens, sounds buzz and crackle and entire ship lights up. A screen centre stage sparks into life and reveals the face of* **The Showman**, *a gauze transformation bringing his face into focus.*

The Showman This is The Showman calling. This is The Showman calling. May I introduce you to the only creatures still willing to participate in voyages of inter-galactic discovery, to go boldly where no man has been before. Only the most steadfast heroes of fairy tales will man our missions now, zooming into the unknown in frozen animation, to colonize new planets and take the message of true love and happy ever afterings to the rest of the universe.

Planning ahead

Good organization is of paramount importance when planning sound effects for a play.

If everything has been well thought through, clearly marked up on the sound script and well rehearsed, then there will be none of the panic and sweaty, stressful moments that can occur if the approach has been sloppy.

Ensure when you mark up a play script that you mark clearly not only the actual effect but also the moment when you need to prepare the effect in order to be ready in good time.

In theory, although one hopes it will not be necessary, a properly organized sound crew should be able to hand over their script at a moment's notice to someone new in an emergency and everything will be easy to follow.

This should be the 'order of play':

1 Read the play script and highlight clearly whenever particular sound effects are needed.

2 Discuss requirements with the producer and any technical staff involved (for example, thunder and lightning would mean coordination with the lighting team too, and extra personnel might be needed in the wings for on-the-spot sound effects).

3 Check what music is needed for pre-performance, linking scenes and during intermission.

4 Research all the possibilities on how to achieve these effects.

5 Make a sound plot, showing what is needed when.

6 Attend rehearsals to check out appropriateness of ideas and incorporate into the sound plot any changes or additions that occur during the development of the play.

7 Check that all the sound equipment is in good order. Borrow, buy, make or organize the renting of any extra effects or equipment that is needed.

8 If using taped sound, mix sounds as needed and make up a tape or tapes, plus back-ups, with the various sound effects in correct order. Then mark your sound plot clearly to indicate the final positions of each sound on the tape.

9 Supervise all the sound effects at the dress and technical rehearsals.

10 Make any necessary adjustments. Finalise coordination with the stage manager and the rest of the backstage team.

11 Be there early on the performance nights – in good time to check that everything is in order and to have apt welcoming music playing in house as the first members of the audience arrive.

Music is a vital element in creating the right atmosphere and will help to set the mood from the moment the audience enters the hall. It will also encourage them to relax as they settle into their seats.

Cueing sound effects

Sound effects can be created manually as and when required – or can be pre-recorded and played back at the appropriate moment. Either way, a copy of the script will need to be marked up appropriately.

It is important to allow sufficient time on the cue sheets to allow you to locate the right effect on the tape – or pick up the piece of equipment required if the sound effects are manual and being done at the sound depot rather than offstage. So although you will probably highlight the actual effect as described in the play script, you also need to mark the script clearly, ahead of the effect, so you are aware of the moment when you need to get ready. Nothing sounds more amateur and ridiculous than a sound effect that arrives after the event, so it is vital to be organized and ready in good time.

Volume of sound

Volume also needs to be carefully considered. The sound of waves washing on a shore, birds singing in a wood or rain drumming down will certainly establish an appropriate atmosphere but this rain sound may be very distracting and reduce audibility of the dialogue if it is played at full gusto throughout a quiet scene.

It is generally best to begin with the sound loud and clear to establish in the minds of the audience that the wind is howling, or whatever, and then to gradually fade the sound away to an acceptable level and perhaps fade it out completely once the scene is running.

If required, the sound can be reintroduced now and then during pauses or when someone goes outside or when the drama of the moment demands.

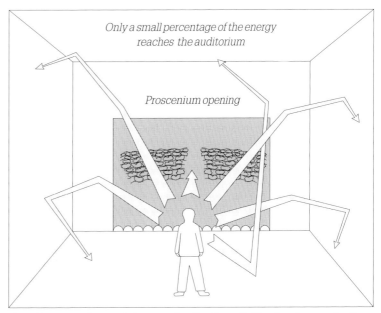

Only a small percentage of the energy reaches the auditorium

Proscenium opening

Sound bounces all around the actor. It will reflect off all hard surfaces and will carry on doing so until, finally, it is absorbed. So only a small percentage of the sound energy of the voice is actually projected into the auditorium

On the spot sound effects

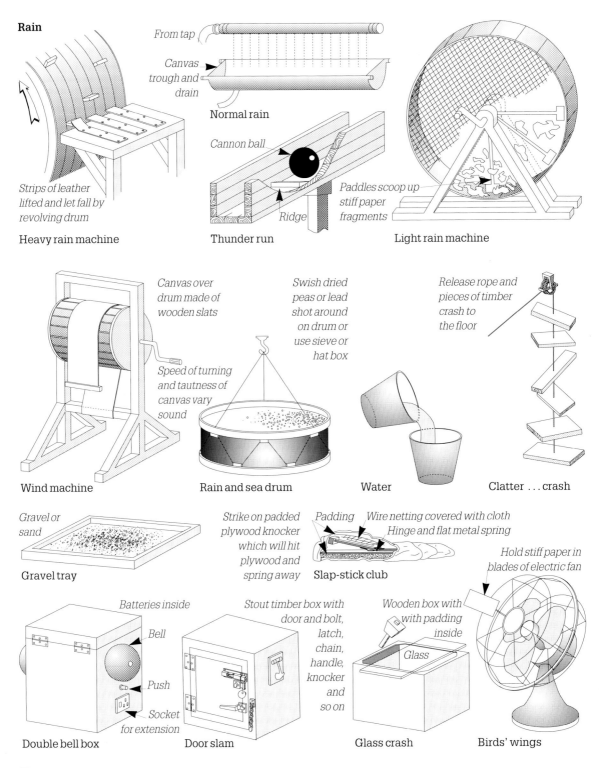

Rain

Heavy rain machine

Strips of leather lifted and let fall by revolving drum

From tap

Canvas trough and drain

Normal rain

Thunder run

Cannon ball

Ridge

Paddles scoop up stiff paper fragments

Light rain machine

Wind machine

Canvas over drum made of wooden slats

Speed of turning and tautness of canvas vary sound

Rain and sea drum

Swish dried peas or lead shot around on drum or use sieve or hat box

Water

Release rope and pieces of timber crash to the floor

Clatter ... crash

Gravel tray

Gravel or sand

Slap-stick club

Strike on padded plywood knocker which will hit plywood and spring away

Padding

Wire netting covered with cloth

Hinge and flat metal spring

Hold stiff paper in blades of electric fan

Double bell box

Batteries inside

Bell

Push

Socket for extension

Door slam

Stout timber box with door and bolt, latch, chain, handle, knocker and so on

Glass crash

Wooden box with with padding inside

Glass

Birds' wings

On the spot sound effects

Creating live sound effects backstage or in the wings may seem old-fashioned and unsophisticated, but sounds created on the spot can be very effective and are especially appropriate to certain productions such as pantomime and melodrama. Moreover, there are some manual effects which cannot be bettered on a recording. For example, a live human scream is always more chilling than any recorded voice and so it is always better to have someone in the wings primed to let rip at the right moment.

Moreover, any on the spot sound effect is reliable because it is not prone to technical hitches and may be less complicated to do in time especially if the actors skip a page or so, or start going in circles through the script.

Audibility can be a problem, especially if the curtains are very heavy or there is any other barrier which muffles the sound.

A microphone and loudspeakers will be very useful to counteract this sound absorption problem (see also pages 30-33).

Using a microphone for on the spot sounds

There are also many additional effects that can be produced by breathing gently on a microphone or tapping it gently (microphones are delicate instruments) or by using a hairdryer or vacuum cleaner nearby, or rubbing or scratching sandpaper or glass paper.

Rustling leaves
Try shaking some old recording tape or film in front of the microphone for the sound of rustling leaves in trees.

Footsteps in a forest
Crush old recording tape or film rhythmically in front of the microphone to create an atmospheric sound of footsteps in a forest.

Footsteps in snow
Alternatively, you can crush a bag of flour in front of the microphone to create footsteps in snow.

Sea waves
Stroke brushes to and fro across a metal sheet in front of the microphone to sound like waves.

Ship's siren
Blow across the neck of a bottle half filled with water in front of the microphone for a ship's siren.

Fire
Crushing matchboxes or cellophane paper near a microphone can sound like a fire crackling.

Experiment to see what effects you can create. You will be amazed at the range of possibilities, but bear in mind that trying to cram in too many will become complicated and may hinder the flow of the play, rather than helping. So discipline yourself to use only what works best for the play.

All of this can still be enormous fun as the sound personnel or their delegates wait poised in the wings with some of the following:

Rain
Buckets of water to pour into metal containers below
or
Dried peas for rain – in a tin or rolling in a wire sieve
or
Sugar poured down a grease-proof paper chute for an alternative rain sound effect.

Thunder
Flexible metal thunder sheets: Suitably amplified, a good thunder sheet takes a lot of beating – in more ways than one! Actually it is shaken, not beaten, and needs to be firmly fixed so that it can be prevented from thundering in between uses.

Horses
Coconut shells beaten on a bed of sand for horses' hooves.

Wind
Lengths of silk can sound like wind if dragged across wooden boards in front of a microphone.

Creaking hinges or rowing boats
Use genuine rusty hinges to creak and squeak. This can also sound like rowing a boat if combined with dipping a piece of wood in a bucket of water.

Shots
Cap guns and starting pistols: do remember that a gun license may be needed. (See also the section on weapons and firearms, pages 83-87.)

Breaking glass
Boxes full of broken glass to shake.

Bells, whistles and so on
Whistles, bells, gongs, squeaking toys and rattles.

A knock at the door
Door knockers on hunks of wood.

Space can prove difficult if the wing area is cramped. This must be considered and the effects rehearsed well ahead so that you can ensure there is ample room to flex a thunder sheet, break glass in a metal bucket, or whatever, without tripping over the prompt or obstructing anxious actors waiting to enter. The last thing they want to add to their first night stage nerves is

Making the most of the kit

Loudspeakers

to find unexpected obstacles and people in their way when their timing of an entrance is critical.

Musicians

Musicians, if you have any, can introduce a variety of sound effects too. Apart from the obvious accompaniment (such as playing to add background music to a chase scene or slapstick fun), a pianist and drummer can suggest all sorts of bangs, crashes, tinkling bells and cymbals clashing, while today's electric organs offer a splendid choice of background and foreground sounds such as waves washing onto a shore, organs or harps playing and Hawaiian music.

Be positive

Be imaginative

Plan well ahead

Recorded sound effects

Using pre-recorded sound effects gives the sound team the opportunity to draw on a huge variety of exciting sounds. Sound effects can be created specifically for a production and recorded on tape in readiness for the performance or 'bought in' and mixed to fit the play's needs. They are available on record, cassette tape or compact disc in shops and libraries.

The voice

Of course the most important sound in any piece of theatre (except in dance or mime) is the actor's voice. If dialogue cannot be heard, the audience will be justifiably irritated and restless. Moreover, their understanding of the plot may be lost.

Generally, encouraging the cast to be audible is the director's role but there may be occasions, especially in a large venue, out of doors, or for a musical performance, when microphones and speakers may be called upon to help voice projection.

Making the most of the kit

The quality of the sound effects you can record, plus the quality of these and any other sounds when played back, is obviously dependent on the quality of the equipment used – which, in turn, will be controlled by the budget (see also page 36).

The group may be lucky enough to be able to call upon the services of a sound technician who owns expensive equipment, or can borrow it, and is sufficiently enthusiastic about dramatics to allow it to be used for play productions. Or perhaps the society or college is blessed with lots of money and excellent equipment is already installed.

However, whatever the quality of the equipment – and many groups have a fairly basic outfit – the overall end result and the smooth running of the play will depend upon organized skilled handling. Much can be achieved with relatively primitive sound equipment.

The advantages are the wide choice of sounds readily available, guaranteed audibility and more professional final effects than might be possible when recording your own – in most cases but not all. If, however, your needs cannot be met by a ready-made sound, try manufacturing your own sound effect and recording this on to the sound tape for the play (see also page 35).

Whether recording your own or buying in sounds, remember to leave a respectable gap between the various sound effects on your tape, to tape more than you initially think you need so the sound effect never runs out too soon (it is a simple matter to fade it out when no longer needed) and to check volume levels carefully in rehearsal from various positions in the hall so that you do not leave your audience straining to hear, or deafen them by pumping the sounds up too loudly. Remember that a full audience will absorb some of the sound, so you will need to adjust the volume according to the density of human bodies.

Loudspeakers

Any sound equipment that is used has to fulfill the following:

1
Capture the sound

2
Amplify the sound

3
Reproduce it

A basic public address system will consist of:

1
a microphone

2
preamplifier
may be built in as part of the mic or mixer

3
an amplifier

4
a loudspeaker

A theatre system
will probably use a
mixer too, so the set-up
now becomes:

1

a microphone

2

a mixer

3

an amplifier

4

a loudspeaker

Loudspeakers translate the sounds (which are basically electrical vibrations) from an amplifier back into the pressure waves that make up a particular sound.

1 The microphone captures the sound.

2 The mixer can combine a number of signals. Each input on the mixer has a volume control so the various signals can be mixed at the chosen levels before being passed on to the amplifier and thence to the speakers.

3 Most mixers, amplifiers, tape recorders and so on will incorporate a preamplifier. This amplifies the sound to a standard level so that whoever is in charge can control and adjust the sound level more conveniently, altering the volume, bass or treble, and so on, as required.

4 The sound is transmitted to the amplifier.

5 The amplifier magnifies the signal to a level that the loudspeaker recognizes and to which it can therefore respond.

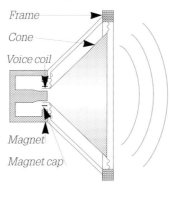

Cone loudspeaker

Frame
Cone
Voice coil
Magnet
Magnet cap

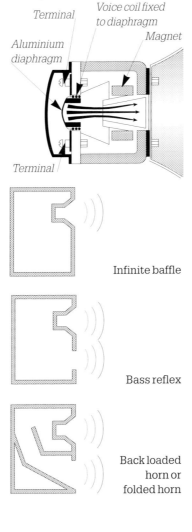

Horn pressure unit

Terminal
Voice coil fixed
to diaphragm
Magnet
Aluminium
diaphragm

Terminal

Infinite baffle

Bass reflex

Back loaded
horn or
folded horn

6 The loudspeakers reproduce the sound and complete the cycle.

Technical hints and tips when using loudspeakers

As a general rule, the larger the loudspeaker (and the more costly it is) the more effective it will be.

Try to have all the same types of loudspeaker so the sound produced will have the same quality throughout and not be distractingly different from one loudspeaker to another.

Do not underestimate the power needed. If a loudspeaker is overloaded it will be damaged or burn out. For example, if you have a 35 watt amplifier, make sure the loudspeaker can cope with a constant flow of 35 watts and the odd burst of 50 watts.

When connecting up loudspeakers, ensure that all the positive connections are wired in exactly the same way (say, to the brown wire) and all the negative ones are consistent also. If you vary this the loudspeakers will work 'out of phase', with the direction of oscillations counteracting each other and thus reducing the bass response and effective levels when a listener is between two loudspeakers.

Long cable runs may mean a loss of power. Make sure you use cables of sufficient size which have a low enough resistance and the problem will be avoided.

Cables will often pick up hum and other electrical interference, especially if the sound system is unbalanced.

A balanced system

An unbalanced system will result from interconnecting cables with one

Loudspeakers

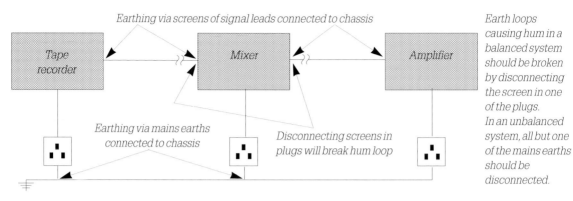

Earthing via screens of signal leads connected to chassis

Tape recorder

Mixer

Amplifier

Earthing via mains earths connected to chassis

Disconnecting screens in plugs will break hum loop

Earth loops causing hum in a balanced system should be broken by disconnecting the screen in one of the plugs. In an unbalanced system, all but one of the mains earths should be disconnected.

conductor and a overall braided screen (a co-axial cable). Unbalanced systems will use plugs or sockets with two pins or connections.

A balanced system is possible if you use two conductors plus a screen (a twin screened cable). A balanced system will use plugs or sockets with three pins or connections.

Positioning loudspeakers

It sounds obvious, but make sure loudspeakers face the audience and are as near to the stage as possible.

Ensure that they are between the microphones and the audience to

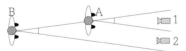

Listener A can easily pinpoint the locations of speakers 1 and 2, but listener B cannot tell the difference

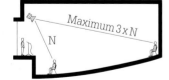

The most remote location covered by an overhead loudspeaker should not be more than three times the distance to the nearest location (N = nearest distance)

minimize acoustic feedback. The ideal position is centre stage but this is rarely practical unless the speakers can be placed directly above the front of the stage.

If you place loudspeakers around a hall there will be a time lag in the production of the sound effect and confusing multiple sounds will then erupt. So attempt to do this only if you can afford an expensive electronic delay system to even out this effect – or if you actually want to achieve the effect of sound moving round the auditorium, probably relaying a pre-recorded tape. This might be used, for instance, to suggest voices coming from a magic flying carpet, gods talk-

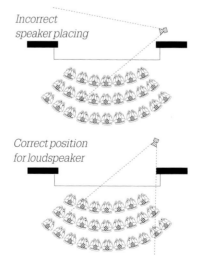

Incorrect speaker placing

Correct position for loudspeaker

ing from the clouds or an aircraft zooming overhead.

Because the high frequencies emitted by loudspeakers are directional the audience will locate their source. So if the speaker is supposed to be creating the sound of a prop such as a television, computer, or telephone on the stage it needs to be as close as possible to this, either built into the scenery nearby or, at the very least, in line with the audience slightly to one side and behind the prop concerned but still facing out front. Heavily angled speakers will sound fine to those of the audience in a direct line but the sound will be blurred and indistinct to their counterparts on the opposite side of the auditorium.

Ensure that nothing is placed in front of the loudspeakers which will muffle the sound. Sometimes this can happen at a later stage when someone ignorant of their function puts something in the way without realizing.

If the loudspeakers have to be masked to become part of the scenery, use a perforated material like hessian, gauze or scrim.

Test out the effect of the loudspeakers from a good variety of vantage points in the auditorium.

Microphones

As a general rule, if the front face of the loudspeaker is visible from a sitting position in the audience then the sound will be clearly audible too.

It is wrong to think that the sound from the speakers will be loudest at the front of the hall. Remember that sound waves are like beams of light and may not 'focus' on the front row at all. In fact you should aim to tilt the speakers so that the maximum sound is aimed at the back of the hall. Then everyone should be able to hear well.

Microphones

Do not use too many microphones.

The rule is to use as few as possible. Then a clean sound will be achieved with the least possible reverberation (multiple echoes) and minimum time-lag between the original sound and its relay to the audience.

Place the microphone as near as possible to the source of sound.

Microphones can be placed at floor level or raised up on stands at the front edge of the stage – the ideal position for capturing the sounds as the actor projects his or her voice in that direction.

In fact, microphones that are placed right on the stage floor can be very effective. This, of course, will work only on a hard stage, not a carpeted

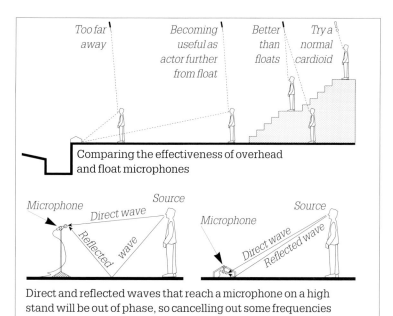

Comparing the effectiveness of overhead and float microphones

Too far away — *Becoming useful as actor further from float* — *Better than floats* — *Try a normal cardioid*

Direct and reflected waves that reach a microphone on a high stand will be out of phase, so cancelling out some frequencies

one. Microphones placed on the stage floor will receive only direct sounds and not a combination of direct and reflected sounds.

Vibrations near microphones can cause horrid noises to be emitted so microphones will often need to be 'shock-proof'! A simple shock-proof mounting can easily be made from thick foam rubber and then secured firmly with rubber straps.

A combination of shock-absorbent mounting and a disciplined stage crew in soft shoes will help to reduce the problem!

Microphones can also be suspended – but only if the microphone can be hung close enough. Actors speak out, not up, and suspending a microphone that is too high to collect the sound is a pointless exercise.

If an actor is at the top of a flight of stairs, for example, a suspended microphone may well be appropriate.

In a musical event it is generally acceptable for the singer to carry a microphone or wear a radio microphone with no concern over disguising this. In fact, in these circumstances a microphone may well

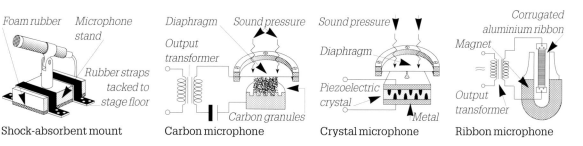

Shock-absorbent mount — Foam rubber, Microphone stand, Rubber straps tacked to stage floor

Carbon microphone — Diaphragm, Sound pressure, Output transformer, Carbon granules

Crystal microphone — Sound pressure, Diaphragm, Piezoelectric crystal, Metal

Ribbon microphone — Corrugated aluminium ribbon, Magnet, Output transformer

Mixing and recording

be used as a sort of prop. However, if this is a production of *Hamlet* or a historical piece, then, of course, the microphones must be as unobtrusive as possible.

Mixing and recording

Mixers

The mixer is the heart of the sound system, so invest in the best that can be afforded. Make sure you choose one that is flexible so that it can be

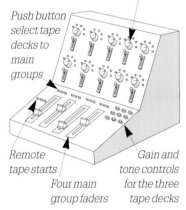

Fourteen loudspeaker circuits with on/off switches and rotary selection to any one of the four groups

Push button select tape decks to main groups

Remote tape starts

Four main group faders

Gain and tone controls for the three tape decks

Sound effects mixer

used with a variety of inputs. Just like video recorders, the basic essential is to make sure it is simple to operate, at the same time as being able to achieve the right technical standards and do the job you want it to do.

Stereo mixers can output to the left or to the right or use a two-way 'fader' called a 'pan' control to output anywhere in between.

There are individual controls which will allow for the adjustment of the

bass, mid and treble sounds.

In addition to the basics, there are many extras which will help to give more precise and/or more sophisticated operation, control echo and reverberation, allow the operator to listen to a particular channel and even to 'fold back' the sound to those on stage, if necessary.

Tape recorders

Despite being 'old-fashioned', tape recorders are probably still the most versatile pieces of sound equipment.

They offer a choice of speeds, but as a general rule, the higher the tape speed, the better the quality of the recording will be.

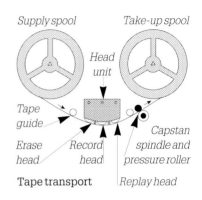

Track configurations

Some tapes have several tracks. This allows more playing time and facilitates the smooth overlapping of sound effects.

It will also enable you to create a 'backing track' and then add layers of other sounds, just as a music group will record the backing of a song first and then add the voices.

One word of warning

When the tapes are divided up into narrow strips in this way, you need to be scrupulously careful about keeping the tapes clean: even the minutest

of specks will cause the tape to drop away from the head and result in a fault in the recording.

Supply spool   *Take-up spool*

Head unit

Tape guide

Erase head   *Record head*

Capstan spindle and pressure roller

Tape transport   *Replay head*

Steps in recording

1 Check that the full spool of tape is on the left and that the free end of the tape is wound around the reel on the right – about three loops.

2 Check that the 'coated' side of the tape faces the magnetic heads.

3 Set the speed adjustment.

4 Set the track selection.

5 Set the tape counter at zero.

6 Make sure the machine is in Record mode.

7 Set Record Gain on the meter at the optimum level.

8 Press Record/Play.

9 Let the machine run for a few seconds before cueing in so that the tape settles to an even speed and to avoid any irritating 'start-up' clicks.

Guidelines to editing a tape

You will need:

1
A stop watch

2
One splicing block

3
A packet of single-edged razor blades

4
One pair of scissors. Make sure they are not magnetized or they will create clicks on the tape. Brass scissors are good or use a head demagnetizer.

5
A reel of splicing tape

6
Reels of coloured leader tape – make sure these have one side matte so they can be written on with a ball-point pen.

7
A ball-point pen

8
A white chinagraph pencil

9
Some empty spools

10
List of sound effects needed

11
The cue sheet

12
You might also need the full script for reference

10 At the end of recording, let the tape run for a few seconds with Record Gain turned down. This will provide a useful quiet pause and make for easier editing.

Always record in one direction only, whether in mono, stereo or multi-track. This will allow you to alter the contents of sections of the tape at a later stage.

Editing

In this process, the aim is to:

1 Select the actual recordings chosen and edit out any unnecessary 'takes' as well as any clicks or interference noises.

2 Cut the effects to the correct length, allowing some extra time for fading in and out.

3 Cut the cueing-in sections to the required length.

4 Splice together any sounds that need to be combined.

5 Place the sound effects in the right order.

6 Then mark all the divisions and cues clearly.

Method

1 Play the tape recording machine and locate the beginning of the first cue.

2 Press the stop button.

3 Very carefully move the tape backwards and forwards by hand (be

careful to avoid stretching the tape) until the exact spot where the sound begins is located.

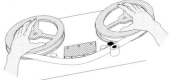

4 When you are sure the sound is at the gap on the relay head, make a small mark with the chinagraph pencil. Do this very gently so as not to damage the head.

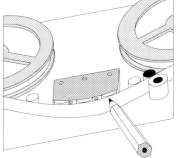

5 Rewind the tape a little and then run it at normal speed to check that the mark is at the right place.

6 If it is marked correctly, cut the tape about half an inch (13 mm) away from the mark. Be sure to do this on the appropriate side. If the mark indicates the start of a cue, cut on the right of the head. If the mark indicates the end of a cue, cut on the left. Do leave a little extra spare tape at the end of each cue in case you need to re-edit later on.

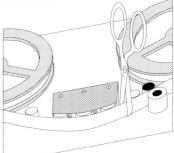

7 Place the required end of the tape in the splicing block. Make sure that the mark is at the centre of the 45 degree cutting guide.

8 Cut off a sufficient length of the leader tape.

9 Place one end so that it overlaps the cutting guide by about one inch (25mm).

10 Use the razor blade to slice the tape gently but firmly. The two ends of the original tape and the leader tape should now butt together neatly, as shown below.

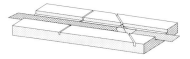

11 Cut off one inch (25mm) of self-adhesive splicing tape and lay this carefully over the two pieces of tape. Make sure that it does not overlap at the edges or the tape may snag and break.

12 Finally, press into position firmly and rub smoothly to remove all the air bubbles.

Before replay

When the tapes are being prepared for replay during a performance, you will need to insert coloured leader tapes as cue markers. During a show, you will probably be working in low light levels so make sure these markers are bright enough to be clearly seen. It can be useful to colour code the markers too so that scenes and/or acts are clearly identifiable. Any other linked sequence of sounds can be defined in the same way.

Always ensure that the matte side of the marker tapes is away from the heads. The cue code – or any other relevant information – can be written with ball-point pen on this matte side only and will need to be away from the heads to be visible during playback.

> Always, always make a **back-up copy** of the final tape.

Other useful equipment

Compact disc players

These are very simple to use for playing professionally recorded sounds. Locating the position of a particular sound is very precise and easy. The CDs are relatively durable and the sound quality is good.

Their disadvantage is that they can be complicated to operate smoothly if you have not used one before. Experiment to see if the equipment suits the way you work. Moreover, recording your own sounds onto a CD requires a CD maker – at present a very expensive piece of equipment. However, the price of CD makers has dropped dramatically recently and perhaps investing in one will become a viable prospect for theatre groups in the not-so-distant future. In the meantime a conventional compact disc player will be an invaluable addition to the sound equipment as a source of sounds for re-recording.

Cassette recorders

The familiar cassette player can be useful too. In a very small hall, their output may suffice, and even in larger halls, a cassette player may be very useful for rehearsal purposes if all the 'proper' sound equipment is not yet up and running.

Choose one which has big speakers, the best that can be afforded.

It is essential to have a counting device so that you know where you are on the tape and can readily locate particular sounds.

Cassette multi-track recorders

These are widely available now at a reasonable price – just like the reel-to-reel recorders – and will be a good flexible piece of equipment to have in the sound department.

Connecting up to loudspeakers

The majority of reel-to-reel recorders, cassette and compact disc units can be connected up to the loudspeaker system and can then be successfully played through this.

However, most of the current so-called personal stereos, 'Walkmans' and so on cannot be used in the loudspeaker system. There are exceptions, but, if this is what is planned, it will be wise to check compatibility early on.

The sound booth

All this equipment will need to be installed in a convenient location where the sound team can see the play without interfering with the view of the audience. Generally this means that the sound booth will be raised up. It may be located in a purpose-built 'studio' but more likely it will be up on a scaffolding tower or set to the back or side of the auditorium.

Make sure everything is within easy reach and that the operator can be relatively comfortable as he or she will undoubtedly be there for the duration of the performance. Contact with other members of the team, especially the stage manager and lighting crew, will be essential and will be helped by internal radio links. A baby alarm system may be a relatively cheap way to achieve this contact.

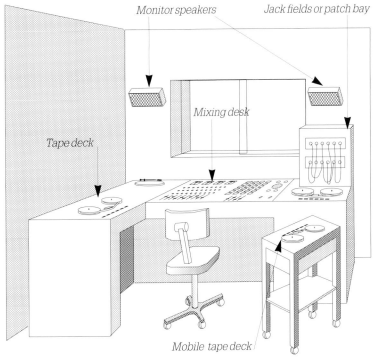

Monitor speakers *Jack fields or patch bay*

Mixing desk

Tape deck

Mobile tape deck

Control room layout with view through a window into auditorium

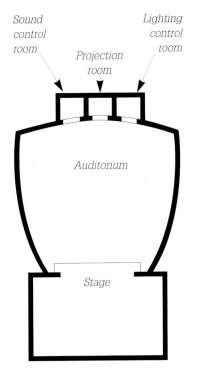

Sound control room *Lighting control room*

Projection room

Auditorium

Stage

Theatre layout showing typical control room positions.

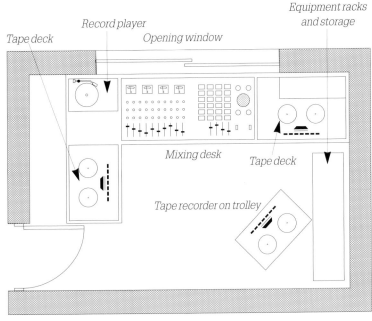

Record player *Equipment racks and storage*

Tape deck *Opening window*

Mixing desk *Tape deck*

Tape recorder on trolley

A typical control room plan

Questions and Answers

What should I look for when choosing a microphone?

Choose a microphone that has the right sort of directional sensitivity for the job you want it to do.

Vocal microphones Ensure there is no 'handling' noise, that it is supercardioid, mechanically durable and that it is comfortable for the actor to hold.

Float microphones A capacitor microphone is generally more effective than a dynamic one. Good sensitivity and minimum feedback are essential.

Fly microphones These need to be sufficiently sensitive to pick up well at greater distances but should not be too directional or there will be hot and cold spots. A capacitor Short Shotgun is ideal.

Why use a radio microphone?

A radio microphone will avoid the need for a cord.

However, they are expensive and can suffer from unwanted interference and inter-reaction. Four or five should be the maximum number used on any frequency. To avoid picking up other transmitter's channels, there is a system of licensing. A license or a permit from the supplier will be needed for most frequencies.

Can the actor hide a radio microphone under his or her costume?

No! Make sure the microphone stays outside and try to avoid contact with jewellery or friction against a costume or lots of irritating rustling noises will be created. The transmitter can be secreted in a pocket in the costume and the antenna strapped down a sleeve or across the back.

What is impedance?

This is the AC resistance of a coil. It is important that the output of the recording and playback unit has an impedance that is evenly matched to the impedance of the mixer/amplifier of the speaker system. Ask your supplier's advice or check the owner's handbook for each unit.

What frequencies are audible to the human ear?

A normal human ear can hear sounds ranging from 16 Hertz to 16,000 Hertz. There have been instances of highly sensitive ears recognizing sounds at 23,000 Hertz, but by the age of sixty, most people cannot hear anything above 6,000 Hertz.

Generally, unaided by any microphone, a human voice will range from 40 to 1,200 Hertz and a piano from 30 to 4,000 Hertz.

What is the Doppler effect?

A sound that is approaching you seems to be higher pitched than when it is going away from you. Whether the sound is emanating from a bus, a train, a siren, or a one-man band – if the sound is approaching you – you actually receive more cycles per second. Recorded sound will often exhibit this change in pitch. Christian Johann Doppler (1803-1853) was the first to explain this effect, hence the name.

What problems does an orchestra impose?

It is vital to get the sound balance right so that all the different instruments can be heard and so that the actor or singer can be heard above the orchestra. Many a fine rendering of a song has been drowned by an over-enthusiastic drummer!

Even if there is only a trio, if the guitar amplifier is adjusted by even the smallest degree, then a carefully structured balance will be destroyed. Consistency among a few can be just as difficult to attain, as within a large orchestra when a conductor is exercising some control.

Also, it is worth noting that any accompanists tend to play progressively louder during the run of a show as confidence in the performance increases. If possible, adjust the sound balance accordingly.

Trouble shooting: what should I check first?

Is everything plugged in and connected properly, and switched on?

Are all the leads and cables functioning properly? Wiggle them, or try a substitute.

Are all the batteries still alive?

Is the tape threaded correctly?

Are the heads worn?

Is something dirty?

> Dirt is one of the main causes of problems. For example, any build up of grime on the capstan will cause 'wow' and 'flutter' (horrid variations in sound pitch) while chirping and squealing sounds may be caused by dust or dirt on the felt pads and tape guides. If in doubt, clean everything and try again. To minimize problems with dirty tapes, always store the tapes in their boxes.

Lighting

The designer/technician

In professional theatre there are two separate lighting roles:

1
In the first place, designers design the lighting for plays (a scenographer may, in fact, be responsible for all the aspects of design for a production, including scenery and costumes).

2
Then the lighting technicians organize the electric system.

In amateur theatre, generally, these distinctions do not exist and it is likely to be one person who undertakes the design and the mechanics, works out the lighting plot, scrambles up ladders and scaffolding to fix lanterns and spots (perhaps with a couple of helpers at this stage) and who is then responsible for pressing all the right buttons and switches during the final rehearsals and performances.

This is the person who will be most invaluable when it comes to the creation of special effects – and, in fact, the combination of technical expertise and creative flair in the enthusiastic amateur will contribute enormously to the magic of the special effects. Find an imaginative lighting expert who is willing to experiment and the group will be well on the way to success in this field.

To contribute fully, the lighting expert will need to appreciate the nuances of the show's plot and mood in order to do full justice to the production and use the lighting effects sympathetically. It is important for the lighting team to be involved at the earliest possible time in order to plan ahead any special effects that are needed.

It is rare that any special effect works in isolation, and actors, producer, set designer and stage manager will need to work together closely to achieve a well integrated effect.

Special effects can be great fun but must always be seen as part of the whole and not override visibility. Wild enthusiasm to create special effects and to light particular areas of the stage for dramatic moments, may result in the emphasis of the lighting for the general scenes being overlooked. The result of this can be that if actors move too far in one direction, their faces are plunged into shadow. Attention must be given to the entire stage and overall result.

Special lighting effects will:

Add dramatic emphasis
Creative use of colour and light will underline the action and mood.

Suggest the time and season
The time of day – from dawn to dusk and dead of night – can all be indicated by the appropriate use of light, as can the glow of summer or the brilliant light when sun reflects off snow.

Create weather effects
This is a special effects forté and a variety of methods can be implemented to create swirling snow, rain, clouds, and lightning. Lighting can be one of the simplest means to achieve good weather effects. Projection and gobos are very useful for this. (See pages 45-53)

Suggest a setting or place
Different levels, colours of lighting and patterned effects will help to establish whether a scene is occurring outside or inside, in a hot or cold climate, in dappled shade, in a palace, a church, a cave ... and so on.

**Planning
which-when-where-how**

1 Read the play and highlight any special effects.

2 Make a list of these.

3 Discuss ideas for creating the effects with producer and, possibly, the set or costume designer.

4 Do any necessary research on the exact effect needed and the means to achieve this.

5 Make lighting plot and highlight any special effects.

6 Check existing equipment to see if it is adequate for the special effect required and in working order.

7 Attend rehearsals and incorporate any changes into the lighting plot.

8 Organize the renting or manufacture of any equipment needed.

9 Discuss requirements and areas of responsibility with other members of the team. Make a timetable showing who does what when.

10 Set up the electrical and special effect equipment as needed.

11 Check safety of all the equipment and focusing of lanterns.

12 Supervise lighting and special effects at dress and technical rehearsals. Check that everything works well and looks as you hoped –

Planning which-when-where-how

and that everyone else involved is happy with the results too.

13 Make any adjustments.

14 Oversee lighting effects throughout performances.

15 After the show, if necessary, take the lighting rig down safely and return or store equipment.

16 Keep a note of any particularly effective special lighting and how this was achieved so the effect can be repeated in future without having to repeat all the ground work research and experimentation.

For each scene, the lighting expert will need to analyze . . .

1 What is the particular effect (or effects) required?

2 What time of day is it?

3 What is the mood of the scene?

4 Will a colour filter help to create the right effect?

5 Where are the actors standing when any particular special effect is needed?

6 Will any specially set lanterns or spots be required?

7 Who else will be involved in making this particular effect work?

8 Does any new equipment need to be bought or hired?

Lighting angles

The angle at which any light is used is very important.

Up lighting

Up lighting gives a very eerie effect as faces take on strange shadows and hollows. Footlights were the earliest form of theatre lighting, so if you're staging an historical or Restoration piece, a Victorian play, melodrama, or pantomime, up lighting will be very much in keeping with the original style of lighting used.

Silhouettes and dramatic shadows

A simple silhouette effect is achieved by lighting just the background and nothing else on stage. Anyone or anything in front of this will then appear as a dark shape or as an outline only. Alternatively, gauze or material can be back lit. Then there is less ambient light to bounce around and the image outline will be that much sharper.

If a smoke screen can be back lit this will create a brilliant effect as the silhouette appears projected into the smoke.

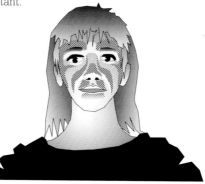

Uplighting creates eerie shadows

A silhouette effect with high backlighting

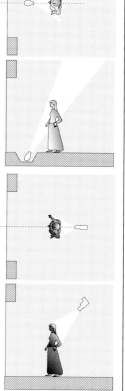

Back light

If the stage is to be filled with strong colour but you do not want the actors to have red or green faces, or whatever, light the stage area with back lighting and the actors with front lighting. The actors may still have a halo of colour on their head and shoulders but this can look quite effective

Top or down light

Using light from above will expose only certain protruding elements of the body or costume so it has a strong sculptural effect. This can be very dramatic, high-lighting, for example, an Edwardian lady's parasol and sweeping hat or an alien's tentacles, webbed hands and space artillery. An angel's wings and harp might be lit, or a soldier's helmet, armour and sword.

Focus

Lighting can also be sharply focused or soft-edged – and this too can reflect the feel of a scene or the overall style of the production.

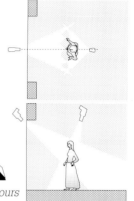

Combine back and front lighting if strong colours are used on set and actor is to look normal

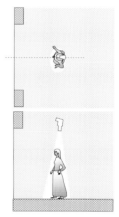

Top lighting is dramatic and highlights the shapes and outlines

Sharp focus

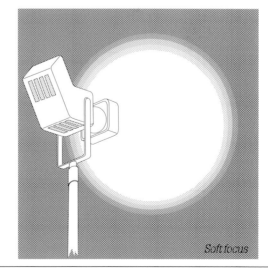

Soft focus

Colour

Do experiment: the effect of colour gels will vary according to the colours of sets, cycloramas or backcloths onto which they are directed. Also the colours of the lights may change the colour strengths of costumes.

Try out the following gels

Warm daylight
103, 159, 205, 206, 212
and open white

Cool daylight
117, 201, 202, 203, 218

Moonlight
143, 161, 174, 183

Indoor light
103, 151, 152, 153, 154, 162
and open white

Numbers used by gel manufacturers such as Lee

Countryside and woodland scenes will need a composite of ambers and golds. Sunsets, of course, will need reds and pinks. Greens and reds will give dramatic emphasis for special scenes and would quite naturally be considered for musicals, ballet, opera and so on but, used more subtly, colour changes can work well in conventional plays too. The warmth or coolness of the atmosphere in a scene – not just the physical weather conditions but the mood – can be emphasized by sympathetic lighting.

Mixing colours with pigment and mixing them with light are two very different things as the following illustrations show:

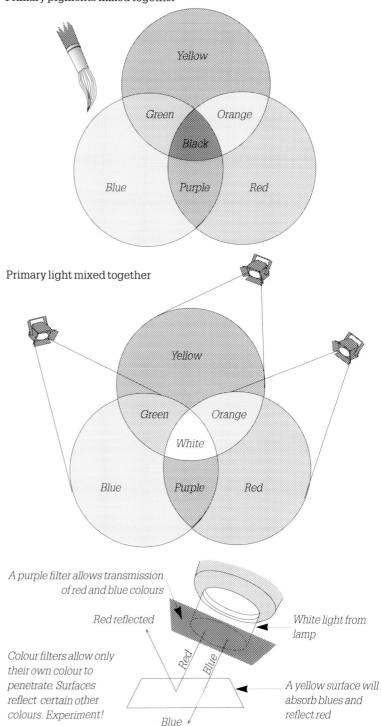

Primary pigments mixed together

Yellow

Green · Orange

Black

Blue · Purple · Red

Primary light mixed together

Yellow

Green · Orange

White

Blue · Purple · Red

A purple filter allows transmission of red and blue colours

Red reflected

White light from lamp

Red

Blue

Colour filters allow only their own colour to penetrate. Surfaces reflect certain other colours. Experiment!

A yellow surface will absorb blues and reflect red

Blue

A colour wheel will allow circles of different coloured gels to be turned in front of a lamp. Having several of these can be cheaper than renting an equivalent number of extra lamps and dimmers, but setting up and synchronizing them can take a good deal of time, so do allow for this.

Using colour to change sets

Colours change under certain lights and can disappear completely and appear again when a different filter is used. This can be used to create changes in a scene, the change of light colours falling onto the same set mutating its appearance. For example, a tree through the seasons could change from full spring blossom back to bare branches in winter if the right colour paints and the right colour lights are used.

For more subtle colour changes see the chart that appears on page 113 in the costume chapter.

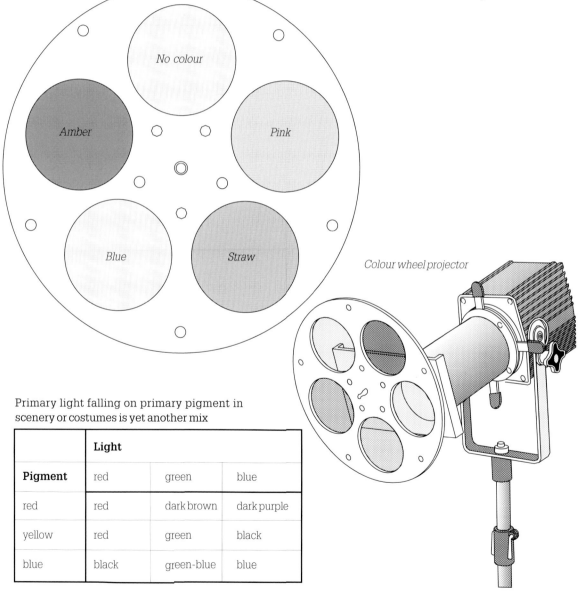

No colour

Amber

Pink

Blue

Straw

Colour wheel projector

Primary light falling on primary pigment in scenery or costumes is yet another mix

Pigment	Light		
	red	green	blue
red	red	dark brown	dark purple
yellow	red	green	black
blue	black	green-blue	blue

Special lighting effects

Special lighting effects

Gauze (or scrim)

Stunning magical effects can be created by gradually reducing front light on a gauze (or scrim) and simultaneously bringing up back light on a scene or person behind. Solid walls simply melt away and a new scene or a character appears. This can be great for suggesting ghosts or someone who is far away, or in another scene altogether, faces appearing on a television or monitor, or characters in a dream or a different time zone (a gauze transformation might create just the right special effect for a look into the future, as when a character visualizes what might be).

The position of the lighting and where actors must stand or move has to be carefully planned, especially if space is limited, and will need careful adjustment and rehearsal when everything is in situ in the final stage of rehearsal.

This is really one of the most simple of special effects but is also one of the most stunning if done well.

Tips for using gauze effectively

The steeper the angle of light illuminating the gauze, the better the effect.

Make sure as little as possible of the front lighting can pass through the gauze; you do not want to light up any upstage areas before the transformation or the effect will be diminished.

It may be helpful to hang black fabric behind the gauze that can be drawn or flown away immediately prior to the effect, especially if – when actor(s) are taking up their positions behind the gauze or stage hands are changing the scenery – their movement or shadows might be detected.

The characters or scenery behind the gauze will need to be lit by equipment rigged upstage of the gauze. The timing should be very precise so that the lights are brought up on the new upstage scene at exactly the same time as the lights on the gauze in front are dimmed.

The gauze (or scrim) can be painted to blend in with the rest of the scenery, if required, so that the audience have no forewarning that this magical change will take place.

The gauze itself comes in two commonly used types of weave. An open-weave gauze is the best for disappearing completely, but because of its open texture, it is harder to paint effectively. A black open gauze is often used untreated. Closer woven sharkstooth gauze is easier to paint and can be made virtually opaque – but is less transparent and harder to 'dissolve' completely away. It all depends on what the specific effect and the lighting angles are.

The thinner the gauze or its surface painting, the steeper the angle of light required to make it opaque.

Bring up light C on the ghostly figure of the boy and dim lights A and B so that the gauze 'disappears' and the boy can be seen clearly

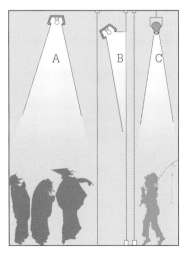

Light B can light the gauze in front for a silhouette effect prior to ghost appearance

Gobos

A gobo is a metal plate with a pattern or shape cut out or etched from it. You can buy or rent a whole variety of these – or you can make your own from thin metal cut just a few inches taller than the gate of the luminate. (Printers' lithoplate is excellent but aluminum 'pie plates' will do if cut very precisely!)

Use a very sharp knife, trimming blade or box cutter. Do not cut too near to the edges or focusing will be difficult.
◆

When a pierced or cut gobo is fitted in front of a profile spot, textures and shapes are projected onto the stage or a drape. Some will project purely abstract 'break-up' patterns while others suggest dappled woodland light, a mountain range, windows, brickwork, fences, jail bars, clouds, leaves, a distant palace, New York's skyline, a castle, Moorish arches, birds, fish and so on. Soft focus is often most effective.

Using gobos is an excellent way of changing a very basic set from one scene to another when fast changes are needed – provided there are enough lights available.

The gobos become very hot very fast so they cannot be changed 'ad lib'. Gloves, or a cloth, will be needed when handling them, even after a very short use. ◆ Moreover the lights may be set up very high or in view of the audience, so this will limit how many gobos can be changed and when. However, if there are enough lights to set up to use in succession (or just a few are required to switch to and from as the action moves back and forth between settings) the gobos will be most effective.

Foliage   *Bushes or scrub*

Bare branches   *Tree glade*

Abstract geometric   *Moon and stars*

Splash!   *Galleon*

Special lighting effects

Spiral swirls

Romantic castle

Geometric swirls

City skyline

Flames

Lightning

Jagged wheel

Rippling waves

Gulls

Church

Arched window

Tiger

Gobos can also be useful in a situation where stage hands are changing scenery in front of the audience: a dappled light effect will 'break up' their outlines and be visually interesting.

Multi-coloured gobo images

Again, much depends on the quantity of the lights available for special effects, but it is fun to create a beautiful multi-coloured lighting effect. Several gobos with different shapes cut out and lit with different coloured gels can be used to light the same place and make up a composite image (in the same way that a printer prints different coloured inks on top of each other or a lino-cut is created from several layers of images or shapes in different colours).

So it is possible to create a stained glass window with different coloured glass – a national flag, dappled leaves in russet and gold, a Christmas tree with coloured lights, and so on.

Chasing gobo images

As well as making interesting patterns of light, you can try using a series of slightly different gobos on different lanterns and flashing each one in turn so that they 'chase' each other to create moving images (like making an animated flip book). This method can be used to suggest any repeated pattern – such as a cascading fountain, wildly waving tree branches, or a ship tossing in a storm.

Glass discs

Moving images can be simulated with painted glass discs set in front of a projector. These can be purchased if their use is likely to be frequent – or rented, if only a one-time requirement. They will create effective clouds, snow, water, rain, smoke and fire (also see pages 50-53).

Green *Yellow*

Blue *Red*

White *Total image*

Cut out a window shape with a modelling knife

Skies

Skies

Cycloramas

A cyclorama is, ideally, material that is hung across the rear of the stage to use as a straight or curved backdrop which can be lit in many different ways. (There is more information on the various ways a cyclorama can be hung in the Sets and Scenic Effects section on page 67.)

If you do not have room for a cyclorama, even a plain white wall can be lit effectively with different colours and effects to create the impression of space and light. The main problem with walls is that bright light will show up every imperfection on the surface and any bubbles, bumps and cracks will undermine the spatial effect of a clear blue sky or seem odd in the middle of clouds.

Sunsets and sunrise

Bottom light on a cyclorama can be used to create very effective sunrises or glowing setting suns. Because the most intense light focuses on the base of the backdrop, a very convincing illusion of distance can be created. Use a ground row piece of scenery set just in front of the cyclorama to conceal the lights and light this area. If, say, three different colours of light can be set there then it is possible to light the sky at different times to suggest sunrise, daylight and sunset.

Make sure a sunset spot is less powerful than the sun it is replacing, and arrange to darken the sky too.

It is also possible to achieve a good sunrise effect by placing a flood on its back (or more than one for a bigger effect) and simply laying strips or solder

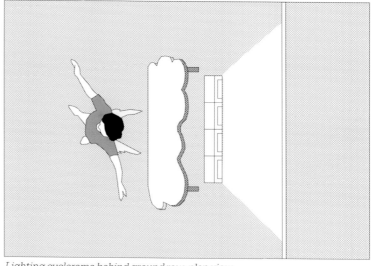

Lighting cyclorama behind ground row: plan view

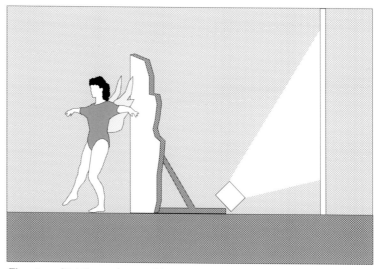

Elevation of lighting and set positions

Three colour wash arrangement

across the top of the flood to turn it into a gobo with a sunburst pattern of rays streaking out. (See also Light boxes on page 56.)

Lightning

Often this is most simply achieved by a few staccato flashes of white light from an overhead batten.

Strobe bulbs (plugged into a strobe unit) or photoflood lamps will work very well, as they both give off a brilliant white light.

There is also a forked lightning effect available which uses a flicker wheel and a slide. It is possible, by using complicated turntables and pivoting in a stand, to make the forked lightning flash in different places, but usually one good forked flicker plus the photoflood flashes and a loud roll of thunder from the sound department works really well. Considerable time can be consumed in trying to perfect multiple forked flashes, time which is out of proportion to the value of the finished effect. Keep it simple – and get it right!

These photoflood flashes also will be most effective if you need a flash before a blackout – say for a transformation scene or whenever you want to 'blind' the audience for a brief moment. A very bright flash beforehand will make the blackout even more effective.

Stars

Stars can be imitated by a gobo or a star slide in a projector but check distances and ensure that the stars do not end up grossly oversized.

Alternatively, tiny pea bulbs or clear Christmas tree bulbs can be wired up and then pierced through a 'star cloth' hung at the back of the stage. Be sure to leave enough space around the bulbs so that they do not overheat and go out. A gauze hung downstage of these will produce a wonderful shimmering effect.

A galaxy of hanging stars can be suggested by suspending clusters of foil balls on black thread and then lighting these by side, top or back lighting. A narrowly slotted profile spot will crosslight these well. They will then twinkle very effectively as they move

in any slight air movement. Make sure they are not exposed to any gale-force draughts, though, or your galaxy will end up in a confused tangle!

Holes may be cut out of any dark drop or piece of scenery. If you then brightly light a pale blue cyclorama close behind it, a starry sky will glow on a darkened stage. You might also try using strips of foil or tinsel behind the drop so that the stars shimmer – or hang behind each hole tiny mirrors which will move in the air current and twinkle beautifully.

Fibre optics can also produce a myriad of very pretty stars from a central source. Fibres can be sewn onto a drop or set on scenery covered in black velvet.

Shooting stars or comets

To create the impression of a moving celestial body, rig a light box unit to slide down a fine metal cable. Flashing lights can be powered by a motorcycle battery. If the sky is filled with smoke and a par light (see page 18) shines from the rear end, a trail or tail can be created. (Page 56 gives more information on light boxes.)

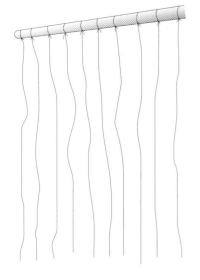

To make a twinkling starry sky, attach lengths of strong black thread to the stage bar. Create a galaxy by twisting aluminium foil around these threads and then make a pleasing random effect by looping up the threads to crisscross so the stars are scattered

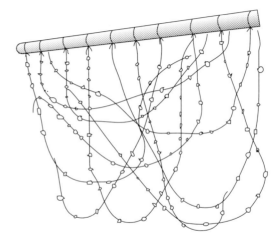

Skies

Moons and moonlight

Moons can be created by projecting through a gobo cut to the appropriate moon shape. Make sure the angle of the projection is correct, especially for a full moon, so that the moon is properly round and does not assumed a squashed egg shape. (See also Light boxes on page 56.)

If possible, for some degree of realism, make the moon rise on the opposite side of the stage to wherever the sun was supposed to be. Meanwhile, the sky can be made to appear somewhat blacker by adding just a little blue, but keep it minimal.

If moonlight has to pour in through a window, it is generally best to make this a 'special' light rather than trying to make it part of the general rig. Then you will be able to adjust angles and colours to achieve exactly the effect you need.

If you are trying to achieve a parallel moon beam in an outdoor scene, a single Fresnel without its lens may work well. Although of a low intensity, moonlight is actually very white and cold and creates strong black shadows. If the scenery can be black and white too this will add considerably to the black and white effect.

Clouds

Fine mesh can be used in gobos to create a fascinating speckled effect that is less bland than a straight cut-out shape. This can work very well with clouds.

Mesh used with a cloud gobo

A suggestion of clouds moving uses the gobo 'chasing' technique outlined on page 47, where similar images follow each other in quick succession.

Professional moving cloud effects (the clouds are painted on a glass disc) can be purchased or rented and then projected. The glass, painted image is turned by a motor inside the special effects unit – which is fitted to the front of the projector before the lens is fixed in front. The effect is beautiful as clouds move across the sky drop. If two projectors can be used, with one running at a slightly faster rate than the other, then the clouds will move across each other and give a very realistic three-dimensional effect.

Ensure angle of projection is correct so the moon is properly round, and not oval

Fluffy clouds

Streaky clouds

Simplistic clouds

Cloud outlines

Cloud effects are available in a variety of forms – there are fluffy pretty summer ones, storm clouds and thunder clouds. You may wish to combine the first two.

Fleecy clouds work best on a blue backdrop and should be run fairly slowly. Stormy ones may run a little faster. This three-dimensional effect can be further enhanced, if stage space allows, by placing a gauze (or scrim) just downstage of the back cloth, cyclorama or back wall. The projected images will then show on both layers – the gauze and cyclorama, as the light passes through the gauze mesh. This looks terrific!

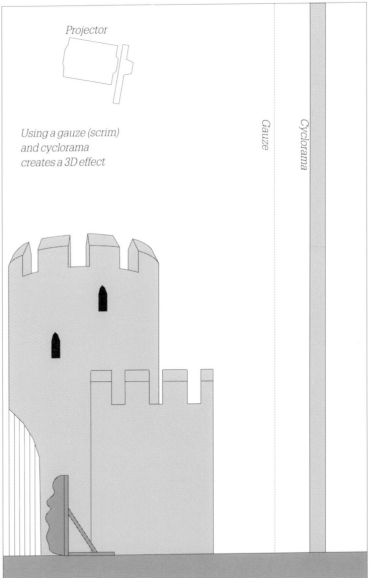

Projector

Using a gauze (scrim) and cyclorama creates a 3D effect

Gauze

Cyclorama

Skies

Clouds and moons

Quite often a moonlit scene will be given even greater impact if clouds can appear to pass across in front of the moon. However, if the moon has been created by a conventional profile spotlight with a gobo, then any projected clouds will not work as they cross the moon. You will need to make positive and negative masks of the moon shape from card or lithoplate.

(For the negative one, paint the moon onto clear acetate so this can be easily taped into position). Combine these with identical cloud effect discs.

Two projectors are needed. One projector with the positive mask will project the moon and the clouds that pass in front of it; the other negative one will project the clouds that cross the surrounding 'sky'. Fit the masks to two projectors that are lined up per-

fectly so that the positive and negative moons are projected into exactly the same position and overlap precisely. The images of the clouds from the two projectors may not always match exactly at the points where they meet the moon edge but the effect will still be convincing.

If the positive moon projector is set at a higher intensity than the negative one, the result will be even better.

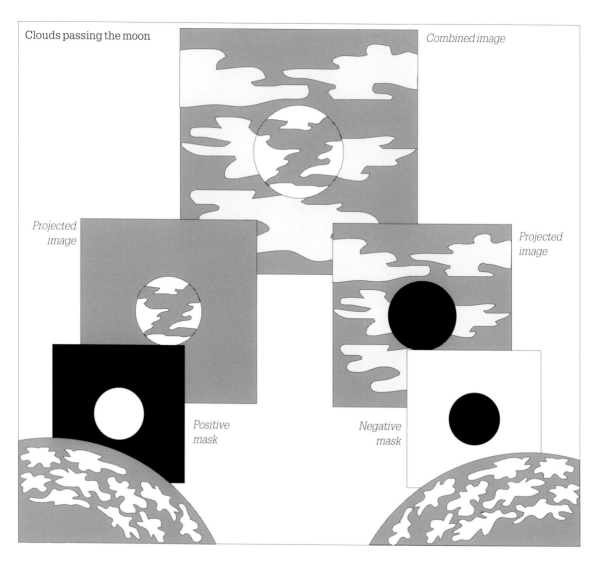

Clouds passing the moon

Combined image

Projected image

Projected image

Positive mask

Negative mask

52

More projected effects

As well as clouds, similar effects units can be used to simulate fire, waves, running or rippling water, snow falling or smoke. These are all fun and very effective. They can be projected onto a cyclorama or any drape so will work very nicely for scenes set halfway upstage or even in front of the tabs. Much depends on the colours, inevitably, and these effects can look very different against light and dark backgrounds.

Of course, mechanical snow effects, as opposed to lighting, work very well indeed (see pages 94-95) but lighting effects do have the advantage that there is no cleaning up afterwards!

It is always worth experimenting with these effects at various speeds, with different colour filters, onto all sorts of surfaces – as well as running them upside down and sideways – to see what can be achieved. Interesting abstract patterns emerge which might be useful to note down for future use.

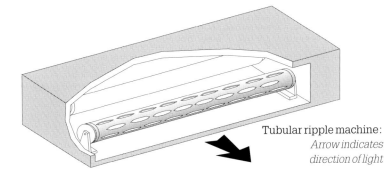

Tubular ripple machine:
Arrow indicates direction of light

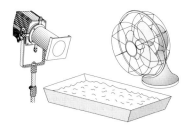

A fan rippling water and the right lighting angle will make the ripple effect reflect onto the stage

A few tips on projected effects:

Snow

A high definition lens will help to give sharper images of snowflakes and will work well on a black background.

The snow looks more convincing if it falls at a slight angle and will work very well on gauze.

Avoid wide-angle lenses on a snow effect or the snow may end up looking like tennis balls!

Wave and water effects

Do not take wave effects right up to the horizon or the scale will be wrong and begin to look very odd.

Remember that a running water disc can be used vertically or horizontally.

Over and above projecting water effects on discs, a ripple machine might also be used. This is a special projector designed specifically to create rippled patterns. A light is directed to shine through a rotating metal tube into which ripple patterns have been cut. This is especially good for rivers and streams.

A wave machine uses fluted glass pieces that move up and down within this special effects unit to give the impression of gentle waves rising and falling on the surface of the sea. This will work well on a backdrop or on the stage floor.

A very cheap way to achieve ripples is to use a tray of water, direct a fan onto this so the water undulates gently and aim a spotlight into it. If this effect can be reflected onto the stage, it will work very well.

Rain

Simulated rain effects are achieved by a disc that is largely black but with a few scratches in the black surface to let light through. This effect is best confined to a small area.

If it is necessary to fill a larger area, use narrow beam lamps with blue filters, pointing straight down, to achieve the most convincing effect.

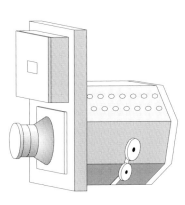

A projected sea wave effect works especially well on the stage floor

More projected effects

Flame and smoke

Flame effects usually include some smoke so there will be darker areas of patterning too. A bright light is vital to make the flame areas work well, so, just like the rain, this effect works best used in a small area with a good reflective surface.

Flame discs can run at different speeds, so experiment first to see what speed best suits the effect you want.

A motor-driven flickering flame disc can be used on a Fresnel spot to suggest a fire in the distance or off stage.

A high speed drum with a 1kw lamp will work well for a flaming effect when space is tight and the effect has to be very close to the object on fire.

Some discs purely create the effect of swirling smoke. These should be run quite slowly.

Try running a smoke disk sideways for a good fog effect. This is especially effective when played onto a gauze.

Projecting slides

This can be an exciting way to give a professional flourish to a production. Make sure the projector can be fixed safely, without dangerous trailing cables, especially as it may need to be rigged up high and at an angle so as not to shine on the actors. It goes without saying but let's say it anyway: if you are using slides in a carousel, make sure that the transparencies are all in the correct order – and the right way up!

Back projection is easier and can be very effective, but small stages do not often have the available space.

Large-scale 'slides' can be created by painting with a suitable ink or a photographic 'painting-out' substance such as 'Photopak' onto thick Perspex or glass. Alternatively some coloured Cinemoid, gel or plastic can be cut to shape like a collage and built up into whatever design is appropriate.

A few tips on projection

Make sure the images are crisp and bright. Use as powerful a projector as possible and avoid too dark pictures.

If possible, use a wide-angle projector lens and large slides so that the projector can be closer to the 'screen' and will give a brighter, bigger picture.

Beware of light spill from elsewhere diminishing the effect – slides will work best of all in a dark setting.

Experiment with angles to avoid distortion of the images.

A projection system can be very good for duplicating actual televisions or monitors – for example, in a space ship, images of other craft or galaxies might appear, or messages might be displayed; for introducing emotive images relevant to a play, such as World War One photographs in *Oh, What a Lovely War* or illustrations from *Alice in Wonderland* for a play about Lewis Carroll; for displaying the words of a song for the audience to join in and sing, or Boo and Hiss signs for a villain in a melodrama. At the top end of the scale, if you are lucky enough to have a generous budget, superlative equipment and lighting expertise, entire sets can be created with projection!

Entire scenic backdrops can be created by skilled projection

Dedicated special effect lights

Ultra-violet light

This can be combined with fluorescent paint on the sets or costumes or fluorescent make-up to give magical effects. Be careful that there is no light spill onto the stage from anywhere else and use only a stage UV light (Never use a medical lamp which may damage skin or eyes.) ◆

There are many exotic possibilities. White skeletons glow and perhaps remove their bones one by one, fairground lights sparkle in the dark, ghosts dance in a churchyard, animals' eyes appear gleaming in the jungle and a huge spider's web radiates out of a nightmare scene. Scenes can change magically as normal stage lights fade out and invisible fluorescent painted images suddenly glow under the ultra-violet light.

Do not flood the stage with intense ultra-violet light or all sorts of unwanted fluorescence will occur, especially newly washed clothing as the light picks up fresh detergent! One 125 watt lamp will suffice for a small stage and two for a larger one. Footlights can be used for this.

Surfaces painted in coloured fluorescent paints glow in rich luminous colours under ultra-violet, so this can be used as a decorative effect too – in which case high intensity lights can be used.

Fluorescent paints can be used to make part of a scene or a prop glow in a situation where conventional lighting is difficult – for example, if back projection is being used and front lighting spill would kill this effect, a carefully positioned UV light will light only what is required and has been painted accordingly.

The Indian Rope Trick can be simulated against black drapes by painting the lower section of the rope in fluorescent paint and the top in black so that the climber appears to be in mid air beyond a certain point – or might disappear altogether if dressed in black with fluorescent strips and then moving out of the ultra-violet lit area as he or she ascends.

Spotlights and follow spots

Isolating an actor in a spotlight is always very dramatic. Its most obvious use is when a solo artist is singing or a strong character or a pair needs to be set apart form the rest of the scene. But spotlights can work in many other ways too. Switching from one actor to another by lighting each individual in turn can change a conventional scene into something very dramatic. It can become very stark, as black and white contrasts highlight the drama. Alternatively, more and more faces might be lit until a veritable crowd is gradually lit and accumulated. Or coloured gels can give a different emphasis altogether: the good fairy in pantomime or children's theatre is conventionally lit in soft pink and the demon in eerie green or fiery red.

A follow spot is simply one that is able to swivel and can be moved by the operator during performance to follow a particular actor – or perhaps to pick out members of the audience!

Flashlights (torches)

If a complete blackout is possible, actors or dancers dressed from top to toe in black can achieve magical effects with coloured flashlights that swirl and mingle, sparkle out from the blackness or flash off and on.

Strobe lighting

This can be used only for a short period of time as it effects the sense of balance and may induce epileptic fits in those who are susceptible. (A warning about the use of a strobe and the timing of this will need to be displayed in the foyer and put in the programme so anyone who might be affected can take evasive action.) ◆

However, handled responsibly, the flashing strobe light can give a very dramatic result, seeming to make actors move in a very rapid jerky way, as in an antiquated silent movie.

This can be used to add to the humour of a scene or indeed to mimic an old film. It can also serve to have a generally disorientating effect and might be very effective in a shipwreck storm scene, a battle scene or in a thriller to add drama to a murder, such as a silhouetted 'stabbing'.

Overhead spotlight highlights central character in a lit group

Dedicated special effect lights

Light boxes

Special light boxes can be created to achieve all sorts of optical effects restricted to a small area.

The light box is generally a wooden or metal box with a lamp or lamps wired inside it and the front cut out to make the shape or pattern required.

Cool strip lights will work best if the box has to be narrow. Pearlised or silver-topped (reflector-topped) bulbs will help diffuse the light if domestic light bulbs are used.

It is best if the front of the box is made of strong cloth and then different fronts with cut-outs from wood or black card can be attached to this so it becomes a really versatile piece of special effects equipment.

A neon sign might be simulated by using coloured bulbs or coloured gel set between the light source and the front of the box. A frosted gel will help avoid hot spots.

The cut-out might be a simple circle for a sun or a moon effect, or the large star over the Bethlehem stable in a nativity play.

The box might be concealed within the scenery if it is going to stay put throughout the scene, or it can be hung behind and right up against the cyclorama.

The effect of a setting sun could then be achieved by lowering the box slowly as the colours are made to fade from, say, light yellow to golden amber. In the same way, the moon could rise in a night sky!

Light curtains and lasers

A light curtain

A light curtain can be produced by a row or batten of Par lamps rigged close together and at a steep angle to give an intense sheet of light. Smoke can then be wafted into the 'curtain' to give it a really dense appearance. Meanwhile, any dust particles that are floating in this curtain of light will make the effect even more solid and so create a veil behind which scenes can be changed or through which characters may materialize as if from nowhere – a really magical effect.

If you have the space and the necessary number of Pars, a row of light curtains, one behind the other can be used, each in a different colour.

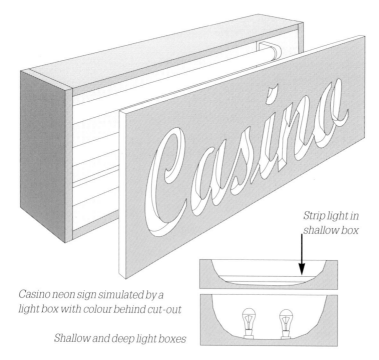

Casino neon sign simulated by a light box with colour behind cut-out

Strip light in shallow box

Shallow and deep light boxes

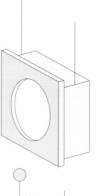

A moon box: A diffuser cloth in front of the light box stops the lamp filaments showing. The moonbeam can be made soft- or hard-edged by setting the cloth at varying distances from the light box

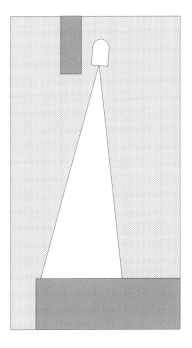

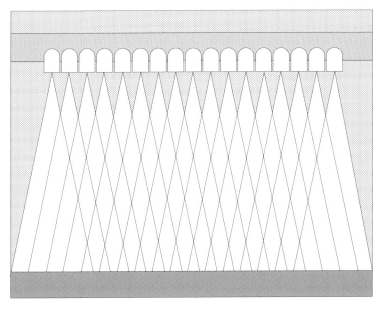

Side elevation of light curtain and front view of a light curtain

Lasers and holograms

Lasers produce a narrow, intense, parallel beam from a low wattage and compact laser 'gun'. Mixes of laser beams in different colours have long been the stuff of pop concerts and work extremely well when used to simulate the music rhythms visually. When lasers are used to record three-dimensional information onto a photographic plate, then a hologram is created.

◆ High-powered lasers can be used only by experienced operators and there are health and safety regulations controlling this. Your local Health and Safety Department (or the Federal Food and Drug Administration) will help and advise.

The less powerful kinds of laser, however, can be used by amateurs, provided the instructions are followed carefully. Used sensibly they are safe – and do give stunning effects. So far as most groups are concerned, at present lasers remain an exciting possibility for the future, rather than part of the conventional lighting schemes. But they're well worth considering for a spectacular finale or as a way of creating a fire effect when filled with red swirling smoke.

A few points

Small neon lasers are inexpensive and easy to secrete within a set.

They are either switched on or off, so they work best in short scenes or if their introduction can somehow be veiled by, say, a light curtain.

Smoke or dust will be needed to capture and reflect the light.

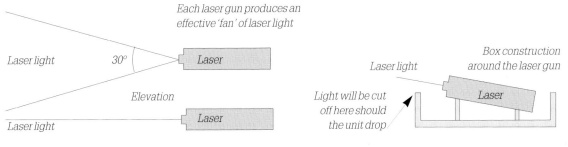

Plan view

Each laser gun produces an effective 'fan' of laser light

Laser light   30°   Laser

Elevation

Laser light   Laser

Laser light

Box construction around the laser gun

Laser

Light will be cut off here should the unit drop

Shopping around and safety

Shopping around

Christmas tree lights and other useful paraphernalia

Many effects can be achieved with simple 'household' articles. It is worth exploring stores that sell electrical goods, hardware, do-it-yourself tools and automobile spares to see what might be needed at some time. You may not be in a position to purchase speculatively, but make notes of what is available and the relevant prices for future reference.

Disco mirror balls

Suspended centre stage and then lit, these multi-faceted balls cast glittering patterns over the stage below and are excellent for suggesting fairyland, for ball scenes, grand finales and any other celebrationary events.

Check out:

1
Long tubes of chasing lights: great for space ships, fairgrounds and so on

2
Fibre-optic effects

3
Christmas lights of various kinds

4
Flashlights (torches)

5
Candle-shape bulbs

6
Glow-in-the-dark effects

European wiring

Yellow green
or
bare copper
Earth wire

Blue
Neutral wire

Brown
Live wire

Black Neutral wire
and
Red Live wire
not used on appliances
but still used for circuit cables

USA wiring

Green
or
green and yellow striped
or
bare copper
Safety ground – earth wire

White
or
natural gray
Neutral wire

Black
Hot-live wire still used for circuit cables: second hot wire may be red or blue

Safety factors

Check and service cables regularly. Make sure they are in good order and fully insulated.

A planned programme of inspection and testing of all equipment should be undertaken regularly and records kept of this.

Phase terminals, and any other such equipment, should be covered to prevent anyone touching the live parts.

Metal casings or exposed metal parts of any equipment should be electrically connected to earth to ensure that they are safe.

Protect circuits with the correct size and type of fuse or circuit breaker.

Always use the correct type and rating of fuse in all the equipment.

Do not overload the system. Always check the capacity.

Check how heavy a load your dimmer/wiring system is designed to carry: it may be no more than 5 amps. You might, for example, need a separate dimmer and cable to control a projector. Never run a 2000W load through a 5 amp system. You may damage both cable and connectors and overloading increases fire risk.

Ensure the cables used are the approved kind and can carry the required current loading.

Label all plugs clearly.

Check the lights are securely fitted.

Make sure safety chains on lights are properly in place.

Keep all cables well away from any heat sources.

Use good safe ladders or scaffolding when rigging. Never balance precariously.

Sets and scenic effects

Scenery makes a huge contribution to the setting of a play and is a vital element – not to be overlooked when thinking through potential special effects and how to create them.

During the eighteenth and nineteenth centuries panoramic cycloramas and trick scenery, often involving huge machinery, were considered a major theatrical attraction, while today's musical productions like *The Phantom of the Opera* and *Les Miserables* are renowned for their exciting visual effects, not to mention the spectacular staging often used in operas and ballets. Small stages impose limitations, of course, but it is amazing what can be achieved by an imaginative set designer – even in a tiny space or in street theatre or festival productions. There are many excellent books on set construction for further reference and, hopefully, inspired by some of the ideas suggested here, most companies should be able to find ways to introduce a fresh vitality into their scenic effects.

In the beginning

Using the team effectively

The most magical changes on stage are generally a combination of scenery, lighting, sound and often props as well. Rarely can the lighting team or the set designer achieve the best results in isolation. And if special effects are to work well, then the combined efforts of many of the backstage team will need to come together at the right time in the right way.

A good producer will be aware of this and will have highlighted the areas in the script where this sort of special magic is required so that before the set designer is let loose on the initial plans, he or she will have been thinking about these special effects, discussing them with the producer and other relevant back stage personnel and asking these sort of questions:

Does a special colour have to be used on the background for this skeleton dance to work properly?

Do we need to use gauze for this transformation scene or does the actual scenery need to move to effect a swift change?

How can we make the beanstalk grow? And is this beanstalk the set designer's overall responsibility or is it up to props?

Are we going to paint a night sky or use a starry sky lighting effect?

> Often the scenery will need to serve practical purposes as well as adding to the atmosphere, especially if special effect devices have to be concealed on stage. The questions may well include something like the following:
>
> **1**
> Will we need the smoke machine for the witches' scene?
>
> **2**
> If so, can it be concealed on stage behind the cauldron?
>
> **3**
> If it is set behind the cauldron, will the witches' moves be restricted in any way?

Too often these sorts of questions are asked too late in the day and problems have to be resolved in a piecemeal way, with the added risk of friction between the various departments who suddenly find their needs vying with each other.

Plan ahead early enough so that the team pull together happily and take pride in achieving a truly dramatic special effect.

How to begin with a special stage effect

No two plays are ever alike, and certainly there is a vast amount of difference between a drawing-room drama box set and the scenery for a ballet, opera or musical.

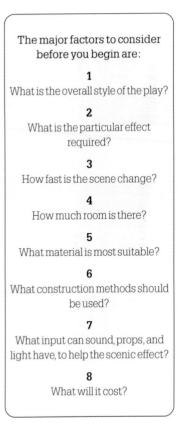

> The major factors to consider before you begin are:
>
> **1**
> What is the overall style of the play?
>
> **2**
> What is the particular effect required?
>
> **3**
> How fast is the scene change?
>
> **4**
> How much room is there?
>
> **5**
> What material is most suitable?
>
> **6**
> What construction methods should be used?
>
> **7**
> What input can sound, props, and light have, to help the scenic effect?
>
> **8**
> What will it cost?

Evaluate the specific requirements of each production.

In the beginning

Plan of campaign:
Ideas and structure

1 Read the script and, if possible, take another look at the venue. It is vital to understand the entire play and the demands and restrictions of the environment where it will be staged.

2 Discuss ideas with the producer. Investigate the themes and concepts before planning any special effects – as these must reflect the overall approach and style.

3 Research useful information and illustrative material.

4 Sketch out rough ideas.

5 Build a model of the set. The designer will need to present a general overview of the set and encompass into this how any special scenic effects will look and work, considering the technical aspects as well as aesthetics. A scale model will prove invaluable for demonstrating and discussing these ideas, especially as special effects will invariably involve other aspects of production, in particular sound and lighting. Being able to work everything out on a model first will make for easier communication between all those involved and there will be less risk of error.

6 Special effects in detail: it may be useful to do drawings of any complicated procedures so that the producer, stage manager and others involved can have copies of these.

7 Order any materials necessary.

8 Construct the special effects scenery along with the rest of the scenery and paint them. The designer will need to implement – or oversee the implementation – of the structure and painting of the scenery. It is vital to ensure that any plans are carefully structured so that the sets and special effects work as a whole.

Safety

Remember that all special effects must be practical, and above all, safe. Take into account fire regulations and the security of all elements.

9 Double-check the progress in other fields.

It is essential to coordinate with the producer, the props team and all the other members of the backstage crew, to check if anything they are doing will affect your special effect and, by the same token, to consider whether the development of your plans will alter theirs. For example, it is no good designing a piece of scenery that blocks a lighting effect.

A coordinated effect on the stage is essential, and if that magical castle or oak tree is to rise from the ground it will need space to do it, with no lights in the way. Similarly, if the crowd are permanently waving huge banners which hide all the backcloth, there is little point in wasting time creating a splendid starlit sky behind them.

A compromise may be needed, but iron out any such conflicts well ahead of the production week.

10 Ensure that stage manager and backstage crew are aware of any set-change details.

11 Technical rehearsals: Special effects can need a lot of rehearsal to work smoothly, so be prepared to give these time.

12 Performances: Give the audience – and yourself – something to remember!

13 Strike and store scenery. Some special effects equipment may need to be returned or stored carefully so that it can be used again.

Special effects can be wonderful. Create scenic magic and it will be enormously satisfying as you bring to life an illusory world on the stage in an exciting and stimulating way. It is fun to stand at the back of an auditorium and share the audience enjoyment of a special effect for which you have been responsible.

Fast changes

An integral part of many productions, a swift change of scene stimulates the audience interest. By the same token, a slow ponderous change will kill interest and break the flow of a play. Fast changes can be achieved in various ways. Try some of the following:

A variety of levels

Changing the levels of height can create the effect of different scenes and will be much more exciting to look at than a flat stage. Different levels stimulate interest and help the producer to group actors in a greater variety of ways. Functional sets can be built with scaffolding and ladders and lit in different ways for different scenes – or areas might be curtained off and revealed in turn. As the scaffolding itself will be permanent for the duration, it may need to be combined with mobile pieces of staging. Care must be taken for the safety of the actors appearing in the raised sections who may be clambering up to make their entrances in unlit or dimly lit areas.

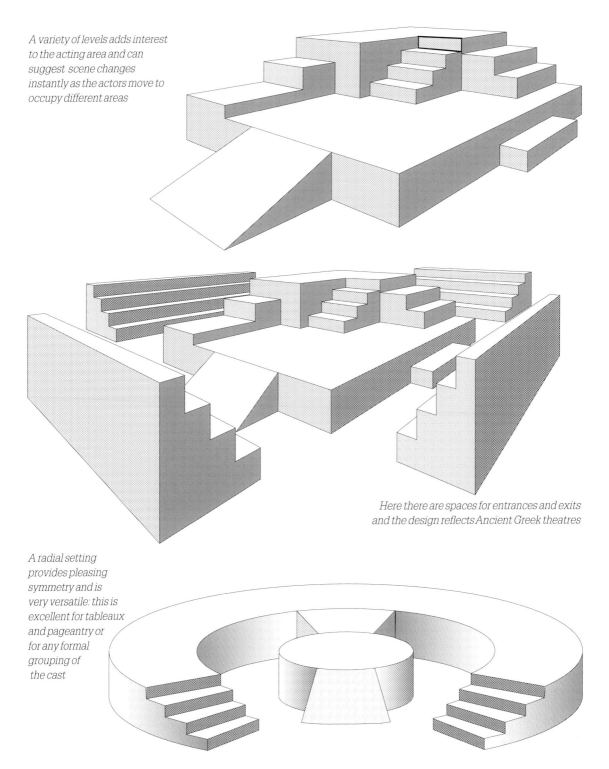

A variety of levels adds interest to the acting area and can suggest scene changes instantly as the actors move to occupy different areas

Here there are spaces for entrances and exits and the design reflects Ancient Greek theatres

A radial setting provides pleasing symmetry and is very versatile: this is excellent for tableaux and pageantry or for any formal grouping of the cast

Fast changes

They will need to have secure footing and may need help from stage hands if it is very dark. ◆

Consider the use of raised areas (rostra) and split levels, trucks (mobile platforms set on castors), blocks, platforms, bridges and steps of various shapes and sizes – both on the stage and leading up to it. Simple arrangements and then rearrangements of these can symbolize in turn palace interiors, castle battlements, a ship's bridge, a courthouse, or whatever.

Simply changing the lighting to focus on a different area may be enough to change the scene or the rearranging of rostra and steps can create an entirely new setting quickly and transform the action from one place to another. Moreover, this is the kind of change that can often be accomplished in front of an audience. Projecting appropriate patterns or designs with a gobo can add enormously to the impact of this kind of setting (see page 45).

Fast changes:
Drapes and hangings

Curtains and drapes can be used in combination with flats and can be very useful for special effects and for fast changes.

A cyclorama or skycloth might be a stretched backcloth (curved or straight) which can be lit interestingly, or a smooth plastered wall. A change of lighting – colour, texture or intensity – on a cyclorama is one of the fastest ways to change a set.

One of the advantages of backcloths and drops is that they can be quickly hung, drawn, or best of all, 'flown' – if there is sufficient ceiling space above the stage and there is a sound struc-

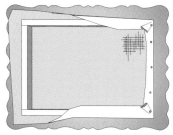

Stretch gauze over a picture frame. Fix with a batten nailed into place

Paint the picture or design on the downstage side

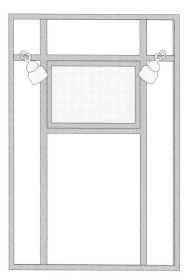

Fit the picture frame to a door flat with filler flats at the side

A light-proof curtain will prevent light spill spoiling the effect

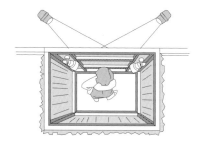

Plan view of transformation 'booth' showing lights fixed out front and above character who is to appear

Images appear and disappear as the lighting switches from front to back. See lighting chapter for more details

ture capable of supporting the extra weight. This can facilitate a fast change. (See page 67 for more ideas and information on cycloramas.)

Gauzes (or scrim) which let light through will allow for 'transformation' scenes and ghostly effects (see page 44 in the lighting section). These can be painted as part of the set and become translucent only when lit from behind. A gauze in front of a backcloth can work very well with special lighting effects and might also be combined with smoke or a light curtain for truly dramatic effects (see also pages 44 and 57).

Glitter curtains give a superb sparkling effect. Different colours are available, or the silver ones can be lit in exciting ways and will change hue beautifully under coloured lighting. Their reflective quality and shimmering movement opens up all sorts of possibilities. Hung right across the sides of the stage, they can also be used instead of wings so that the entire stage is shimmering. They may

need drapes behind them to conceal actors waiting to enter. Check the sightlines carefully. Glitter curtains are marvellous for fast changes. They can be simply hooked up in front of an existing set and create a totally different atmosphere. A witch's cave instantly becomes a palace – or a drawing room turns into a night club.

Aluminium foil can also be used to create a reflective set, especially if you can find the heavier weight varieties that are less likely to tear. Even the least expensive versions become relatively sturdy once glued firmly to another surface. Some glues take a while to dry – so be patient, or use a generous amount of double-sided adhesive tape.

Festoons and swags

If rings are sewn onto vertical rows down the back of a curtain or drape (or its lining) and lines threaded through these, then as the cords are pulled the tabs will rise into a very pretty 'Austrian blind' effect. Pulling the lines at different times and in different

combinations can create a variety of shapes and contours.

Experiment with this beforehand to decide what works best for the particular scene or for an opening.

If the rings run in diagonal lines then the curtains can he raised in the classical swagged manner. They may be flown as well, which looks very effective, but this flying can prove more difficult if space is restricted and the drapes are too heavy or bulky. It can work beautifully with soft muslins and scrims.

Canvas or other cloth

This might be on a roller that can be dropped or it might be flown. It can even be drawn across on a curtain rod or rings.

Paper

Heavyweight paper, such as the kind which is used for photographic backgrounds, can also be implemented. It is available in a choice of colours and widths and can be painted if required.

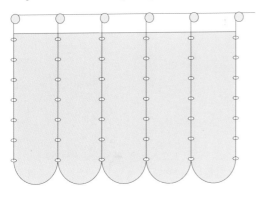

A festoon curtain: lines drawn through rings can be pulled simultaneously or in pairs or groups

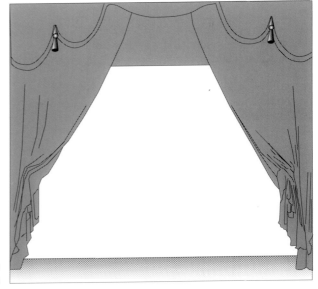

Classic-style swagged tabs frame the stage beautifully as they are drawn back and up

Fast changes

Fast changes with flats

Rotating flats

These are flats that are hung and so can swivel. If they are fixed only at the top and hung from sturdy timber or onto an industrial track, as shown in the illustration, flats can be spun around very quickly indeed for a most effective fast change.

Layering flats

Layers of lightweight flats can be quickly located onto pins on the main base flats. This will work for the rotating flats as well and allow multiple changes rather than using just the initial two surfaces.

Revolves

These are similar to rotating flats but have three surfaces and are in effect triangular columns that are mounted onto a central pivot and can be turned on their own axis. There might be an entire row across the back of the stage or just a single revolve to change one section of the scene – for example, a disappearing door or bookcase, a bed that vanishes when the irate wife arrives to find her husband with his lover, a secret safe – and so on.

Obviously a three-dimensional structure occupies more space than a basic flat, but if the revolves are being run across the back, then the more that are used, the less depth they will need to occupy. However, matching up the parts of a design across a set like this can be difficult, so the results will depend very much on the type of design involved. If it is a row of vertical shapes – like pillars or trees, skyscrapers, panelling or coloured stripes – these revolves can work very well. Moreover, the sharp edges, rather than the flat surfaces, might also be used to create an interesting three-dimensional zig-zag pattern.

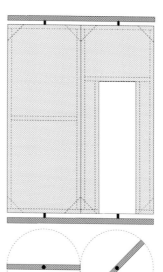

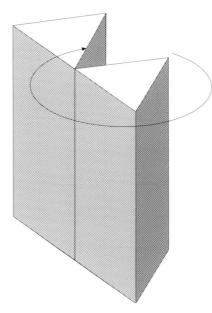

Rotating flats allow for fast efficient scene changes and are very economical on space if you have a shallow stage. They may be hung from an industrial track. Always ensure the flats are left to hang; the bottom pin should be for location purposes only

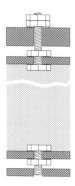

Rotating flats can be hung from sturdy overhead timber, using double locking nuts and bolts with washers

Above MDF board can be a suitable material for the rotating flats. Here the flats are used in conjunction with 'U' aluminium extrusion

Revolves allow for instant scene changes as the three different surfaces are turned to present a fresh facet to the audience. Alternatively, if the sharp edges face the audience, an interesting zig-zag effect can be achieved

Sliding flats

Flats can be set onto on runners so they run like sliding doors.

Hinged flats

Rather like an old-fashioned screen, a hinged set of flats can be painted with scenes on both sides and folded in different ways to create a great variety of scenes. Obviously, after each change, it must be secured firmly with battens, wedges or clamps.

Interior scene: make sure the central hinged flats join neatly. Use an extra strip of canvas on one side to make the join flush. Simply fold back the hinged flats to reveal exterior scene

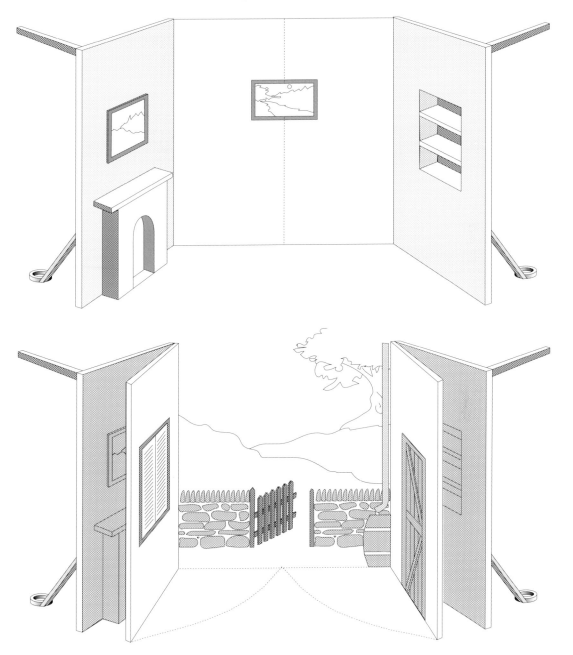

Fast changes

Trucks

A trucked four-sided unit (a truck is a mobile platform set on castors) with each face presenting a different scene can be quickly swivelled around so the appropriate side faces out front.

Filler flats

Mobile flats secured between more permanent ones can be reversible so that one side is for example, a fire-place, and the other a shop counter or a window, a door, a throne, a kitchen range, a bookcase – and so on. A range of these that fit the particular slot might allow for a pair of scenes in each act to be changed very simply and quickly indeed.

Cut-outs and ground rows

Independent cut-outs can also suggest a specific scene. These are straightforward to make and are especially useful in brief front-of-curtain scenes – for example, forest trees, a hedge, a wall, a milestone or signpost, prison bars.

Trees are particularly useful and seem to crop up in all sorts of productions, so they are worth making well and storing for future use.

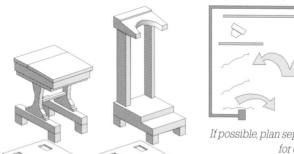

A single platform truck can form the base for a whole range of stage pieces

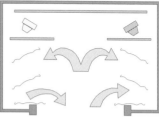

If possible, plan separate entrances for cast and scenery

One wheeled truck can carry four separate scenic devices. Marry up the outlines and paint the interior black to help any silhouette effect

A four-sided truck can be lit from inside. Allow room for access and use ample cable so the unit is mobile

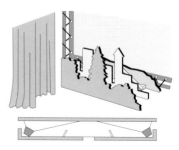

Ground rows can be quickly interchanged to alter a scene

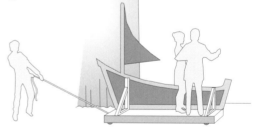

A simple boat shape can be set on a truck and then pulled across the stage by a strong cable – and a strong stage-hand!

Cycloramas

Cycloramas are used as plain backdrops with no scenery painted on them and are often called skycloths because they can be lit to create varying sky effects, horizons, and times of day or weather. They create a magical feeling of space and depth. Generally they are made of canvas which is fairly strong and a good surface on which to paint. Sometimes muslin is used. Avoid seams, as these will totally destroy the feeling of a real sky or space and distance.

The cyclorama may be set into a metal framework and is hung at the top and sides with tapes attached to it or from eyelets inserted into the cloth. Canvas will shrink when sized so do not attach the fabric too tightly before doing this. It can be made taut and adjusted later to create as even and smooth a surface as possible.

Sets should be kept as simple and uncluttered as they can be. Aim to create silhouettes and basic shapes that act as a framework to encompass the sky or lit background, lending form without distraction. This is literally the canvas on which you will paint time and dimension with light.

Kinds of cyclorama

Cycloramas (or skycloths) can take various forms:

The cyclorama might simply be the back wall of the stage painted white.

The cyclorama can be fabric hung straight across the back of the stage.

A wrap-around cyclorama literally wraps right around the stage, encompassing the sides as well as the back.

A tented cyclorama will provide for the same effects from the audience viewpoint as the wrap-around one, but has vertical splits in the lower sections which can be disguised by 'tenting' the material round them. The upstage end of the 'tent' is pulled offstage and the downstage edge is pulled onstage. This 'billowing' of the material disguises the gaps created. These gaps make for easier lighting from the sides, as the lighting equipment can be conveniently masked behind the 'tents'.

Lighting the cyclorama

Lighting the cyclorama in different ways creates brilliant sky effects (See the lighting chapter for more details.) Sunsets, moons, stars, clouds and projections of all kinds come into their own. Any pieces of scenery that are set in front of a cyclorama, such as arches, pillars, building silhouettes, rooftops or trees, should be lit from behind, whenever possible, to give the best effect and sense of space.

Curtains can be combined with cycloramas to create an even greater variety of settings. The drapes may be drawn partly across into different positions to make the changes, hiding and revealing areas of sky, different colours or projected images.

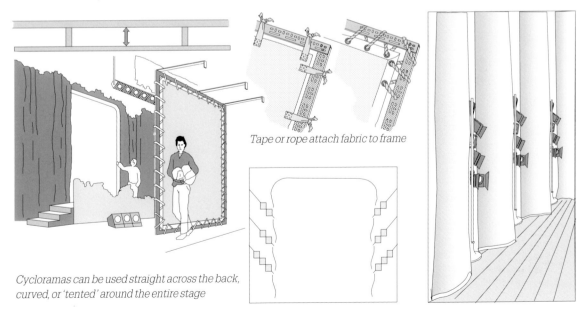

Tape or rope attach fabric to frame

Cycloramas can be used straight across the back, curved, or 'tented' around the entire stage

Tripping, tumbling and flying scenery

Tripping, tumbling and flying scenery

Flying scenery does require overhead space. Traditional theatres have galleries above and at the sides of the stage for securing scenery and lights and for the mechanics for the raising and lowering of these. However, this is not to say that it is impossible to move scenery upwards into a smaller space.

It can be achieved by tumbling and/or tripping, rather than flying. This means creating a system of rolling (tumbling) and folding (tripping) cloth so that it can be kept out of sight in a smaller area. Certainly, some ingenuity may be needed, but here are the basic requirements.

A grid

This is a metal or wooden criss-cross framework, constructed up above the stage, that provides a secure structure for suspending scenery, lights, any props that might need to fly and all the mechanical bits and pieces – such as lines and pulleys – needed to raise and lower these.

An olio back cloth

This device can work well when headroom is limited. Canvas is sandwiched between wooden battens which are suspended from the grid superstructure above the stage. A simple lightweight roller is made by fixing battens onto discs of wood and then the lower edge of the canvas can

be rolled around this long cylinder and held in position with tacks – once the fabric is even and taut. Slim battens or rods can be inserted into the cloth in various places so that it can be lifted from different positions and tripped (folded) if required.

Ropes and pulleys can then lower and raise the backcloth. Using counter weights as well will make the whole process easier, especially if just one person has to handle the change, and do it quickly!

Since the top of the backcloth remains in a static position, no extra headroom is needed.

For flying people, see page 147 in the Special Projects chapter.

Typical pulley arrangement

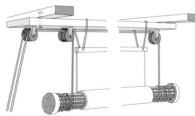

Here rope is slotted into the roller

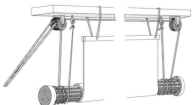

Ropes, knotted to eyebolts screwed into the batten, are then passed around roller

Tripping cloth or gauze will allow it to be both raised and folded away out of sight if overhead space is limited

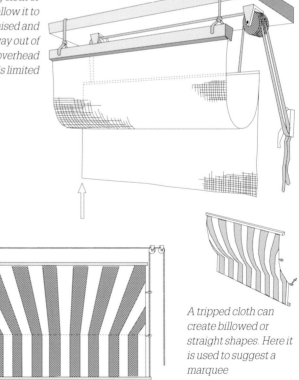

A tripped cloth can create billowed or straight shapes. Here it is used to suggest a marquee

Hints about design and painting

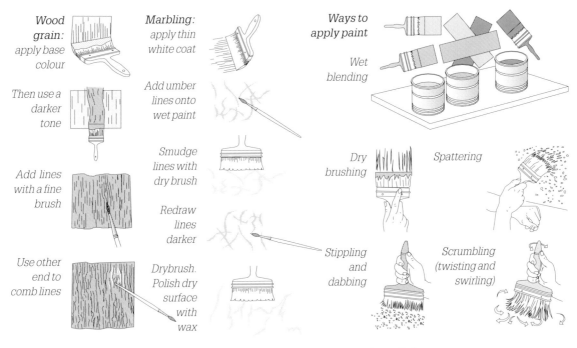

Wood grain: apply base colour

Then use a darker tone

Add lines with a fine brush

Use other end to comb lines

Marbling: apply thin white coat

Add umber lines onto wet paint

Smudge lines with dry brush

Redraw lines darker

Drybrush. Polish dry surface with wax

Ways to apply paint

Wet blending

Dry brushing

Stippling and dabbing

Spattering

Scrumbling (twisting and swirling)

Hints about design and painting

Simple scale drawings

A scale drawing will provide the best starting point for any set design.

1 Measure the area to be painted.

2 Draw the area on paper, say, one tenth of the actual size: complete the drawing within this area.

3 Photocopy or trace this drawing and then the copy can be squared up with a grid (like graph paper), with each square, say, one tenth actual size.

4 Give the flats a white coat of paint When the paint is dry, place the flats on the floor.

5 Then use a chalk line – taut string coated with chalk; this can be bought at a hardware store. Stretch the cord across the flats at the appropriate intervals and pluck it. Lines of chalk are transferred onto the flats to divide these into squares.

6 Mark both the scale drawings and the flats like a map grid – with numbers along the top and letters down the sides so that those doing the drawing can locate which squares to work in. It is then relatively easy to reproduce a rough outline of the drawing, square by square, in pencil.

If you can provide several copies of the squared-up design, then several people can be busy at any one time.

7 The designer can alter or improve this guideline, if need be, before setting about the painting proper.

If time is short, helpers can fill in an outline with paint under the guidance of the set designer – not unlike painting by numbers.

Paint

Water-based paints such as matte household emulsion (or latex) paint are probably the simplest to use. Special colours can be mixed in do-it-yourself stores or paint suppliers.

Be careful if using gold paint or sprays. It can look black under certain lighting angles and may work from only one viewpoint.

Masking with tape

Tape which can be peeled off when the paint is dry is a useful way to make stripes or divide up areas of different colour. This is great for creating panelled doors or fencing, oak panelled rooms, or chequered effects.

Be bold

Do not be afraid of colour or daunted by the size and scale involved in stage scenery. If an effect is to be effective, it may need to be overstated to be appreciated by an audience all the way to the back row.

Perspective

Perspective

A common scenic problem is conveying the right sense of space and distance on the stage, especially a small one. Any company with limited resources staging *My Fair Lady* or *Cinderella* is likely to cry: *How can we achieve the effect of a huge ballroom on our tiny stage?*

This is where perspective, the age-old theatrical device, comes into its own. It is one of the most useful scenic tricks to master and exploit. Used properly, perspective can suggest much greater space than is actually on the stage. Even on a small shallow stage, rooms can seem to have great depth; a library, for example, might have shelves that appear to stretch a long way back; a landscape of hills suggests countryside that rolls away into the distance; archways lead from a palace out into vast gardens.

Moreover, the setting becomes three-dimensional and far more realistic because of this.

The designer must first establish the eye level of the viewer. Is the audience sitting below or on raised seating? Where do you want their eyes to focus? In an outdoor scene, the designer must also establish the position of the horizon.

In the real world, when you look into the distance, parallel lines appear to converge until they meet at what is termed the vanishing point. So using converging lines – for example railway tracks or an avenue of trees – will create the effect of perspective.

But be careful about the immediate foreground! If the perspective is overdone, the actors who stand at the back will look like giants. This however, is something that might be used to your advantage if indeed there is a giant in the play. His height can be exaggerated by this technique, provided no-one else of supposedly conventional stature stands in the same place!

Before you start creating any perspective you must understand the three drawings below.

The starting point is always the eye level or horizon. When making the decision as to where the eye level should be, always take into account both the audience's and the actors' eye level.

The second consideration is the centre of vision which can be anywhere along the eye level. This is marked so that everything vanishes to that point.

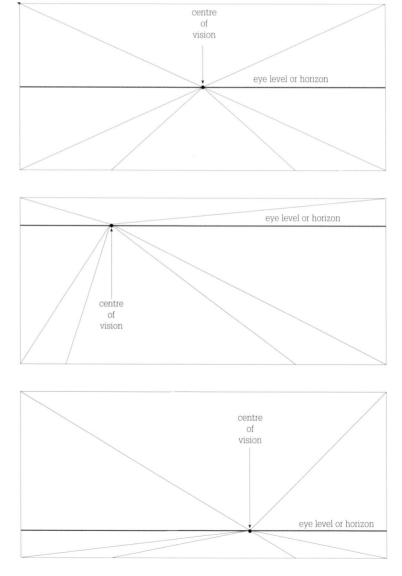

Creating a tiled floor

Before you begin creating the tiled area, mark up the vanishing point at the chosen eye level. Draw ceiling perspective lines from the vanishing point to the top corners of the backcloth, as shown.

Now refer to the numbers in the diagrams for these steps:

1 Sketch out lightly a full-size 'upright' tile, with its vertical line on the centre line of the base of the backdrop.

2 Mark off all the tile widths across the baseline of the backdrop. From these points (points 2 on diagram) draw lines to the vanishing point at the chosen eye level.

3 Sketch out a diagonal from the bottom corner of the backcloth to pass through the top right corner of the 'upright' tile to establish point 3.

4 Now draw parallel horizontal lines. These should be placed so as to pass through the points where diagonal 3 crosses lines 2 – those going to the vanishing points .

5 In order to continue dividing up the backcloth higher up and further back, you need to sketch out another diagonal. This should run through the top and bottom corners of the tiles in the last three rows, as shown, and then be continued on to establish point 5.

6 Now draw further parallel horizontal lines. These should be placed in order to pass through those points where diagonal 5 crosses the lines created at stage 2.

Repeat actions 5 and 6 as required.

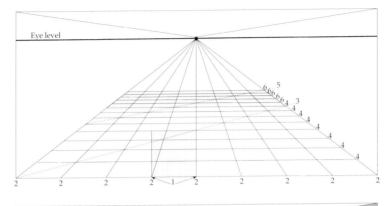

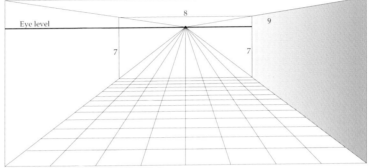

Remember this is the backcloth. If the design is to be continued on to the stage, perspective lines must be followed on the flats or side panels

7 Draw the verticals to form the back wall of the room.

8 Now draw the horizontal line to complete the end of the room where lines 7 meet the ceiling perspective lines.

9 Fill in the side walls with gradated colour to give an appropriate effect of distance.

10 Paint the tiles. Here they are simply black and white; other patterns and colours can be used.

Perspective

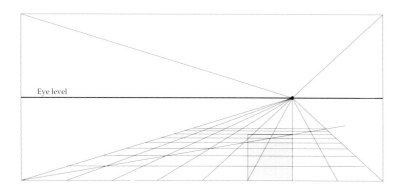

Eye level

If you wish to create a different patterned floor, use the square tile guidelines as created in 1-9 on page 71, but then design your pattern – in this case a central design – to flow out from the centre of the floor area.

Curved lines can be created by using the square grid.

Here the vanishing point has been shifted further stage left.

Establishing the vanishing point and the correct lines of perspective is important when drawing any background scene

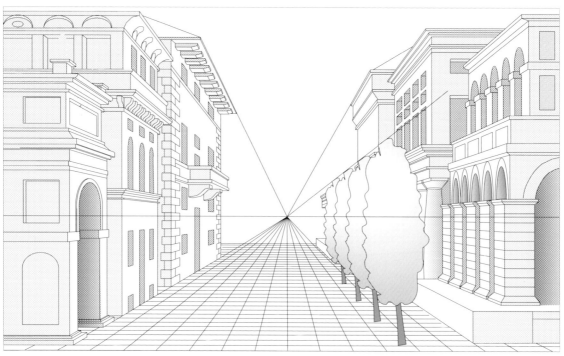

Illusion

Three-dimensional relief effects

As well as perspective in the overall scenery, using relief effects will help enormously in the detail of sets by helping to create a good three-dimensional effect in, say, panelling, doors, columns and walls.

The trick is to draw a clear framework with carefully executed vertical and horizontal lines for the geometric shapes so that these are convincing and then to create shadows in the right places.

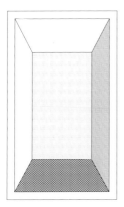

The basic shape for a book case, cupboard or corridor, with centre of vision clearly defined.

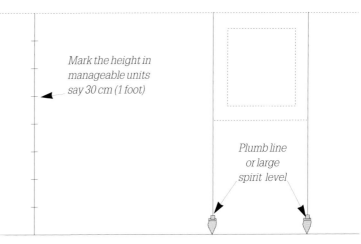

Mark the height in manageable units say 30 cm (1 foot)

Plumb line or large spirit level

1 First draw the outlines. Use a large spirit level or plumb line, measuring up from the stage floor.

2 When drawing windows, recesses or book cases, always use the same eye level and centre of vision.

3 Decide where the main light source is coming from and be consistent in suggesting that source.

4 Treat round windows or circular architectural features in the same way, remembering that if they are on a side wall they must also be in perspective (see arches illustration on page 72).

5 Choose the base colour you want the item to be (say, green for a panelled door). Put some of the colour in two pots. Add a small amount of black and blue paint in pot 1 and a little more in pot 2. This will give you two depths of shadow.

6 If it is felt necessary, a yet darker line can be added to sharpen up any detail – especially a positive edge. If you are not competent with a small brush, use a straight edge and a thick felt-tipped pen.

Above and left Illustrations show how simple it is to create an intricate cornice or moulding.

Illusion

Painting 'in relief'

1 First, identify the imaginary light source so that all the shadows fall in the right direction.

2 Mix plenty of the base tone colour needed. This will be used for the lightest areas.

3 Now make a shade tone by adding a little blue and black – or brown and black – to some of the base colour. (Straight black will make the shade too 'dead'.)

4 Mix a darker tone for the areas of deepest shadow. There may be only a little base colour in this if the

shadows are meant to be very dark.

5 First paint the light-toned areas that are supposed to be facing the light source.

6 Now paint the shade tones, and finally, the areas of deepest shadow, as shown in the illustrations.

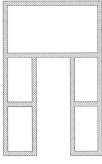

Reverse of door flat. A rail across the door frame carries the hinges

When screwed to rail, shelves should fit neatly inside doorway

Here shelves are below a window

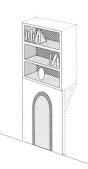

Now the shelves are above an inset fireplace

Three-dimensional leaves

A simple box construction that is very lightweight can be used within a door frame flat to create a simple but fast and effective scene change.

Set a rail across the door frame to which the hinged unit can be attached. The box leaf should be secured with a small bolt or twin latch. Ensure that the overall supporting structure is very firmly secured and braced so that the swinging movement of the construction can be supported

Properly painted, a flat leaf (as shown on right) can assume three dimensional qualities and then be used in the same way to swing on hinges and change the set.

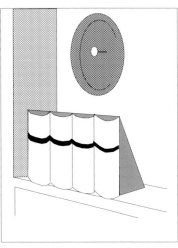

Paper plates and artificial book spines can be used to save time

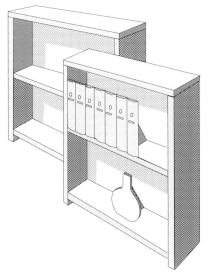

On a flat leaf, paint the shadow effects first and then add the specific items on the shelves. Highlighting the items may help the 3D illusion yet further.

Backpainting for glowing effects

If there is space and opportunity to light a backcloth from the rear as well as from the front, then interesting effects can be achieved. This is especially useful if there is to be a lit area that needs to appear to glow softly – such as a window, fire, sunset or sunrise, moon, stars, and so on.

Coat the back of the cloth with a dark opaque colour, leaving clear those areas through which you want the light to glow. If the backcloth material is very heavy – and there is no objection to its being tampered with ! – it may help to cut out the sections concerned and replace them with muslin or calico that will let the light through more easily.

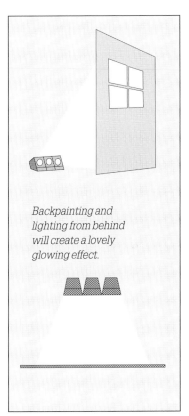

Backpainting and lighting from behind will create a lovely glowing effect.

Textures

Texture can be added for real by applying some other material to the scenery and then painting over this. Check if fire-proofing is needed.

Wood chippings and shavings

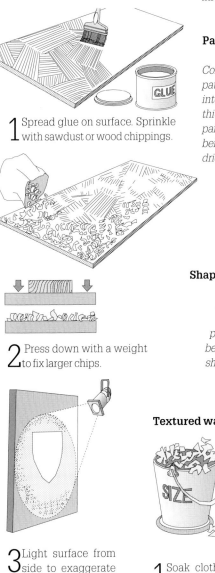

1 Spread glue on surface. Sprinkle with sawdust or wood chippings.

2 Press down with a weight to fix larger chips.

3 Light surface from side to exaggerate texture and shadows.

Sparkle or glitter, gold and silver stars, and so on, might be added to a finished painted scene and can be very effective. For example, a door can be given an instant studded effect by applying gold coloured circles and this can be much quicker than painting them. 'Stick-ons' like this may need extra glue if they are to stay on throughout the show.

Paint textures

Comb patterns into thick paint before it dries

Shape patterns

Interesting collage patterns can be made with shaped wood

Textured walls

1 Soak cloth or paper in size.

2 Arrange pieces on surface.

Illusion

Textures and patterns

Rollers and stencils can greatly speed up the application of textures and repeat patterning. Rollers can be cut into patterns (say, random leaves) or rags wrapped around them for creating interesting irregular tones. Masking tape can also be circled around a roller for making striped patterns. Whether the effect is brickwork, bark, or rows of fleur-de-lis, valuable time can be saved by preparing stencils, blocks or rollers beforehand – and then, several helpers can be working at once.

Moiré patterns

Moiré patterns are enormous fun: all sorts of optical effects are created when stripes and zigzags move across each other. It is possible to do this by painting stripes or radiating lines onto gauze sections and then moving a painted diagonal area of stripes behind this. You can either slide a section to and fro or spin a pivoted circle of radiating lines. This is practical only in small areas but can still look like strange eyes whirling in a forest, wheels turning or dizzy movement in a nightmare scenario.

In fact, all on its own, gauze can create moiré patterns. If one stretched section of gauze is moved in front of another, shimmering patterns ripple across. Once again, experiment. Try using similar gauzes and then those with different textures against each other and see what happens.

Fire and water with fabric

Imaginative use of fabric can create stunning dramatic effects.

Billowing fabric can create the feeling of clouds, water and fire. Rippling

Cut away pattern from stencil card

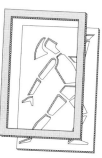

A card frame prevents damage to stencil

Place accurately; then paint through shapes

Repetitive patterns are easy to apply with stencils and look very pleasing

Brickwork: paint light colour and mortar joints

Apply darker patches

Add even darker tones so surface seems uneven

Make designs with pre-cut rollers

Rags around a roller give a random effect

Masking tapes help make even stripes

Illusion

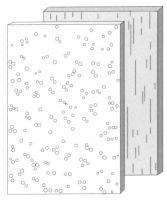

Glue polystyrene to plywood. Draw design with a thick pen

Apply thick paint between lines. Trace lines with hot wire or poker ◆

Or melt unpainted sections by passing over over a naked flame ◆

Roll paint over surface

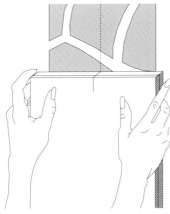

Press painted block down firmly

Make a block of polystyrene 'brick' shapes to print stonework effects

lengths of horizontal fabric across the width of the stage can represent a river or waves in the sea while people and/or props can move across between these swathes – which might be lifted up and over them, or slid away, by stagehands at the side. This idea was used brilliantly in the film of *The King and I* when the king's wives put on a play. The billowing fabric was suddenly stretched taut as snowflakes fell and the river turned to ice. And in a stage production of *The Royal Hunt of the Sun*, the Inca courtiers who wore pointed crowns and had huge cloaks, suddenly turned their backs to the audience, spread these capes wide and then were lit in silhouette to represent the outline of the Andes mountain range. So simple – and so dramatic.

Strips of silk can create a brilliant flame effect when agitated by a blower and then lit from beneath. This can be used on a large scale and still look very good where some lighting effects might appear to be spread a little thin. And scorched blackened strips can look like the after-effects of fire.

Smoke

Real swirling smoke can be used on stage and is created by dry ice, fired smoke puffs or by a special smoke machine. (The techniques are discussed in more detail in the Pyrotechnics chapter.) As smoke rolls across the stage, the scene can be set for misty moorland, the supernatural, the launch of a spacecraft, or whatever. But, beware! If too much smoke is pumped out and the audience are very close to the stage, they may become engulfed as well, so make sure the effect is not overdone or the first few rows will be too busy coughing and wiping their eyes to appreciate the drama of it all! ◆

Moving and mechanics

Moving and mechanics

Most small societies perform in relatively unsophisticated theatres but can still achieve stage effects which add enormously to the impact of the production. There are a number of mechanical aids which are useful and relatively inexpensive for any group to consider, such as trucking scenery on wheels, using overhead tracks to move suspended scenery – as well as a whole range of tabs and drapes. If you do not have room for a trap or lift, borrow the school trampoline and the genie can be projected into mid-air from the wings!

If you are lucky enough to have a stage that is raised sufficiently high, all sorts of mechanical aids can be accommodated which will help move actors and/or scenery into position as if by magic. Combined with a blackout and perhaps with a few pyrotechnics thrown in – flashes, bangs, or whatever – a witch, fairy, genie, ghost or demon can be raised on the lift to appear suddenly from below stage or to disappear again in a flash!

Lifts, traps and moving sections

Lifts

A lift is a means of raising a platform. It may be worked by a motor, such as a scissors lift, where the supports are pivoted like joined scissor blades and so can raise the height when the 'legs' are moved closer together. Industrial chains and sprockets might haul the lift up and down, or it might be a Screw Jack lift that is driven by a system of threads and gearboxes. Obviously the lift must be sturdy and mechanically sound and should be checked over and tested thoroughly before a production commences. ◆

Traps

A trap is an opening in the stage floor. A solid rostrum can be raised to fill this opening and bring the actor into view or lowered so that an actor disappears. An actor may even be projected up into the air if there is enough room below for a decent speed to build up!

Bridges

Bridges can span the entire stage or link sections of this. In effect a bridge is an elongated lift and may or may not be motorized.

Sloats

Sloats are narrow slots allowing scenery to be raised from below stage.

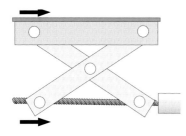

A scissor lift on a screw thread. Moving scissor legs closer raises lift

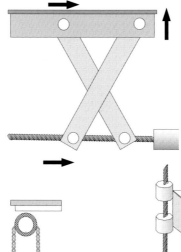

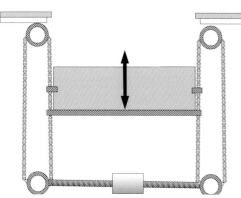

A chain on linked sprockets can raise or lower this lift

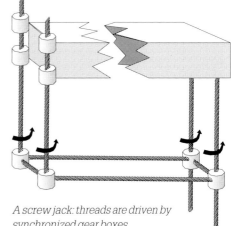

A screw jack: threads are driven by synchronized gear boxes

Moving and mechanics

Travelators

These are moving 'conveyor belt' sections of flooring like flat escalators or the kind of moving floor area found in airports. Even a very small travelator will enable a person to run on the spot, and this can work particularly well if a diorama of moving scenery can be set in motion going in the opposite direction behind the actor.

Panoramas and dioramas

A panorama is a painted scene that crosses the width of the stage. A diorama is a large painted backdrop of scenery which can be lit from behind and which may be moved across the stage. Just like running a film behind the actor, this can add to the impression of movement and changing scenery.

Tracking and rails

Everyone considers tracking as standard for the hanging of drapes and curtains, but these can also be considered for the moving of flats and scenery. Many different arrangements of pulleys and hanging devices exist, and it is best to procure a good catalogue from a supplier to decide what best suits your purposes.

A diorama 'send-up'

If a conventional panorama or moving diorama is too ambitious a structure or beyond the budget (and for a not-too-serious production!) try using a static head-height piece of scenery that traverses the width of the stage: actors can run concealed behind this and carry appropriate cut-out profile pieces of scenery or properties that appear to pass by at great speed. These might be stars or comets for a space scene, cars and buildings for a city scene or desert island palm trees and seagulls for a sea scene.

If this is vaudeville, pantomime, comic revue or the like, the whole thing can played with a vengeance as both the performers in front of the scenery and the hidden actors behind rush on ever faster, the buildings or palm trees eventually overtaking each other.

Space saving bed

A narrow bed in which actors stand saves precious stage space and can be stored flat when not in use

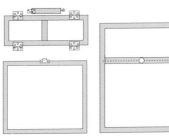

Stage bed is in three sections. A batton and hook link headboard to foot of bed

Magic carpet

A fun diorama: a trucked magic carpet carries actors along in front of scenery

Scenery on the move

Hidden stage hands run with scenic pieces behind scenery that is just above head height

Special Properties

Organization

Generally, when a production is underway, the properties department is busy gathering together coffee tables, cups and saucers, artificial flowers, cushions, umbrellas, buckets, brooms, standard lamps and the like. Props people coax friends and neighbours to part with whatever minutiae of life happens to be needed to dress the particular set or for the actors to handle during the drama.

Special effects would seem to have very little to do with this.

However, along with all these other mundane items, nearly every play needs some complicated or special prop. If the production is a pantomime, farce, musical or revue, then the properties are likely to include all manner of objects that do not exist in the everyday household, such as exploding cakes, collapsible swords, disappearing top hats, giant-sized beanstalks, and magic wands.

Even a conventional thriller may well need secret doors and drawers, guns, knives, or bits of human body! Historical productions cry out for fires and braziers, cauldrons, flaming torches, statues, thrones, firing cannon and so on.

This is when the property department can come into its own and be truly creative. Some help may be needed from lighting and sound departments too, of course. As with the other areas of production, it cannot be stressed enough how vital it is to relate to the other disciplines and to ensure the best teamwork possible. It is important to start making everything in plenty of time, to check if extra help is needed and whether it can all be done within budget.

Before beginning on any specific special property, a few questions need to be asked:

1
What is the style and period of the play?

2
Are there any fast scene changes that complicate life?

3
What will the special props cost to procure, hire or make?

4
Is there anything 'already in stock' that is suitable or which can be adapted?

5
Is such and such a property really part of the set or lighting design? Should I check it out with these other departments?

Plan of campaign for special props

1 Discuss ideas for any special effect props with both the producer and set designer.

2 Research relevant information and illustrative material.

3 Sketch out rough ideas for any special props.

4 Buy any materials necessary.

5 Make or organize the renting of special properties.

6 Ensure that these are approved by producer and/or set designer.

7 Supervise special properties at dress and technical rehearsals.

Check everything looks fine from out front. As with a magic trick, using a special effect prop may take considerable practice by the actors.

8 Organize properties before, during and after the show so everything is ready for the next night, and check that special-effect properties remain in good working order throughout performances.

9 After the show, gather in everything safely, clean and repair as necessary, and return any rented items.

Hints and tips

Make the props fun! Especially in a pantomime or comic revue, absurdity will not go amiss. Then the properties should be colourful, oversized and as humorous as possible.

Be imaginative and resourceful and you will find that you do not need to spend too much money.

Do not waste unnecessary time. Keep outlines and decoration simple and uncluttered. Few things on stage are ever seen that close up.

Check through party shops and joke shops for useful items.

If there are any friendly local conjurors, see if they are willing to join you or to lend their expertise to your group. (See also the section on magic tricks on pages 89-91.)

And,
to help fast scene changes . . .

Be well organized – with every property carefully noted in running order.

Whenever possible, keep properties fairly lightweight so they are easy to move quickly – but always make sure they are stable.

If some part of the property is static and is not moved during the show (say, a row of bottles and jars on a shelf) then these elements can be glued on so that only one integral item has to be moved.

Any properties not being used can be glued in place to save time setting the scene. Leave the ones to be used free, of course

Make plans of the stage and map out property positions carefully, marking the stage floor with sticky tape for fast but accurate positioning. This can be especially important for magical effects when correct positioning and the relationship to audience viewpoints will be vital.

Dramatic changes

This is where the real fun begins. All magicians refer to sleight of hand, deceiving an audience with nimble fingers, and it is a well-known fact that this is best accomplished by first distracting the audience, diverting their focus of attention before the trickery, making them concentrate on the wrong areas.

So it is with special stage effects. Ask the director to suggest that the witch wave her wand in dizzying circles on stage left if you have an awkward manoeuvre with the cauldron on stage right.

Of course the director might opt to plunge the stage into a black-out or screen the mechanics with smoke or flashes of light. All to the good, as these are dramatic effects in their own right and will help to build the atmosphere of magic. Of course, it is vital then to bring the audience attention back to the trick that is being effected, wherever this is taking place. Distract from the 'cheating' element but then focus back on the magic.

Percussion instruments will help, as well. A good drum roll, or cymbal crash can add drama or humour and the sound may usefully cloak the noise that any pulleys, cord, or wheels might be making.

It often pays to capitalize on any problem that arises. For example, the squeaky descent of the large Bethlehem star dropping into place above the stable will make the audience cringe and ruin the magic. Whereas if this squeaking is disguised by the sound of tinkling bells – effectively making the starlight audible – this will add to the effect beautifully instead of detracting from it!

A rising cake or snake

Flat folded fabric can be unfolded and so extended – up or along (see page 82). Also, three-dimensional objects such as a birthday cake or a boa constrictor can be built from fabric stretched over hoops. These hoops will lie neatly on top of each other when collapsed inside the cake tin, snake basket or whatever is appropriate. However, once the hoops are lifted by wire or cord over pulleys, it is surprising just how tall or long an object can grow. If the basket is set over a trap in the stage floor, an even longer snake can be secreted below there. Add a few sound effects, explosions, smoke and flashes to suit the occasion and then enjoy the audience's whoops and laughter!

If the whole operation is sped up and the object is not fixed at the base, the snake or cake might be flown out of its container and right away out of sight. Extra lines fixed from the base of the snake will allow it to be pulled flat again as it reaches the flies and disappears from audience view.

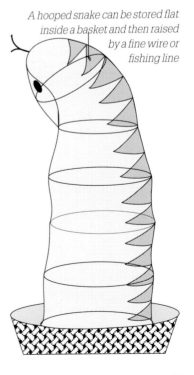

A hooped snake can be stored flat inside a basket and then raised by a fine wire or fishing line

Dramatic changes

Making Jack's giant beanstalk or a magic tower

Things that grow are often effected by tripped or concertina-folded fabric or scenery that rises out of a trucked box that has been painted to look like part of the set, a garden, woodland, or whatever. Hoist the beanstalk, tree or tower by a black cable or fine strong fishing line that will not be obvious to the audience. Properties such as a beanstalk or tower that has to rise from the floor can be created by painting or building up 'collage' on gauze or scrim which, if lit properly, will provide a sound structure but one that is not really visible to the audience. A well supported rope ladder can be slung behind the scrim if Jack has to climb the beanstalk or the prince must scale Rapunzel's tower. Make sure this is securely fixed from a strong vantage point and then the climber can grip this ladder behind the fabric, with hands and feet, from the front. ◆

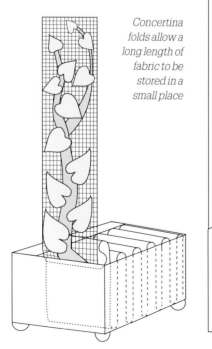

Concertina folds allow a long length of fabric to be stored in a small place

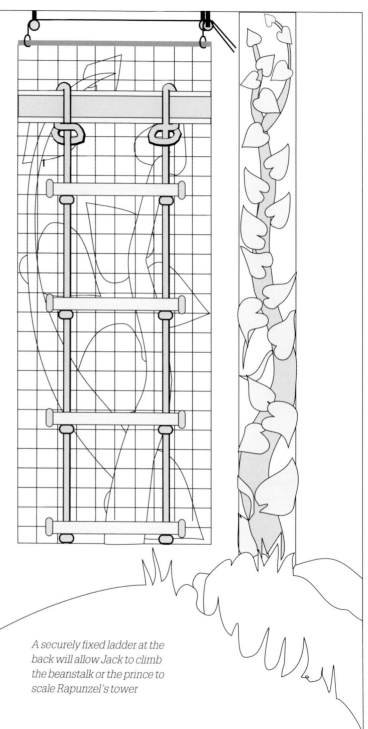

A securely fixed ladder at the back will allow Jack to climb the beanstalk or the prince to scale Rapunzel's tower

Smashing things!   Weapons and wounds

Smashing things!

Explosions

Refer to the pyrotechnics section for information on the actual explosion effects and always follow any instructions carefully. Meanwhile, whatever the prop might be – an oven, an apple pie, throne, army tank or parcel – it will need to be constructed of fairly light-weight material in sections that are designed to fly apart on cue.

Larger items may require the synchronized flying of sections; smaller ones can be held together under tension by elastic bands which will need to be released at the appropriate moment. Velcro sometimes works but only if used in very very small sections so that it pulls apart quickly enough and if its very distinctive noise can be cloaked. Paper fixings can be surprisingly strong but, as any chain is only as strong as its weakest link, are easily broken at the right moment.

Fine twine or wire can be tied to hold the components together and then untied to release them or cut through quickly. In all these cases, human interference is needed. The actors may initiate the breaking up of the prop, or someone secreted behind the set or in the wings may be able to do this, especially if this is a 'strung-up' object: organize the wire or twine release mechanism to be able to be slipped undone or cut from an extension of twine that feeds into a convenient vantage point offstage. Make sure this is where the props team can see what is happening on stage and time the effect accurately.

It can be useful to enclose some kind of 'debris' inside the exploding object or bomb that will fly out once released

and add to the effect. Try crumbled cork or lumps of cork, polystyrene, cornflour, coloured sparkle, ribbons, confetti, vermiculite, peat – anything suitable that is light enough to whoosh out in a cloud – but which cannot hurt either cast or audience. If the explosion device is shallow but with a wide top, then the explosion effect and debris will travel outwards over a wider area.

Breaking furniture

Find a suitable chair, ladder, or whatever and decide which bits need to break. This operation needs to be carefully controlled as undoubtedly some poor actor is going to land on the floor and does not want an unexpected rung or chair leg slicing into his or her arm! Safety must come first. ◆

Separate all the joints and make sure all traces of glue are removed. Decide which parts you wish to fly apart and put these together loosely, by merely pressing into place or using a very light glue. Then make absolutely sure that the rest of the components are very firmly fixed together, because they will come under considerable strain during the 'accident'. This effect will need to be thoroughly tested with the actor concerned to make sure it all works as planned.

Furniture that is not actually going to be used much prior to breaking can be replicated in lightweight materials so – if there is a fight in a cowboy saloon and chairs have to be smashed – these pieces could be made of brittle balsa wood or plywood.

Glass

Trick glass bottles and glasses can be bought that can be safely smashed. These are quite expensive but are

hard to reproduce yourself – and splinters of real glass on the stage is certainly something to be avoided.

Sugar glass products designed to break easily on impact include beer bottles, cola bottles, whisky bottles, wine bottles in clear or green sugar glass, as well as various shapes of wine and beer glasses.

Pseudo glass might be cast in fine transparent wax but this will not make the right sound, so will need to be combined with a suitable well-timed sound effect to attain any semblance of realism.

Weapons and wounds

Slapstick weapons

The word 'slapstick' is originally derived from an actual stick that was used to slap other unfortunate actors! This was a wooden bat, shaped like a sword, that was designed to make a good deal of noise, while actually causing no injury at all. Harlequin beat the heads and bottoms of other actors with a slapstick which had a split or cleft down the middle to amplify the sound. During nineteenth century performances, gunpowder was inserted into this cleft to add to the effect!

While *we do not recommend the hazardous use of gunpowder*, it is certainly worth experimenting with various whacking and smacking noise effects (talk to the sound department) and then creating resonant oversized but harmless instruments of torture and/or safe explosions. (See the pyrotechnics section on page 125.)

This is assuming a humorous approach, but if, say, someone has to

Weapons and wounds

be beaten, whipped or caned on stage during a serious production, much rehearsal will be needed to create authenticity without injury. The actor may need to be suitably padded or protected under the clothing if real contact is intended or is a risk. Nothing looks more amateur than a supposed injury or fight when it is patently obvious that no contact is being made at all. So if the weapon can be made of foam rubber, expanded polystyrene, or the like and actually touch the victim, this will work much better than any 'near-impact' tactics. It can be painted to look authentic and heavy. Good timing of appropriate sound effects, suitable reactions by the victim and blood effects if necessary (see pages 87 and 101-2) will make the whole effect convincing.

If the weapon is not as sturdy as you would like and you are uncertain of how it will withstand repeated batterings, night after night, you might ask the producer or director if it is possible to do a 'slow-motion' or 'stop-go' effect with suitable rhythmic staccato sound and lighting, and then the impact can be quite gentle, while still looking very dramatic.

Custard pies

Classic comedy, circus clown or pantomime slapstick is bound to lead to the hurling of custard pies at some poor souls on the stage. While real custard, meringue or soft whipped cream can indeed be used, it is more likely that the property department will be using an aerosol foam of some kind or another, squirted onto paper plates. While real custard or cream can be a dire mess to clear up and means repeated laundering of costumes, it is at least safe to throw into actor's faces. It is essential when using any substitutes to think about the actor' eyes and make sure nothing astringent is used. Always check the can instructions carefully and do remember that, however tempting simple shaving foam might be, it can sting the eyes unmercifully and be a real health hazard. ◆

All things considered, it is best to buy spray cans of custard pie foam from a theatrical supplier.

Sci-fi and space weapons

While fun ray guns can be readily bought from toy shops, they can also be made from all sorts of household items. This may help ease a tight budget. Keep toilet-roll and kitchen-towel tubes for the basic gun barrels, onto which papier maché can be built if necessary. String or cord wound around will look like 'turning'.

Paint over with shellac mixed with metal pigment – or a suitable metallic spray can be applied. Expanded polystyrene packing comes in all sorts of interesting shapes and sizes that can be cut off to suit your needs. Some glues and paints 'melt' polystyrene, so check the directions carefully and/or experiment on a small area first.

The ray gun can then be decorated with as many knobs and buttons as required and sticky gummed shapes in bright metallic colours can be used for a final flourish.

Conventional guns and rifles

If these are to look authentic as modern weapons or an appropriate historical period, do some research first to establish the basic outlines and proportions. These are the kinds of props that may be used time and time again so they justify some expenditure – of time and energy, as well as of materials.

Every gun has three main components: the lock, or firing mechanism, the barrel – the metal tube that contains the charge and bullet, and the stock – the wooden framework that supports these working parts.

Locks

You may be able to buy a complete lock from a dealer. Otherwise, make one in wood or metal. You can also use the curved section of a plastic coathanger, a curtain hanger, the end of an old key or a bolt (without its nut) glued and threaded onto stout wire.

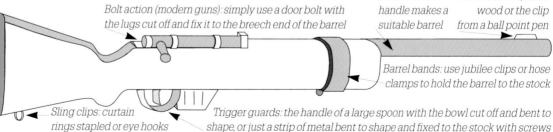

Bolt action (modern guns): simply use a door bolt with the lugs cut off and fix it to the breech end of the barrel

Dowelling or an old broom handle makes a suitable barrel

Sights made from hardened felt, balsa wood or the clip from a ball point pen

Barrel bands: use jubilee clips or hose clamps to hold the barrel to the stock

Sling clips: curtain rings stapled or eye hooks

Trigger guards: the handle of a large spoon with the bowl cut off and bent to shape, or just a strip of metal bent to shape and fixed to the stock with screws

Weapons and wounds

The trigger mechanism for a modern rifle can be constructed from a door bolt with the lugs removed.

Bend a loop of metal to make the trigger guard; or use old scissors handles, D-rings glued together, or pipe wall brackets. You might also cut sheet aluminium or tin but be very careful of the sharp edges. ◆

Stocks

These can be made of wood and need to be cut and styled to suit the period. A scrap table or chair leg might well be adapted.

They might be decorated with dressmakers' frogging which provides the right sort of swirly patterns, coiled string or scrap metal fragments – suitably painted.

Barrels

Barrels can be made from the following materials: doweling, broom handles, conduit, metal pipe, gas tubing or bamboo.

The barrel can be fixed to the stock with jubilee clips or hose clips.

Shorten the barrel and attach a funnel to make a blunderbuss.

Toy guns can be very convincing and should always be considered as a simple option. Cap guns make a good loud noise, even if used purely for the sound effect in the wings, simultaneously as a prop gun on stage.

If you are using a starter pistol or the like, you will need to conform to all rules and regulations and will probably need a license. In the interest of safety, check this out before you are committed to using a gun.

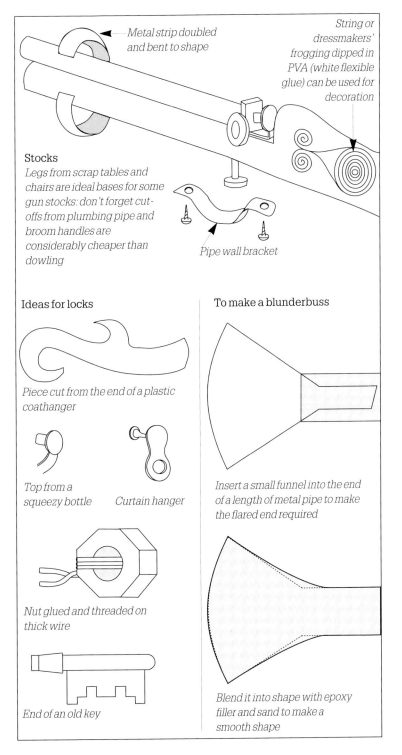

Metal strip doubled and bent to shape

String or dressmakers' frogging dipped in PVA (white flexible glue) can be used for decoration

Stocks

Legs from scrap tables and chairs are ideal bases for some gun stocks: don't forget cut-offs from plumbing pipe and broom handles are considerably cheaper than dowling

Pipe wall bracket

Ideas for locks

Piece cut from the end of a plastic coathanger

Top from a squeezy bottle

Curtain hanger

Nut glued and threaded on thick wire

End of an old key

To make a blunderbuss

Insert a small funnel into the end of a length of metal pipe to make the flared end required

Blend it into shape with epoxy filler and sand to make a smooth shape

Weapons and wounds

Swords and knives

Rapiers, scabbards, swords, cross-bows and the like can all be made from wood and painted to look realistic. Just as with the guns, all manner of household items can be called upon to embellish the basic form – several thicknesses of wire strands wound together, beads, bolts, plastic bottle edgings, felt, plastic mouldings for woodwork, cord and string. Of course papier maché is ideal for creating very specific forms.

Single thickness of wire, or several strands bent with pliers; tape to ply

Front

Nut, threaded on wire and built up with pulped papier mâché

Back

Beads, nuts or shaped pulped papier mâché

Heavy cord dipped in shellac

Front

Thin layer of laminated papier mâché

Glue on a sandwich of cardboard, then cover with papier mâché

Cut a ball in half, or make a chicken wire frame and cover with papier mâché

4mm (¹/₄ inch) ply. Divide in half and paint one half a shade darker

Scabbard

Glue on interior edging at the top using a scrap of plastic cut from a bottle

Leather strap or shellacked felt

Shellac and metal pigment or metal gloss spray

Piece of wood to strengthen base

Making a cutlass blade

Folded litho printing plate with shape of blade inscribed. Cut out and glue together

Handle for sword

Fix two pieces of wood (same width of blade) to the blade with glue or insulating tape. Gilt picture frame wire is bound around the handle to resemble gold

Inflicting a wound

Having made the knife or sword, it may be necessary to appear to inflict a wound with this. A narrow pipette or eye dropper containing artificial blood can be taped against the back of a knife or dagger with a bulb at one end to pump out the blood. This bulb needs to be close enough to the top of the shaft to be easily depressed by the assailant's thumb at the appropriate moment; a steady stream of blood will flow as the knife is drawn along the flesh. If the edge of the knife is the least bit sharp, cover this edge with thick cellophane tape so that the victim does not bleed for real! ◆

A bigger bleed

A larger wound, such as might be inflicted by a sword thrust, can be effected by secreting a sponge soaked in artificial blood under the victim's clothing in a plastic bag with holes at the top. At the right moment, this can be squeezed by the victim, supposedly clutching the wounded area in agony or shock, so that blood floods out through clothing or fingers.

Plunging a knife or sword into a body can be simulated by using a weapon that collapses in on itself or which slides up inside the protagonist's sleeve. Give this weapon a piece of decoration or paint a different colour at the end – and then duplicate this section in a sheaf or tube that will slide up the weapon as it is apparently thrust into the body. This will add to the effect enormously, as the end of the shaft will then seem to be moving inwards until the weapon is sunk to the hilt.

To make a retracting dagger

1 Find a piece of plastic plumbing pipe 30mm (1.2 inches) to make the handle.

2 Cut the blade from modellers' plastic sheet or thin plywood or very stiff card board to the same height as the inside of the handle and shape the end. It should run smoothly inside the handle.

3 Use two plumbing nuts from a plastic pipe bend and glue them at each end of the handle.

4 Cut four semi-circles out of plastic card and glue at each end of the handle as guides.

5 Spray blade and handle silver, keeping them apart.

6 Wind string or gold picture wire around handle.

7 When stabbing someone, the blade should glide through the handle to be hidden in the actor's sleeve.

A non-retracting dagger using an eye dropper or pipette that contains artificial blood

Fire and flame

Indoor and outdoor fires are commonly needed in plays. In order to make them appear to glow, generally you will need to work in close conjunction with the lighting department to ensure that this is practical and that your fire has the necessary components, space and a suitable site on the set to allow for this.

A simple fire

This can be a basic construction in softwood mounted on a heavy block-wood base. Use red or orange fireproof gel or plastic filter material for the sides. Leave one side free for access. Screw in a light bulb socket and switch. Insert a battery attachment.

A pyramid shape will make a good campfire if then covered with sticks or logs that should be glued into place, leaving chinks for the light to glow through from inside. Cloth-backed tape can be useful for this and the colour will blend well into the background. An indoor household fire should be built in the same way, using or mocking up coal, logs, or whatever fuel is suitable.

Orange and red tissue can be lightly oiled or varnished, which makes it semi-transparent, and then used to look like flames. These flames might be on the top of a pseudo flaming torch which is actually an electric flashlight or torch hidden in a cone made of rolled card.

Flickering fires

Check with the electrics department and ask for their assistance to achieve this effect. Flickering lights can be created by using fluorescent starters and wiring these in series with different coloured light bulbs. Change the wattage size of the bulb or the starter to alter the speed of the flickering.

If one bulb is kept on constantly there will be a continual glow as well as the flickering effect – a combination which will be very realistic.

Candles

Flickering candles are wonderfully atmospheric but real ones will not be approved by local fire prevention officials. Special candle shaped bulbs can be purchased which will be useful for artificial candles, of course, but also for chandeliers. Discuss what shadow effects might be possible with the lighting department: for example, flickering shadows will create the same eerie atmosphere. The candles themselves can be made very simply from white tubing – the sort that is used for plumbing – with wires fed through inside the tubing to a battery. This battery may need to be disguised in a tray or saucer. It is also possible to buy or rent stage candles that flicker by means of having a pair of bulbs built into the flame or one bulb that is suspended on a tiny gimbel.

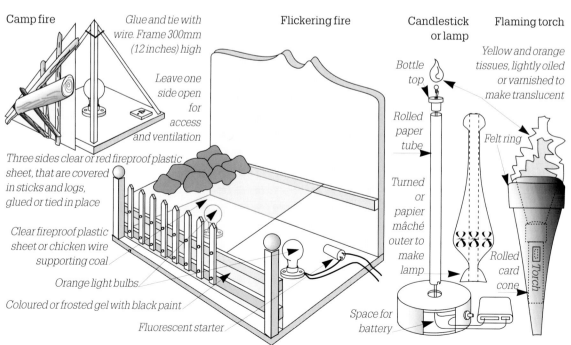

Camp fire

Glue and tie with wire. Frame 300mm (12 inches) high

Leave one side open for access and ventilation

Three sides clear or red fireproof plastic sheet, that are covered in sticks and logs, glued or tied in place

Clear fireproof plastic sheet or chicken wire supporting coal

Orange light bulbs

Coloured or frosted gel with black paint

Fluorescent starter

Flickering fire

Candlestick or lamp

Bottle top

Rolled paper tube

Turned or papier mâché outer to make lamp

Space for battery

Flaming torch

Yellow and orange tissues, lightly oiled or varnished to make translucent

Felt ring

Rolled card cone

Torch

Visit your local library for books on magic tricks. The children's section is often a good place to begin. You will discover all sorts of useful ideas that can be applied to the creation of illusion on stage. A couple of useful tricks are described here and may form the basis of many a good special effect on stage, but the scope is enormous: a few hours' research and making careful notes for potential future use will pay great dividends.

Disappearing props

Sometimes the script demands a magic disappearance on stage, or for one object to be substituted by another. If there is the opportunity for a black-out then a secret panel in the set immediately behind the object may allow it to be removed or replaced in a flash. Or a capacious sleeve or pocket in one of the actor's costumes might provide the answer. This is really the realm of the professional magician but screening an object by covering it with a cloth allows for sleight of hand. For instance, a teapot might be glued to a tray. Cover the tray with a cloth, at the same time slipping under the cloth a wire frame which is the same shape as the teapot on the tray and suggests that the teapot is still in place. Flick the tray down so that its base faces out front, with the real teapot hidden behind it and no longer visible. Whip away the cloth and collapsible wire frame: the teapot will seem to have vanished. Speed is all important. Do not give the audience time to think!

Props that stick to the actor

A magic wand, a lightweight cane, a candle, or whatever can be made to appear to be stuck to an actor's hand, without any visible means of support.

1 Slip a length of fine dark thread through the ring on the top of a fishing weight.

2 Thread the thread through a needle, making sure the weight does not slip off.

3 Make a stitch through the actor's trousers or skirt (which ideally should be the same colour as the thread) sewing from the inside out and then back inside again.

4 Tie the ends of the thread securely together so that the weight hangs on a loop of thread hidden inside the actor's clothing.

5 Slide the wand – or whatever – through the loop.

6 The weight will keep the thread taut and the wand will appear to cling to the actor's hand unaided.

7 The actor should try moving his hand around, so making the wand appear to cling first to one hand and then to the other.

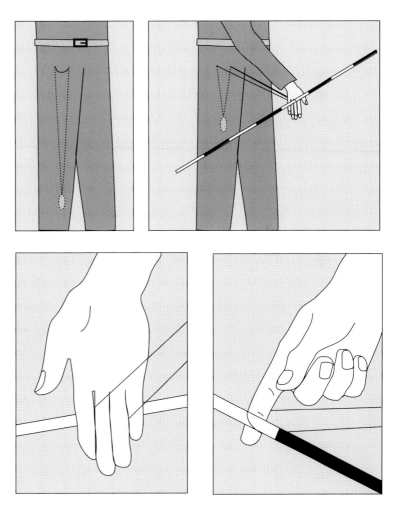

Magic

The floating body

A body can appear to float across the stage all on its own.

1 From card, cut out 'shoe' shape forms that will fit firmly inside the shoes of the person who is going to appear to float.

2 Fix these shoe forms securely onto the end of two broom handles. Use doweling or something solid so that the 'feet' remain firm and upright, at right angles to the broom handles.

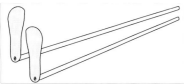

3 The 'body' puts his or her shoes onto these vertical shoe shapes and then holds the broom handles horizontally, with the ends tucked under the armpits for support.

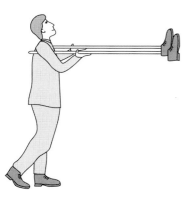

4 Someone else will need to help now and drape a sheet or fabric over the two broom handles so that just the actor's head and the shoes remain in view.

Now the sheet-covered actor can simply walk across the stage and his or her body will appear to float across the stage.

There are all sorts of possibilities to which these kind of illusions can be applied.

The magic empty bag

An empty bag can appear to undertake all sorts of magic tricks. The main factor in tricks of this kind is to have two bags, in fact – one hidden inside the other.

1 Find two paper bags, one just slightly smaller than the other.

2 Place confetti in the bottom of the larger bag.

3 Cut a 2cm (1 inch) section off the top of the smaller bag so that it is shorter than the other.

4 Cut holes in the bottom of the smaller bag.

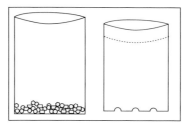

5 Place the small bag inside the larger one and then glue the two bags together neatly at the top edges so they appear to be as one.

6 Show the apparently empty bag to the audience.

7 Drop sections of tissue inside the top bag.

8 Screw up the top of the bag, leaving a small gap and then inflate the bags by blowing inside.

9 The holes in the smaller bag will open out and expand so that the air fills both bags.

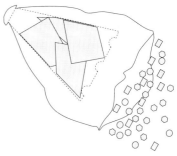

10 Burst the bag and the confetti will tumble out, appearing to have been created magically from the big pieces of tissue paper.

Alternatively, one might put a length of ribbon in the bigger bag. Then, in front of the audience, cut up another

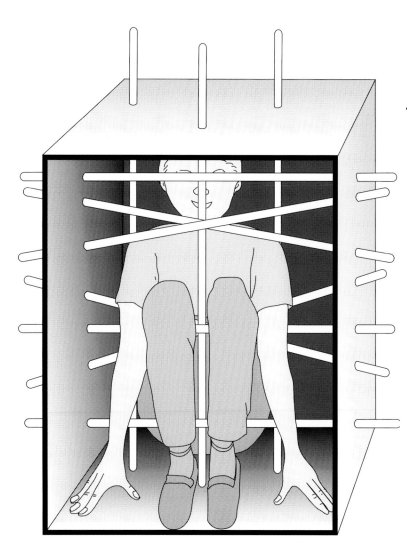

→ *Audience on this side*

practice directing the blades the right way so that the swords pass harmlessly in front of the assistant's body.

The swords are then removed, the victim swivels back to face out front and steps out of the box to thunderous applause!

Human bodies

Shop dummies are always handy and if you see any being replaced in a shop by newer models, it is always worth asking if the old ones are available for you to borrow or purchase, or swap their use for free advertising of the store in the theatre programme!

Human heads and masks

Heads crop up surprisingly often. Ideally, you need to take a cast of the actor's head (if the character appears in the play at any time in his or her entirety). Dental moulage is applied over the actor's face (see pages 92-3), leaving the nostrils clear. This sets very quickly and captures fine details, so a good likeness will be achieved. Another mould is cast inside this first 'negative mould', using plaster (or clay.) You might use this plaster mould as your base, adding a wig of hair and so on, but it is better use of the time

length of the same colour ribbon and drop this into the smaller bag. When the bag bursts the cut ribbon will be hidden and the full ribbon revealed, seeming magically whole again.

Magic sword box

This classic magic illusion is always very effective. The magician will sit a victim inside a box or cabinet and then apparently plunge sharp swords or blades through the box from one

side to the other and apparently, at the same time, through the poor assistant's body inside!

The trick is to convince the audience that the victim is sitting facing the audience, which he does initially. Once out of sight, he turns sideways, so that he is out of harm's way.

The large cardboard box needs to be carefully prepared with holes in the right place. The magician will need to

Human bodies

involved if this mask can be kept as the basic mould for generating any number of masks in the future which will fit that particular actor. He might need to be turned into a werewolf or an alien in the next production!

To create a full round head, you will also need to make a cast over the back of the actor's head and then, when both are finished, join these two sections together before painting.

Alternatively, a back section can be created by building up papier maché over a clay form, a wire mesh base, or over an inflated balloon.

Using a balloon you will need

1
One balloon

2
Brown paper

3
Newspaper

4
Paper towels, or tissue

5
Wallpaper paste

6
Water

7
Shellac

8
Bucket

If you prefer, you can use cloth and carpenter's glue instead of paper and paste.

Optional
Balloons or plastic tops or cups for features

Using a balloon

1 Inflate balloon to the size required and stand on a cardboard collar.

2 Securely tape in place anything being used to make ear or nose shapes (for example, other small balloons, polystyrene cups, plastic tops, or shaped clay).

3 Coat the whole balloon surface with petroleum jelly.

4 Cover with papier maché strips.

5 Leave to dry.

6 Let out the air when the papier maché has set.

7 If necessary, trim away any excess material to fit.

Alternatively, a balloon can be surrounded with a network of criss-crossed string that has been dipped in carpenter's glue.

This string and glue method can also be used to create crowns and headdresses. Once the basic network has been established, the final surface layer can be designed to use the string in interesting patterns.

Making a mould

Masks and heads can also be constructed on top of a mould.

These moulds might be made of clay or plaster, or created directly over the actor's face so that the fit is excellent. You can use dental moulage applied over the actor's face which sets into a rubbery material and reproduces minute details.

You will need

1
Straw and cotton wool

2
Swimming cap

3
Alginate

4
Bandage impregnated with plaster

5
Dental plaster

6
Water

1 Cover the actor's hair with a swimming cap and the facial hair (do not forget eyelashes) with gauze stuck down with petroleum jelly. Make sure the air spaces – mouth and nostrils – are kept clear: plug the nostrils with cotton wool or straws and insert a straw in the mouth. Tell the actor to keep still and to keep the eyes closed.

2 Mix and melt and then apply the alginate moulage, working fairly quickly as it sets fast.

3 When the alginate is dry, build up a good layer of strips of plaster cast bandage – or your own mix of plaster and scrim – over the alginate.

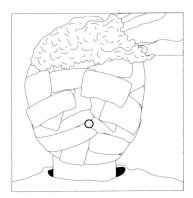

4 Remove the mould a few minutes later, once the plaster has dried.

5 Mix up some dental plaster and fill the negative mould.

6 Once the plaster life mask is cool and set, remove it from the moulage (which can be used again) and leave it to dry for 24 hours.

7 Using this mould, further masks can be formed, the interior surface of which will then fit the actor perfectly. The new masks, whether of clay or papier maché can be modelled with all sorts of new features like huge noses or bulging eyes.

8 Paint it with shellac. If a back head section is needed make this in the same way or from papier maché.

9 Once dry and firm, join the two halves together. Add features and hair. Paint as required.

10 Add any other appropriate details such as blood and gore.

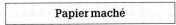

Moulds can also be made with a substance called Flex Wax.

For a much quicker method, the actor's face can be covered with petroleum jelly, with tissue carefully covering any facial hair, and then two or three layers of small wet plaster bandage squares should be smoothed directly on to the actor's face to fit all the contours closely. This mould will set in about ten minutes and can then be used to create a positive cast in plaster of Paris.

Alternatively a head can be created using the 'isopon' mesh and the sort of paste more generally used for repairing the bodywork of cars or patching up a vehicle's rusty areas. This is a very good flexible medium and works well.

Papier maché, of course, must not be overlooked. Good entire heads can be made from this when an exact replica of an actor is not required. Gradually build up into the shape required, paint the head sympathetically and give it appropriate hair.

Papier maché

Papier maché is excellent for making all sorts of stiffer shapes and body parts and is made from wallpaper paste and paper; glue and cloth; sizing and paper; or flour, water and paper.

Paper will need to be torn up into irregular shapes and cloth cut up into strips. Larger pieces can be used for bigger structures but, generally, the smaller the pieces, the better they bind together and the smoother the final finished surface.

Always leave to dry in a well-ventilated room. Paint with shellac or emulsion and seal, if required, with varnish or lacquer.

Newspaper, brown paper, tissue or toilet paper and kitchen towel paper can be used. It is best to start with brown paper and then newspaper, followed by tissue and toilet paper to create a strong smoother finish.

The paper and wallpaper paste method is as follows:

1 Soak the paper in water.

2 Make up the paste.

3 Ring out excess water from paper and then immerse paper in paste.

4 Crush and squeeze until the paper is completely impregnated.

Papier maché

5 Squeeze out surplus paste.

6 Shape the pulp as if it is plasticine.

7 Apply it to the mould or base.

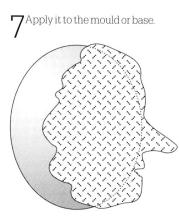

A balloon makes a good base for a head or mask.

The glue and cloth method:

1 Cut cloth into strips, diagonally across grain. Canvas and cheese-cloth are good materials.

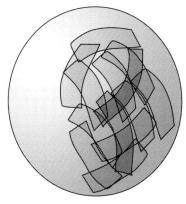

2 Make up some carpenters' glue: dissolve glue block or granules in a small bucket of water which is standing inside a larger metal bucket containing boiling water. Stir well and keep glue as hot as possible.

3 Soak cloth strips in glue solution until it is completely impregnated.

4 Squeeze out any surplus glue. (Wear rubber gloves.)

5 Apply cloth in overlapping strips to the mould or base until two or three layers thick.

6 Put some unsoaked paper in the glue solution and then apply this in the same way. Use small pieces for the final layer to give a smooth finish.

Paper can also be soaked in hot size and applied to a framework.

Other body parts

These can all be made in the same way as heads, but hands can be very difficult to do well.

It is worth raiding the local fashion shop and joke shop, especially for false arms and hands, noses, eyes and so on, which may be very useful in the properties department as well as in the make-up one! Or find a shop window hand or limb.

Falling objects

Snowbags

Although primarily intended for snow, a snowbag is a useful structure that can drop all manner of things as well as snow – balloons, dust or rubble, confetti, silver sparkle, and so on.

Slashes or slots are cut into the canvas bag so that the rate of smaller objects falling may be quite slow and the fall can last quite a long time.

1 Generally the snowbag is slung between two parallel pipes suspended a few inches apart above the area of the stage where the 'drop' will be needed.

2 The snow is placed in the solid uncut side of the bag.

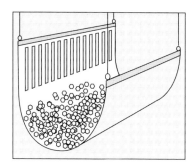

3 On cue, the slotted side of the bag is lowered so that the snow can roll down and slip through the slots.

4 Lower the side further and larger objects such as balloons will simply drop right out.

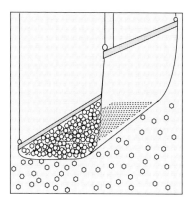

Falling snow can be made from all sorts of things such as torn paper, foam, punched paper from an office, plastic flakes, soap flakes, and crumbled polystyrene. Large salt crystals might be used on the stage floor, window ledges and so on but are too heavy to fall naturally from above.

Meanwhile, a wind machine set in the wings can turn this gentle snowfall into a snow storm.

Rain

'Real' rain water is much more difficult to control than snow. It can be made to run down windows from a trough or hose pipe set above and punched with holes, and there are many new watering systems for automatic watering of gardens that may be used. The problem is stopping the effect when you want to, removing the water as it falls and preventing leaks – not to mention the safety factors with all the electrical wiring around the place. ◆

So, all round, it is probably best to avoid real water and use a projected effect (see page 53).

Dropping larger objects from above

A simple trick release will drop a suspended object from a height. This might simply be a case of nudging the object with a piece of hidden doweling secreted on the set or having a cord that is suspending it released in the wings.

An object, or a whole row of them, may be suspended from a ring or rings slipped over a piece of cable or doweling that is slotted through a fixed set of rings (like those on a proprietary curtain track).

When the rod is removed the rings suspending the objects are released and the objects will tumble down.

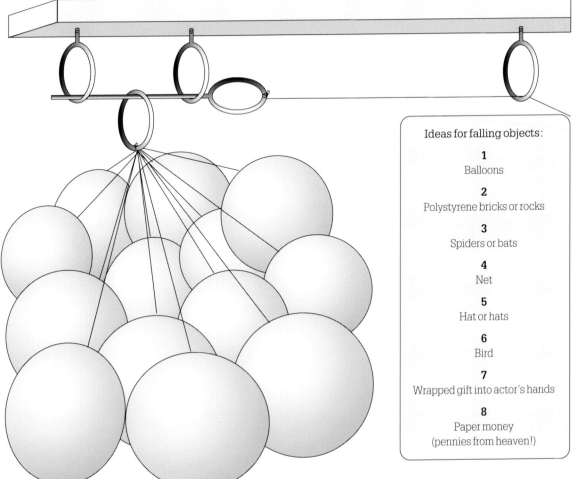

Ideas for falling objects:

1
Balloons

2
Polystyrene bricks or rocks

3
Spiders or bats

4
Net

5
Hat or hats

6
Bird

7
Wrapped gift into actor's hands

8
Paper money
(pennies from heaven!)

Special effect props for finales

Special effect props for finales

Finish with a flourish! If staging a revue, musical, old time music hall, pantomime, pageant or the like, it is important to finish with a lively finale that the audience will remember.

How do you get all these items onto the stage? It is important that everything happens quickly and to keep the momentum going.

It may be a simple matter of the cast arriving for the finale carrying the necessary batons, torches or whatever. If so, arrange for the props team to be primed and ready to hand out the right items to the right people at exactly the right time – and without getting in the way! Easier said than done, especially as a large number of people will probably be involved and some members of the cast may have to contend with a very fast costume change in the wings too.

Some items, like balloons or coloured balls, might be simply thrown onto the stage from the wings.

Other light items, such as balloons, can tumble down on cue from a net suspended above the stage.

It is also possible to fly objects over the audience's heads or across the stage, using a simple system made from nylon fishing line.

Whatever effect is chosen, the main intention is to achieve a stunning final effect. Many of these items are relatively cheap if bought in bulk from a theatre or party supplier. Obviously balloons and the like are expendable. Other items, such as the tinsel batons and bunting, can be used time and time again in a variety of ways. These are worth the investment and should be taken care of after the performance. They may need to be rescued quickly from an excited cast or audience!

Try using some of the following for a special effect at the end:

1
Balloons

2
Confetti balloons

3
Flags or bunting
Flowers and garlands

4
Maracas,
whistles and/or
other noise-makers

5
Colourful, glittering
or fluorescent masks,
hats, wigs, fans
or feather boas

6
Streamers or banners

7
Lengths of silk, chiffon,
shimmering foil or ribbon

8
Party poppers,
blow-out trumpets
and trumpets

9
Fibre optic torches

10
Tinsel baton twirlers

11
Bright coloured throw balls
to toss at the audience

12
Chinese lanterns

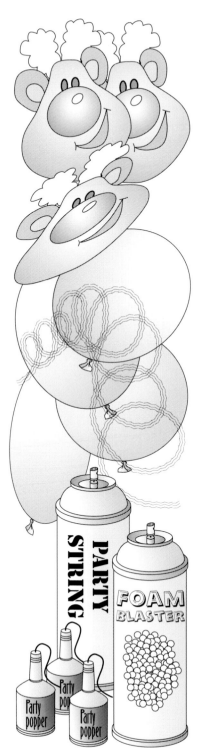

Make-up

An enthusiastic and imaginative make-up artist will revel in special effects, in bringing his or her skills to the exciting aspects of character creation and ways of making an immediate effect on the stage. There are oodles of excellent books on the subject of conventional make-up, but the aim in this chapter is to discover the tricks of the trade in the more unusual forms of make-up and in dramatic stage situations such as transformations, fast changes and moments that need a very strong visual impact.

Moreover, when lighting special effects are being used, often the colour will be drained from actors' faces and then the make-up needs to be especially strong.

So good make-up helps both cast and audience to believe in the characters and will underline what is happening on stage.

Try not to overdo the effect, however. As with any other kind of special effect, some restraint may be needed so that the special effect is suitably dramatic but does not go 'over the top' and become ludicrous.

Planning ahead

The make-up needs to be well organized. The play should be studied, and special characters or changes discussed with the producer and individual actors. A plan of campaign should be devised for the performances, taking into account, especially for the more complicated make-up, just how much time is required prior to 'curtain-up' or a par-

Make-up will:

1

Define characters

This in turn will:

2

Instil confidence in the cast

---

ticular entrance. Will extra help need to be recruited?

Plan of campaign for organizing the make-up

1 Read the play: analyze characters and special effects.

2 Discuss style and aims with producer and actors.

3 Research background information and how to achieve effects.

4 Make a plot of timing, noting any fast changes.

5 Attend rehearsals: check out ideas; incorporate any changes or additions.

6 Check through stock: buy any new make-up required.

Special effect make-up adds dramatic impact to character roles

7 Organize rental of any special effect make-up or wigs as needed.

8 Organize any extra help: plan who is doing what when.

9 Practice any difficult special effect or new make-up.

10 Supervise special make-up at dress rehearsals.

11 Check every effect out front and make any adjustments.

12 Pre-performance – allow plenty of time for particularly complicated special effects make-up.

13 During performance – be well organized for quick changes.

14 After final performance, tidy up and collect everything: note items which need replacing.

15 Return any rented make-up items or wigs.

16 Make notes and keep drawings and photographs of special effect make-up.

What to use to create special effects

What to use to create special effects

Use shadows and highlights

Make-up depends on light and shade, on its sculpturing qualities, rather than just colour. For example, lines alone will not age a face convincingly. Instead use shadows and highlights to create the effect of sagging jaws, eyebags, or wrinkles. Light and shade will emphasize the contours of any three-dimensional shape, including the face.

Shadows and highlights create three-dimensional effects

Use optical illusions

1 Horizontal shadows and lines will widen and flatten a face.

2 Vertical shadows and lines will narrow and lengthen the face.

3 Lots of little divisions make a line look longer. So, in the same way, accentuating eyelashes with mascara makes eyes look wider.

4 Light areas always look bigger.

5 Dark areas always look smaller.

Use glitter

1 A little sparkle or glitter gives extra impact to a glamorous make-up.

2 Lots of sparkle will add to the magic of a fairy.

3 A red sequin on the centre of each eyelid will give a vampire, demon, wizard or genie an occasional extra fiery flash of light.

Optical illusions

Black absorbs light so dark shapes seem smaller than light ones. This effect is exaggerated if a black shape is surrounded by white, and vice versa

Identical line lengths can appear shortened by enclosing them in angled lines and longer by using opening-out angles. Eye make-up reflects this

Little transversal dividing lines make the right half of this line seem longer

A face can be broadened by horizontal lines, whether in make-up or costume, and narrowed by vertical ones, as shown in these two characters

4 Metallic body make-up looks very dramatic and is wonderful for statues, robots and aliens as well as any magical or fairy-folk character. Never cover the entire body, however; leave some areas of the skin free to breathe, be on the watch for any side effects, and do not wear body make-up for extended periods. ◆

Glittery eyelashes are also available for an exotic effect.

Use tooth enamel
Use proper black tooth enamel in order to black out teeth convincingly. Anything else will not adhere properly to the tooth surface and will wash away or rub off.

Use plenty of adhesion
Make the special effect last! Wigs, beards, moustaches and false noses need to be stuck on very firmly. Do not skimp on spirit gum, hair clips or whatever.

Use the extremities
Never forget to make up the neck and hands. They add much to a convincing effect. Nails, noses, ears and hairstyles too should be give appropriate attention or exaggerated to create a strong character or effect.

Use a hairdryer
Many special effect make-ups involve drying between layers, or before applying the final make-up. A hairdryer can be invaluable for speeding up this process.

Ageing

Generally using the sculptural qualities of shade and light to create a thinner appearance will suggest old age, especially when combined with a white or steel-grey wig and a pale

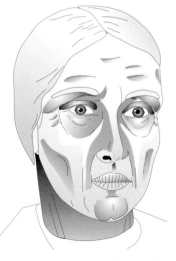

Light and shade will sculpture a face

complexion. Do not forget to make up the neck and hands.

1 First apply a pale sallow foundation to the face and neck.

2 Add shadows to eye area, until the eye seems to sink into the socket.

3 Shadow the temples and the cheek hollows.

4 Thin the nose with shadow down the sides.

5 Add further shadows to create jowls on the jaw, and lines and hollows on the throat.

6 Use a clean brush to add highlight to all these shadows, emphasizing bony edges and heavier folds.

7 Stipple on a few broken veins.

8 Put wrinkles on the lips.

9 Whiten brows and lashes.

Eyes

Eyes are our most striking feature, in that they convey emotion very strongly. Special attention should always be paid to making up eyes effectively, whether for a glamorous make-up, or, as here, for some less conventional forms of eye make-up.

Blindness

Blindness is most simply effected by using flesh coloured fabric-backed adhesive tape. This releases the actor from the strain and concentration required to keep the eyelid permanently semi-closed.

1 Cut out a D-shape from the adhesive tape.

2 Apply to the partially-closed eye lid. When properly in place the tape will comfortably hold the lid almost shut, allowing a narrow slit so that the actor can still see.

3 Shade the edges of the tape away with make-up.

4 After the performance, remove the tape gently, lifting the top edge and easing downwards.

An alternative is to make a moulded eye in clay and paint latex over this. To allow vision, a hole would need to be cut in the eye and then disguised with gauze on the back.

Eyes

A disfigured eye

A disfigured eye can be simulated by using an oval shape cut from gauze bandage and then painting this appropriately.

1 Cut a piece of gauze to the same size and shape as the eye socket.

2 Paint the gauze with a closed eye, an open staring eye or whatever disfigurement the character requires. Let this dry.

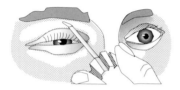

3 Check the size and effect work well. Then paint spirit gum in an oval around the eye area. Be extremely carefully to avoid lids and lashes – and the eye itself, of course. ◑

4 Position in place, allow the gum to dry and then blend the edges of the gauze into the rest of the facial make-up.

A latex rubber piece can also be made to fit over the eye to simulate swelling or damage.

For a real professional effect of corneal damage or a colour change, an optician can prescribe suitable contact lenses, but the cost, and initial discomfort of these to a new wearer, is not generally justified for an amateur or college production, especially as such close-up details are only really necessary for television or cinema camera close-ups.

Black eyes

A swollen, distorted, or black eye can be suggested with sculptural highlighting and shadows, together with appropriate bruise colours simulated with make-up, using purple, blue, reds and yellows. This is described under Bruises and black eyes on page 103.

Oriental eyes

It is possible to purchase made-to-measure eyelids in rubber, but these will be expensive. Why not try making your own from either fine chamois leather – glued on with spirit gum – or from adhesive tape?

1 Cut off a piece of tape or chamois leather about 2 1/2 x 1 1/8 inches (50mm x 28mm). Then cut away the curved shape, as shown by the heavy lines A to B and C to D.

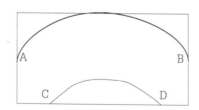

2 If using adhesive tape, apply powder or tissue paper to shaded area E so the sensitive area of the actor's eyelid is not glued.

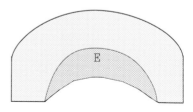

3 Apply spirit gum to area F on the chamois leather lid. Press the false eyelid into place, covering both ends of the eyebrow.

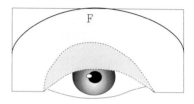

4 Tease out a few eyebrow hairs from under the false lid on the outside edge of the brow.

5 Make up the false lid, and then apply shading and highlighting as shown below.

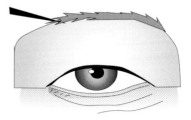

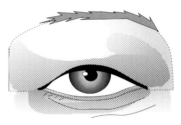

Blood and cuts

How the bleeding is organized depends upon whether or not the injury occurs off-stage so that the wounded victim can be suitably 'bloodied up' off-stage and then stagger into audience view – or whether the inflicting of the wound must take place onstage in front of the audience, a rather more complicated procedure, but very dramatic if you get it right!

Making blood

It is possible to create your own artificial blood by mixing one teaspoon of red food colouring, a half a teaspoon of yellow food colouring and half a teaspoon of water soluble make-up paint into a glass containing one cupful of corn syrup or glycerine. This mix should have the right consistency and opacity, but experiment first by applying it to the hand to see if it runs convincingly and looks right. The main problem will be avoiding staining of skin and clothes.

Blood for the mouth can also be made from red toothpaste.

Mix red toothpaste with the powder adhesive that is meant to be used for securing false teeth and a dried blood effect can also be created.

Types of blood

The blood used depends on whether it is supposed to be from an external or internal wound: blood which must issue from the mouth is contained in gelatine capsules and is a different material, specifically formulated to be safely swallowed if the actor gets it

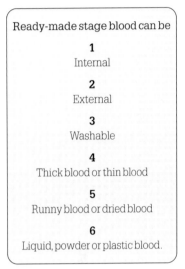

Ready-made stage blood can be

1
Internal

2
External

3
Washable

4
Thick blood or thin blood

5
Runny blood or dried blood

6
Liquid, powder or plastic blood.

Making blood

1 Pour one cupful of corn syrup (or glycerine) into a glass

2 Add one teaspoon of red vegetable colouring

3 Add half a teaspoon of yellow vegetable colouring

4 Add half a teaspoon of water-soluble non-toxic make-up paint

5 Mix well

6 Check the opacity and consistency to make sure that these meet your requirements

Blood and cuts

wrong! *Never allow an actor to use external-only blood internally.* ◆

With any blood preparation, whether home-made or bought 'off-the-shelf', the amount of staining on skin and clothes needs to be checked. Some blood will wash off clothes; others will not and, in the latter case, it may be necessary to use a disposable shirt (or whatever) that is replaced by a new one for each performance.

Instant on-stage effects

Blood capsules can be crushed in the hand or mouth for an instant on-stage effect. The blood will ooze out of the mouth – or the capsule in the hand can be clutched against the supposedly wounded area and squashed.

A knife wound can be mimicked by using a blade with a dropper concealed behind. See page 87 in the section on weapons for an illustration of how this works.

A similar effect can be achieved by using 'Magic Blood'. This consists of two separate chemicals which react together to create a flowing blood-red liquid. One of the liquids is applied to the victim's skin and allowed to dry. The other liquid is spread onto the knife blade. When the blade is drawn across the 'painted' skin the two liquids react with each other and the cut will bleed. This can be very useful in a situation where the blade is too narrow to conceal a dropper.

For a nose bleed, sword wound or injuries resulting from a fight scene, blood can be soaked into a sponge which might be hidden on the stage somewhere until is needed or it can be placed inside a plastic bag, with tiny holes at the top, and then concealed under the actor's clothing (see also page 87). Place the blood as near as possible to the place where the injury is to be inflicted. This blood can then be squeezed out at the appropriate moment.

Cuts

1 Paint the areas involved with spirit gum and let this dry.

2 Spread Derma wax over the wound area and flatten out the edges with a spatula.

3 Using the blunt edge of a modelling scalpel, make a cut and then open out the wound as required.

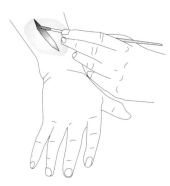

4 Paint the inside of the wound with a dark maroon lining colour. To make it more pliable and avoid damaging the latex, you may need to soften the lining colour with a little cold cream.

5 Paint over the completed wound with a thin film of sealer and leave this to thoroughly dry.

6 Disguise the edges of the wound with make-up to blend it into the surrounding skin.

7 Highlight the edges of the cut to accentuate it.

8 Stage blood can be applied with an eye-dropper or plastic blood squeezed out directly from the tube.

Scars, burns, bruises, black eyes and bullets

**Scars, burns, bruises
black eyes and bullets**

Scars

A scar is a three-dimensional effect so greasepaint alone will not really look convincing.

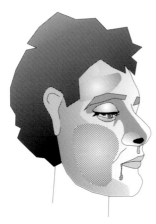

A deep scar can be made with Derma wax or liquid latex

Blood running from mouth and a swollen, bruised cheek effect

One of the simplest ways is to use non flexible collodion which contracts and puckers the skin as it dries. Paint on as many coats as necessary, allow-ing each one to dry before starting the next. Then shadow the depression and highlight the edges to emphasize the scar.

This method can be used only occa-sionally, however, and not for an extended run, as over-use will dam-age the skin and irritate it or leave a permanent mark. Never use collodion close to the eye. ◆

So, for repeated use, it is better to use liquid latex. Shape this on a glass plate with a spatula or orange stick, peel it off the plate once dry, and stick it onto the skin with spirit gum. It can be accentuated with appropriate make-up, scored with an eyebrow tweezer to look like a fresh cut or stippled with a brush when just slightly set.

Always keep the scarlines uneven.

Cotton wool or tissue can be added between the latex layers to build up a larger or roughened surface scar.

Burns

First stipple the area with maroon lin-ing colour or lipstick. A rubber sponge is good for this. Then cover this with a layer of liquid latex or sealer and allow to dry.

White candle wax can be dripped over the sealed area to suggest blisters. To create the effect of peeling skin and broken blisters, rub with the fingertips to break the surface and then make tiny holes in the latex or sealer. Lift small sections away to look like exposed raw patches. Finally stipple black cake make-up or burnt cork as required, to suggest charring.

For a really gory effect, areas of hang-ing skin can be simulated by simply allowing some loose bits to hang or by applying tissue between two layers of latex. Cotton can also be added in this way for creating hanging burnt flesh.

Bruises and black eyes

Bruises and black eyes need layers of lining colour, one on top of the other, but make each successive layer cover a slightly smaller area. Leave the bruise or swollen eye area unpow-dered so it looks shiny and inflamed.

If the area is to be very swollen then build it up first with DermaWax before applying the colour.

Use the colours in the following order

For a fresh bruise:

1
Dark red

2
Purple

3
Blue-grey

For an older 'faded' bruise:

1
A mix of chrome yellow and green

2
Blue-grey and purple

3
Dark red

For black eyes, moist rouge may be added to the inside of the eyelid to make this look bloodshot.

The cheekbone might also be high-lighted just below the eye.

A few unsavoury attributes

Bullet wounds

1 Paint the skin with a circle of spirit gum. When this is dry, spread Derma wax over the top, thinning the edges to merge them into the skin.

2 Now make a bullet hole effect by pressing into the wax with the blunt end of a pencil.

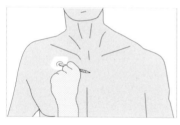

3 To make it look suitably charred and bloody, paint the inside of the hole with black and red lining colour.

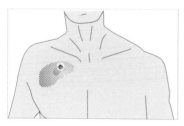

4 Cover the wound with a thin layer of sealer.

5 Add a trickle of dark red plastic blood to complete effect.

Warts and moles

> ### These can be made from
>
> **1**
> Pre-formed latex pieces
>
> **2**
> Derma wax
>
> **3**
> Cotton balls
>
> **4**
> Spirit gum
>
> **5**
> Cereals like Rice Crispies or Puffed Wheat
>
> **6**
> Powdered gelatine mixed with hot water

Add alfalfa seeds for a knobbly surface, or hairs if required, and glue them into place with spirit gum. Add make-up as suits the desired effect.

Huge warts for, say, a troll, witch or toad can be made by using grapes or gooseberries and covering these with latex.

Broken noses

The simplest way is to paint a strong highlight down the centre of the nose in a suitable bent line and then shade the areas to each side of this.

If required, this distorted look can be exaggerated by inserting a nose plug in one nostril.

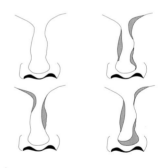

Alternatively, an artificial nose can be purchased or one can be built up from nose putty.

You can make your own nose plugs by cutting out the centre section of a baby's bottle teat (nipple): or use the tip of a dummy (pacifier), pierced with a hole so that the actor can breathe.

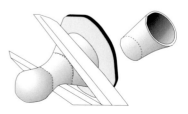

A few unsavoury attributes

Rough skin and wrinkles

Add bran to the make-up.

Or you can use 'fuller's earth'. Add some brown or black face powder to this and mix into a moist paste with water. Ask the actor to pull a suitable exaggerated face and then rub the paste into the skin and allow it to dry.

For rough or wrinkled skin, corn meal, wheat germ or bran can be applied onto a tacky area of spirit gum already painted onto the skin and a latex layer applied over this. Or the roughening ingredients might be mixed with the latex and applied in one go.

Layers of torn tissue over still-damp spirit gum can be applied to the skin and pushed into wrinkles.

Perspiration or sweating

Shield the eyes and then spray the face or body with glycerine or with mineral oil.

Mineral oil or baby oil might be rubbed onto the skin for gleaming body effects.

A greasy sweat can be simulated by adding dark grease make-up to this oily application.

For an instant on-stage effect, the same methods can be applied as for on-stage blood (see page 102) but use a mix of water and glycerine in the sponge or concealed bag – one part glycerine to three parts water will ooze out quickly enough but will then stay longer than ordinary water, which can evaporate quickly in the heat of the stage lights. This glycerine/water mix will need to be discreetly shaken up again if it has been left to settle for too long.

1 Stretch skin; paint with liquid latex or spirit gum

3 Release skin. Then repeat process, if necessary, to achieve desired effect

Dirty teeth

Clean and dry the teeth with a tissue. Apply a layer of brown moustache wax. Once this has set, rub away some of the wax to create a suitably broken pattern of grime.

Hair

Wigs and hairpieces

A full wig can be a very dramatic way to alter the appearance – whether for a man or a woman. A hard-edged wig may need to be combined with the natural hair at the front but, for a lace-front wig, the actor's own hair will need to be flattened and wound out of the way, preferably held with pins, and then covered with cotton gauze or a crepe bandage so that no stray hairs can escape. For extra security use spirit gum around the hair line before applying the wig.

2 Add tissue. Paint on more gum. Dry with hairdryer

4 Stipple with pale grease make-up to accentuate wrinkles

Adding a switch to lengthen hair

A hairpiece or 'fall' pinned at the back

Hair

Toupees, falls, switches and curls must match the natural hair and be fixed very securely. Falls, switches and extra ringlets can be very useful for creating a period hair-style.

Wigs can create a dramatic change, immediately suggesting Ancient Egypt, 18th century excesses or a 1970s punk (or ethnic) look.

Beards and moustaches

Beards and moustaches may be bought ready-made or created to suit specific needs from crepe hair.

To make a beard:

1 Cut the mat of crepe hair into three. Divide the middle section into four equal sections, as shown.

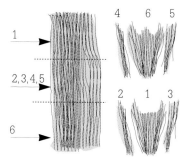

2 Coat the chin with spirit gum and allow this to dry. Remoisten the appropriate section of the face with more gum each time an application of hair is made.

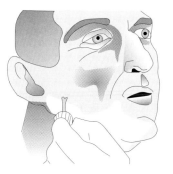

3 Apply section 1 of the hair, pressing firmly into place.

4 Apply sections 2 and 3 to the sides of the jaw.

5 Apply sections 4 and 5 in front of, and just above, sections 2 and 3.

6 Apply section 6 to the front of the chin, just below the lips.

7 Once the beard is all dry, gently stroke the sections together and remove any loose hairs. Trim and shape as needed.

Moustaches

Moustaches are made in a similar way, by layering straight sections one on top of another, each one slightly longer than the one below for a straight moustache, or dividing into horizontal sections for a curled-end Edwardian style moustache.

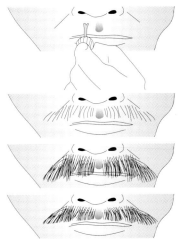

Mutton chop whiskers

Use unstraightened crepe hair, puffed out into fluffy sections, and overlap these like roofing tiles.

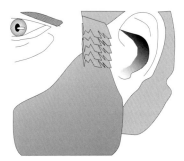

Crepe hair can create various styles

Stubble

Stubble can be simulated by clipping crepe hair into 1/4 inch pieces and attaching this to the chin and cheeks, which have been given a thin tacky film of spirit gum. Pick up two balls of clippings with the fingertips, one in each hand, and apply symmetrically, starting at the sideburns and dabbing down the face. Be careful not to get gum onto the fingers and remoisten the gummed areas if these start to dry out before you have finished.

Apply stubble symmetrically

Receding hair and bald heads

These can look very artificial if they are not well matched to the facial colour, so allow plenty of time to blend in with the make-up. A blender wig with a false forehead section may not need to be made up completely every night, however. If it is thoroughly powdered and removed very carefully, the make-up should last for several performances, with just the join area being retouched.

Bald caps are made from latex and adapt to the shape of the head to fit snugly. Paper-thin ones will work best. The cap should be large enough to cover the ears. Glue the main part of the cap into position and then trim to fit. Roll back the edges to glue these, stretch out any wrinkles and then stick the edges down firmly. Dab on a thin layer of liquid latex to overlap the edges and then, once dry, coat this film with sealer before making up.

Alternatively, create a bald pate by thoroughly soaping down the real hair. Cover it with a nylon stocking and then soap again. Paint with cream stick and powder.

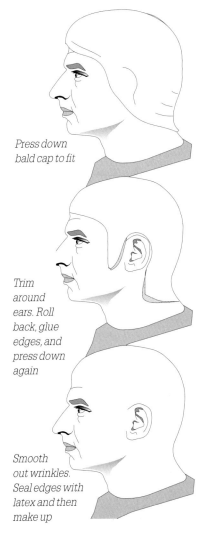

Press down bald cap to fit

Trim around ears. Roll back, glue edges, and press down again

Smooth out wrinkles. Seal edges with latex and then make up

False bits and pieces

False bits and pieces

Pre-made false pieces can be expensive. Ideally, they should be tailor-made to fit, but are light and comfortable to wear and easier to apply and remove than putty or wax, for example. They should be stuck firmly into place with spirit gum before make-up is applied.

False pieces can be used for noses, chins, eye pouches, ears, fingers, as well as the more familiar fingernails, teeth and fangs, and eyelashes of all lengths and colours.

Noses

A false nose can look very effective once it is made up with rubber mask greasepaint, and stippled with a sponge. Set the make-up with translucent powder.

Glue nose in place with spirit gum

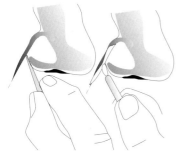

Press nostrils into place; cover join

Nose putty can be built up on the nose into all sorts of interesting shapes. Knead the putty until it is pliable, place it in position, and press and shape, blending the edges to thin away into the real nose. Putty is light coloured, so darker make-up may be needed to make it match the surrounding skin.

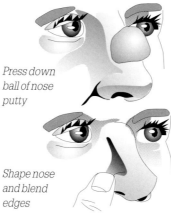

Press down ball of nose putty

Shape nose and blend edges

Derma wax is softer and easier to shape but more easily damaged or dislodged by perspiration. Painting a layer of spirit gum and fluffed up cotton (cotton wool) on the nose first will help adhesion.

Ears

Big ears or long pointed ones for elves or aliens can be made from latex or from adhesive tape in an appropriate pointed shape. Give the ears some rigidity with a bent hairpin trapped between two layers of the latex or adhesive tape – or pipe cleaners can be used. The section that fits over the top of the ear will need a circle of paper

Make elf ears from adhesive tape

folded and stuck inside to make a shell that will sit comfortably over the real ear. Colour with greasepaint and attach to the real ear with spirit gum.

Cauliflower ears made of rubber can be simply slipped over actors' ears.

A small piece of flesh-coloured cardboard can be stuck at the back of the ears to make them stick out.

Nails

Long fingernails for witches and Chinese mandarins can be made from acetate or old photographic film, glued on with false-nail glue or spirit gum. Complete nasty-looking fingers for witches, with long nails attached, can be bought. These will slip over the fingers.

Fingernails for witches can be bought or made from acetate or photographic film

Teeth

Plastic false teeth and fangs abound in joke shops but may not be comfortable to wear for long periods. Teeth can be inserted into a thin strip of foam rubber. Once the teeth are glued firmly into position, the foam strip can be pushed up under the top lip, in front of the gums.

Insert fangs on a foam strip

A full set of teeth, broken or whatever, can be made from proper dental materials to fit the actor but this really needs professional skills.

Gold teeth

Gold foil, say from a chocolate bar wrapping, can be stuck over the tooth with spirit gum.

Face lifts

Temporary face lifts can help to disguise a sagging jawline, throat or nasal folds. They can be made from elongated triangles of fish skin (T.K.) with the top edge rolled around a section of a hair pin and then firmly enclosed in adhesive tape. Make a loop of cotton at the top, with a tiny elastic band threaded through the loop. A length of button thread through this, in turn, will do the lifting.

The fish skin lifts should be stuck to the face with spirit gum, just below the hair, in front of the ears, but high enough for the hair to hide them. Once the fish skin pieces are really firmly adhering to the face and the glue is dry, the threads can be raised – until the skin is sufficiently lifted – and then tied off at the top of the head and hidden under the hair.

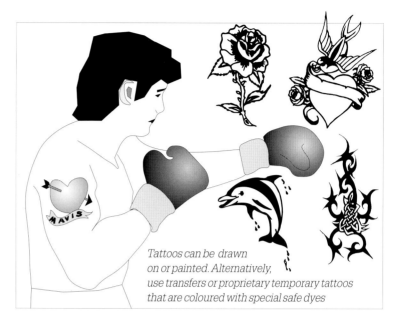

Tattoos can be drawn on or painted. Alternatively, use transfers or proprietary temporary tattoos that are coloured with special safe dyes

Tattoos

Tattoos can be drawn onto the skin with eye make-up pencils. To obtain a pleasing outline, make a paper pattern into which you prick out the lines with holes, using a thick needle. Stick the pattern onto the skin with a film of cold cream and pat black face powder through the holes onto the skin, creating good guidelines for your artistry. If the tattoos do not have to be removed for any changes during the show, it may be much quicker and simpler in the long run to purchase transfers.

Or you can try some temporary tattoos which will last from four days to three weeks, depending on how abrasively your actors wash! A transfer will create the design on the skin, and this black outline is then filled in with appropriate colours. Complete kits are available for this and the effect is very convincing (see the List of Suppliers on page 154).

You will need fish skin (T.K. or tulle netting), fine hairpins, adhesive tape, elastic bands and strong button thread

Lift threads and tie off

Style hair to cover fastenings

Fast changes

Fast changes

The main ingredient in a successful quick change, whether make-up, props or costumes, is pre-planning and good organization.

Obviously a change of costume is a vital factor in a quick change: remember this must be scheduled into your plans (see also page 114).

Plan ahead

Be organised

Be ready on cue

Stay calm

Speed up changes by attaching false ringlets or curls to a hat or bonnet

Decide what is most important so that the make-up can be simplified down to the basics.

1
Plot out exactly what has to be done with clear checklists.

2
Make sure everything is laid out ready and in the right order.

3
Rehearse and time the fast change before performances.

4
In the panic, it is easy to lose things or knock them over. Keep brushes and tubes upright in containers so they cannot roll away at a crucial moment. Avoid spillable liquids or glue their bases to the table with tape.

5
Use make-up that can be applied directly with the fingers, or load up brushes and sponges ready with individual colours.

6
The broader the brush, the quicker the application will be.

7
Cake make-up is good because one layer can be applied over another without removing the first.

8
Code and label make-up items clearly so you know exactly what to pick up.

9
Wigs, hats, spectacles and jewellery can alter an appearance dramatically and quickly.

10
False hair can be attached to a hat or bonnet.

11
Use ready-prepared beards or moustaches. Double-sided sticky tape will allow a quick application and removal of these but position carefully as any readjusting weakens the adhesion of the tape.

12
If there is insufficient time to change details, ask the lighting department to ensure that the face is not brightly illuminated.

13
Do not forget hands and necks. Use appropriate scarves, shawls and gloves if there is no time available to make up these areas.

Costumes and transformations

The costume an actor wears has an immediate impact on the audience and on how the actor feels about the role – so every costume is, in a way, a special effect in its own right. Good costumes will create an exhilarating visual impact through colour and styling, design and flair and will add a little magic to every production.

Moreover, some costumes are directly involved in transformations, quick changes and magical moments when costume tricks may be used to facilitate a special effect on stage.

Plan of action

1 Read the play. Analyze the costume requirements.

2 Discuss ideas with the producer and establish how much is available in the budget to spend on costumes.

3 Talk to the lighting and set departments to see if any special effect requirements should be borne in mind and make notes on these.

4 Research useful information and illustrative material for any special, historical or stylistic effects.

5 Sketch out initial ideas. Discuss these with the producer.

6 Measure the cast. Keep information in a notebook or file.

7 Check through existing wardrobe and buy any materials needed.

8 Make costumes or organize rentals as soon as possible.

9 Try the costumes on the cast and alter them as necessary.

10 Work out a plan of campaign for the special effects and any quick changes.

It will help if you can make a Costume Plot. Show clearly the play's progress, the costumes needed, the times of changes, when fast or difficult changes are due and any other special effect needs. Mark exactly where extra help is needed and set names of volunteers against these times.

11 Supervise costumes at dress rehearsals, checking that everything looks fine out front. Make sure that the special effects work and can be accomplished in time. Now that the play is running, you can also note the times of fast changes and special effects more precisely so that you, and any helpers, are organized to be there at the right moment.

12 Be on hand during the performances to help with any special effects, transformations or fast changes. Have a needle, cotton, scissors and safety pins handy for any last-minute repairs.

13 After the final performance, gather in the costumes and accessories. Clean, repair and return items as necessary.

Be budget aware

An apt and exciting range of costumes is an essential ingredient of a good production, but sometimes there can be a temptation to spend too much. Make sure the budget will not be overstretched.

1 Always keep a record of the costs involved so these do not come as a shock next time around.

*Each costume creates
its own special effect*

Be budget aware

2 Scour jumble or rummage sales and second-hand shops for jewellery, cloaks and capes, tights, baggy trousers to convert into breeches, brightly coloured skirts, aprons, shirts, evening gowns – and anything with sequins, big buttons, feathers, lace, buckles, ribbons, braid and useful trimmings of whatever kind.

3 Old curtains, bedspreads, furniture fabric, hessian, sheets and blankets will provide useful sources of material en masse, net curtaining being especially good for fairy tutus or

Curtain tape can gather sleeves into different styles

wings, 18th-century overskirts and harem pantaloons.

4 Keep an eye out for fur coats – not only for plays set in the times when these were popular but also for making animal costumes.

5 Try to accumulate accessories – such as jewellery, hats, gloves, shoes, fans, umbrellas, parasols and handbags.

6 Keep in a good stock of 'throwaway' clothes such as men's

shirts. Then these can be sacrificed nightly if there is a scene with copious amounts of stage blood pouring onto the garment or a costume that has to be torn apart – or whatever – as part of a special effect!

7 If dresses are made up as separate tops and bottoms they can be more readily adjusted to suit different performers in different plays than can a conventional dress.

8 Make separate collars and cuffs to dress up basic simple-shape tops.

Do not waste unnecessary time or money

Keep the clothes simple.

Do not fuss over details that will not be seen. To convey a particular period or style, concentrate on the shape – on the silhouette of the costume. This is the most important factor.

Use fairly large stitches. These can be quickly undone if a costume has to be altered later.

Use lots of elastic and Velcro.

If time is desperately short, seams and hems can be glued.

Elasticized waistbands mean the costumes will fit a greater variety of waistlines and different shaped actors and actresses.

In the same way, use curtain tape on waists, sleeves and necklines so that these can be gathered in as tightly or as loosely as required. This will allow you to change the size of the costume and the style, as sleeves can be left loose or gathered, necklines low or demure, overskirts left flowing or bunched up shepherdess-style.

Colour and fabric effects

As well as the costumes reflecting the overall style, period, and the location of the play, they may well be part of an overall colour scheme. The wardrobe department will need to confer with the set designer and the lighting designer to check if strong colours or specific colour themes are being used and if any special effect in these two departments requires a costume of a specific type.

For example, if a colour filter is used in a particular scene, it can have a dramatic effect on the costume colours. If a violet colour light is being used, then a green costume will turn pale blue and a yellow one turn pink – which might be very useful for a magical effect. On the other hand, one might not want Fairy Violet's purple dress to turn jet black under a red light. So find out what is happening and be positive about how the colour of the costumes may make the effect even better!

Think colour

Coordinated colour effects will add emphasis and style, especially to chorus and crowd scenes. All too often a hotchpotch of costumes may be flung out to the members of the chorus to see what fits, whereas a coordinated approach would give the final effect an additional and valuable extra dimension. The Ascot scene in *My Fair Lady*, as dressed by Cecil Beaton, will always be memorable for the dramatic effect of those glorious Edwardian dresses, all in black and white. In an amateur production of the same musical, I recall seeing all the ladies' gowns in the Embassy ball scene sweeping through the colours of anemones: various tones of red, purple and deep blue. As the ladies all assembled to be presented in order, the colours gradually mutated from one shade to another. Gorgeous!

Try to work out a suitable theme. One might choose oranges, apricots and pinks for a summer garden theme, or different shades of blue for a play about the sea – or perhaps the strong primary colours where strong divisions mark the play – whatever suits the style and the setting.

Think fabrics

The pattern and texture of the fabrics can all add to an effect on stage. For example, gingham skirts or plain skirts decorated with ric-rac braid are great for the Wild West, for schoolgirls or a country 'peasant' crowd scene.

Glittering fabrics, satins and silks are wonderful for evening gowns but expensive if you are buying new. Curtain fabrics and furniture brocades are a good deal cheaper and make an excellent substitute, especially if you can acquire them as cast-offs or secondhand. Also, the satin-type of lining material is relatively inexpensive and will shimmer beautifully under the stage lights. It will run easily, however, so it may need double hemming and edged seams.

How costume colours change under the lights

Costumes→ Lights↓	Red	Orange	Yellow	Green	Blue	Violet
Red	Fades and disappears	Becomes lighter	Becomes white	Becomes much darker	Becomes dark grey	Goes black
Yellow	Remains red	Fades slightly	Fades and disappears	Becomes dark grey	Becomes dark grey	Becomes nearly black
Green	Becomes much darker	Darkens	Darkens	Becomes very pale green	Turns dark green	Becomes nearly black
Blue	Darkens	Becomes much darker	Turns light mauve	Lightens	Turns pale blue	Turns light mauve
Violet	Becomes pale red	Lightens	Turns pink	Becomes pale blue	Darkens	Becomes very pale

Neutral colours – black, brown and grey – remain almost the same under different lights, apart from a small change in tonal value.

Quick changes off stage

Coarser fabrics such as hessian or sacking, which absorb rather than reflect light, will suggest rustic simple clothing, as for a Middle Ages peasant or monk.

Quick changes off stage

If a play requires fast changes, ensure no poor actor is left to cope alone, panicking to struggle with zips or buttons, knowing his or her cue line is fast approaching. If necessary, several helpers can be waiting in the wings to assist. This needs rehearsal so that everyone knows who is doing what

---

A few tips to speed changes

1

Make sure everything is ready in the dressing room or in the wings.

2

Use elasticised waistbands and cuffs.

3

Use Velcro fastenings which can be undone or done up in seconds.

4

Avoid zips which can jam in a moment of panic.

5

Use masks, hats and wigs to help a fast dramatic change.

6

Use poppers or snap fasteners hidden under 'mock' buttons.

7

Some costumes can be layered, one on top of another.

8

Attach any jewellery beforehand, stitching in place.

---

and in which order, otherwise the poor victim may find three over-enthusiastic helpers twisting one arm in different directions!

ACT ONE SCENES 2/3

TIME: 3 MINUTES

TAKE OFF:

SHAWL

GINGHAM SKIRT

RED SHOES

RIBBONS IN HAIR

PUT ON:

BLUE LONG SKIRT

BLUE SHOES

STRAW HAT

EAR-RINGS

GLOVES

LIPSTICK

Make a checklist in order of priority – so nothing vital is forgotten in the rush but the last items can be ignored if time runs out.

If a rush of people for a musical number or crowd scene all have to change at once make sure the cast are well trained. They need to be responsible for hanging up everything carefully and should keep their costumes neatly organized – on clearly-labelled hangers. If possible, stitch or appliqué onto the costume some numbers, letters, shapes, or a symbol for each person so there is no disputing whose are which. Symbols of some kind, rather than specific names or initials, are good because they will work for later productions with a different wearer. These might be Velcroed into place so they can easily be changed from one set of costumes to another in a later production.

Remember that a change of collars and cuffs can alter a simple shaped top. For example, a T-shirt can be turned into a French Maid's top, a low-necked blouse into the top of a Puritan lady's demure dress, or a man's shirt from conventional day-time office wear to a frilly evening shirt for a night on the town.

Collar, cuffs and sash change a costume style quickly

A variety of layers can be peeled away – or added to as required, without necessarily removing the costume underneath – and so save precious time. This is an especially useful ploy with overskirts, underskirts and capes. In the same way, shawls, scarves, aprons, frills, ruffles, lace and sashes can alter the look of a costume in a moment; while a cape or cloak might incorporate a zip to quickly change it into a skirt.

Transformations on stage

A fast change of costume or character in the wings or backstage can be problematical enough, but sometimes the script demands that this change take place on stage, and that can be even more complicated to achieve smoothly. Much rehearsal will be needed until the actor is completely confident about the transformation and timing. There is nothing more nerve-wracking than dealing with the mechanics of a fast change on stage with the audience watching – and the actor is likely to forget lines or miss cues if his or her concentration is lost because of an impending problem or fear of something going wrong.

Plan well and practice until the whole 'business' is almost automatic.

A few hints about 'on-stage' changes

1 Always provide unfussy clothes.

2 When you can, choose items with elasticated waistlines and/or necklines – or choose clothes that button (or zip) down the front rather than the back.

3 Only use Velcro fastenings if there is loud enough music or sound effects to hide the ripping sound Velcro makes.

4 Shoes can be difficult. Choose the 'slip-on/off' variety.

5 The actor should try to keep as calm as possible. Sweaty hands will add to the problems.

6 Practice and practice until the change is fast and smooth.

Analyze the change

Transformations through costume changes can be undertaken in many different ways. Every effect is different and the play situation should be analyzed before deciding how best to tackle the problem:

Is there bright lighting at the time of the change?

Is there going to be a blackout?

Does the audience see the person who is changing in full view? . . . before, during, or after the change?

Is there to be gauze (or scrim) transformation?

For how long a time and how well is the actor going to be seen before and after the change?

Just how complicated is the change?

What is the shortest possible time it will take, done conventionally?

Do you need to use a substitute actor, and is this feasible?

Is this particular costume change a realistic situation, a magical effect – or a humorous one?

This last question is probably the most important one of all, for how the change is finally achieved will depend on the approach needed.

Comic changes

For a humorous costume change the actor might simply swap hats and wigs and then pop on an artificial beard, or whatever, in full view of the audience – which can add to the comic effect.

If there is sufficient stage area, it can be fun to use cardboard cut-outs, with holes for the faces, like those once common at the seaside or carnivals for photographing visitors as cartoon characters or a deep sea diver. Paint them with the appropriate images to suit the play.

An actress pops her head through a cardboard cut-out

Tunics or tie-on aprons (styled like vinyl humorous ones) can be painted to represent various characters' clothes – and then popped on quickly.

A pantomime dame or a comedienne in a vaudeville show will often do a funny strip-tease – shedding layer after layer of silly clothes and, as she does so, revealing hot-water bottles, cartons of milk, huge bunches of keys, chains and locks, bottles of gin, truncheons, vast corsets – and anything else that will make the audience laugh. The more ridiculous this is, the better. (As there is likely to be audience reaction, cat-calling and so on, make sure the musicians are primed to keep playing for however long the scene requires.)

Transformations on stage

Semi-realistic transformations

An instant transformation is highly unlikely to be realistic, since people do not change clothes or character that fast in real life.

However, there are occasions when, for dramatic purposes, a sudden change is used to create an impact in a relatively conventional play. For instance, this might be a straight play but one where time is compressed so that someone moves forward or backwards through time while still on the stage in view of the audience. Or the actor might be stepping from one situation or setting to another in a matter of seconds, say from home to the office, or from dreaming in bed to reality. In these instances, there has to be a semi-realistic approach.

In farces, too, there are times when people have to dress or undress very quickly, or perhaps do a striptease – but with no actual magic involved.

For a transition through time or some other dimension, it can be very useful if, between any pair of places or supposed periods, the set can incorporate a flat or drapes that will momentarily screen the actor from the audience. The necessary props and clothes for the change can be secreted behind, and, again, someone to help with the change might be hiding there. The change will have to be very simple: a hat and coat can work well, slipped on quickly. Keep the dialogue flowing, meanwhile.

If the actor appears only very briefly after the change, another actor of similar build and appearance, dressed in the new way, might emerge from the screen or flat. If the flats are set upstage and hidden entrances to the stage are behind these flats, then actors and accomplices can slip in and out to appear and reappear in all sorts of guises. Be careful about sight-lines, and check the viewpoint from all possible audience angles – if the audience can see what is happening, then the effect will be destroyed.

Of course the actor might just use these entrances and exits without any pretense, simply walking through a door or arch in one costume and then appearing in another. Once again, a substitute actor may be needed to keep up the pace.

Swivelling or rotating flats (see page 64) can also be very effective and add to the change effect – as well as giving the actor the chance to vanish momentarily.

Magical changes

Using gauze (scrim)

A transformation behind gauze (scrim) is very useful for magical appearances and can either show the actor very clearly or as though veiled in a mist. This misty effect can be very useful in situations where a substitute actor is being used. The behind-the-gauze appearance with another actor portraying a middle stage in a transformation might well provide the link between two extremes, allowing the actor valuable extra time to change, perhaps, from Dr. Jekyll to Mr. Hyde, or into a werewolf mask and costume.

A gauze can help out too, in a situation where an actor is apparently looking into a mirror and then suddenly sees his or her reflection taking on another shape in a different costume.

For more information on gauze transformations see pages 44 and 62.

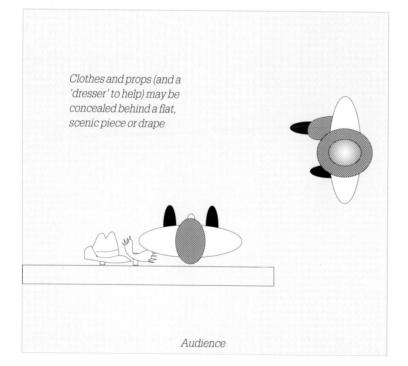

Clothes and props (and a 'dresser' to help) may be concealed behind a flat, scenic piece or drape

Audience

Magic rags-to-riches

Often in pantomime, a fairy-tale presentation, or other children's theatre, a dramatic change of costume has to happen very quickly to have any semblance of the magic it is supposed to be portraying. It is possible, of course, just to close the curtains or send the actor or actress away behind a screen of some kind while the audience have

A costume on a rigid framework may be flown into place

a sing-along, but it is much more fun for the audience if Cinderella can change into her ball gown, the poor urchin Aladdin turn into a Sultan or the Frog be transformed into a Prince – before their very eyes! Much depends on the script, of course, and how much time is allocated but a little

ingenious rewriting can usually adapt the text to suit the situation.

Here is the best method, using the Cinderella change as an example:

1 Find an actress whose height and build is very similar to Cinderella's.

2 It will help if the substitute actress has similar colour hair and hair style to the original Cinderella. However, if this is not possible use a wig and/or a servant's mob cap to hide the hair. The 'real' Cinderella will have to wear the mob cap in the preceding scene if this method is used.

3 On some pretext or another, the 'real' Cinderella will have to leave the stage ahead of the transformation – allowing just sufficient time to change into her ball gown. She might be stepping outside to find the lizard for the Fairy Godmother (as in the original fairy tale) or to admire her new carriage and horses. If the audience can still hear her voice calling back on-stage from the wings, this will help to keep up the illusion.

4 The substitute Cinderella returns to the stage, having donned the ragged costume – or an identical one. She stays near the wings – or whatever entrance suits the change – and keeps her back to the audience.

5 The Fairy Godmother waves her wand, and says the required magic words or spell.

6 There is a bright flash to 'blind' the audience which is followed by a total black-out.

7 During the black-out the ragged substitute Cinderella changes places with the 'real' Cinderella, who assumes exactly the same pose.

8 As soon as the lights are raised again, Cinderella, now in her fine regalia, turns to face the audience and hopefully, thunderous applause!

Flying costumes

It is also possible to fly in a costume from above. It will need to be designed as just a front and sides and made over a rigid structure of wire so it can drop in front of the actor who steps forward to be semi-enclosed in this 'framework'. This is one way that Cinderella might change in full view of the audience. Obviously such a costume would need to be sleeveless and Cinderella cannot turn her back or move to turn side on – or in any way that shows the gap at the back. Many costumes from the eighteenth century had hooped skirts and boned corsets, so the stiff outline is quite in keeping!

See also the Secret Pockets section on pages 121-122. This suggests a method of changing on stage which might well allow Cinderella to slip out of her rags under a cloak provided by her Fairy Godmother.

Reversible clothes

A very quick way to change is to make a reversible skirt with totally different fabrics on the inside and outside. Velcro strips at the side can be undone very quickly and the skirt wrapped around and done up the other way. As noted, sound effects or music will be needed to hide the Velcro 'tearing' noises.

Alternatively, make a generously elasticated waistline and this alone may allow the skirt to be taken off and put on again inside out very quickly. The bottom edge may need to be bound or the hem can be disguised with braid or trimming.

Animals and monsters

Animals and monsters

Animal costumes

The animal (or fish or bird) might be dressed in its entirety in fur, skin, feathers or whatever – or could be an upright humanized character. Check with the director on the approach needed before beginning to make any animal costume.

Although make-up alone can create an animal face, masks and head-dresses are often the most convincing option for an animal head. See pages 92-93 for information on making masks. Whatever the design, always ensure that animal actors can be heard and that they can see clearly where they are going!

Animal bodies

Combined with a mask, headdress or make-up, the animal body may be dressed in human clothing such as baggy trousers or dungarees. A leotard and tights can form a basis for many costumes and all sorts of wings, fur and fabric can be sewn onto these to simulate the particular animal. Or a more 'authentic' animal look might be attempted in fabric that resembles the animal skin or fur.

Useful material for the animal body might be any of the following: fur fabric, old fur coats, woollen coats and capes, terry cloth, jersey fabrics, felt, velvet, corduroy, gabardine, canvas, hessian, leather or suede, vinyl, rugs and bedding of all kinds.

Textures and colours may be painted onto a plain fabric but do not attempt to paint fur fabric unless this is sprayed through a stencil or you will end up with lots of matted clogs!

Three-dimensional bodies

Fabric can be built onto a frame to create a three-dimensional shape that will cover an actor from the neck

Costumes can be built up on a frame or hoops to make a three-dimensional shape

Before beginning, check with the director as to whether or not the animal character is to be 'humanized'

down to the toes or knees. Knee length costumes will allow easier leg movement.

Cylinders can be made of cardboard, or hoops or wire circles might form the frame. This is covered with fabric to create a full-size body section. Smaller cardboard cylinders or cones can be linked to create jointed insect limbs or a dinosaur's tail (see below).

A series of hoops can be linked by a long cylinder of fabric to make a body for a caterpillar, dragon or hippopotamus. With holes for legs, this might be used horizontally by several actors together or simply left to trail behind a single actor.

Wings may be suspended from wrists and arms or fixed on the back

Wings

Bend galvanized wire into shape and then bind the wings together with strong carpet thread. Net, muslin, organdie or plastic cling wrap can be sewn into position or glued onto the wire frame – and then decorated as required. Feathers might be made from paper, felt or fabric.

Tails

Tails are as different as the various animals themselves. Use your imagination and try whichever of the following most suits the particular creature concerned: a feather boa, fabric wound around a wire frame, a sponge roll, jointed sections of cardboard linked together, string, cord or rope, wool, fluffy pompoms, fur fabric (which can hang loose or be wired into shape), stuffed stockings or legs that have been cut from tights.

Claws and whiskers

Claws and whiskers are best made from string that is stiffened by dipping

it in glue. These may need to be reinforced with wire.

The comic horse or cow

Two people are usually required for a horse, camel or cow while any number might be hidden under a dragon or caterpillar's skin.

Make a frame for the head, with holes for the actor to see through. If the actor has to talk or sing, it is better to

leave the face free. Cover this frame with fabric or papier maché and, once this is dry, apply a basic colour paint if necessary.

Add any facial features and anything specific to this animal (for example, a mane made of wool or cord for a horse, a cow's horns, suitable ears or a full mane for a lion).

Make the animal body from fabric, sewing front and rear ends only and

A comic horse costume must usually accommodate two actors

Animals and monsters

leaving a hole for the front actor's head at one end and a small one for a tail at the other. Attach the tail and sew firmly in place.

Use tapes or a hoop to secure the animal body to the actors inside, who will require suitable trousers or leggings to match the costume.

Hints on animal detailing

Make webbed feet from felt built over a ballet shoe or slipper base and wired to hold the shape.

Pull socks over the top of slippers or sneakers to hide them.

Use gloves or mittens to disguise human hands quickly.

Attach claws to woollen gloves or to household rubber ones.

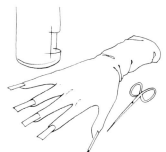

Attach claws to gloves

Check out the local joke shops that generally stock animal masks and accessories.

Make animal costumes from basic fur or skin-type bodies with interchangeable 'heads' or masks so that they are more versatile for future use.

Monsters

The monster's head is the dominant part of his costume, but the head might be achieved simply with make-up or a mask in papier maché and/or cloth maché built up over a balloon or chicken-wire frame (see pages 92-93). The mask might go over the head or the face, or just part of the face. Also, all sorts of horrors like plastic snakes and spiders can be bought at joke shops and then attached to a buckram wig base, a short-haired wig or a bathing cap.

Large-scale heads, or those of giants, can be designed to sit on the top of the head to give more height – like carnival or Mardi Gras parade characters. Be sure that they are well secured and not top heavy. A huge head might rest

Try to build up a collection of masks

Large heads might be supported on the shoulders or a pole

on the shoulders or be supported on a pole by an actor concealed below who is wearing an extra-long costume. See-through gauze can be used as part of this costume to conceal the actor's peepholes, but do ensure he or she can see clearly through these.

If the monster is an amorphous character and you can be as creative as you like, consider the following attributes: hair, slime, scales, strange coloured skin, tentacles, a tail, webbed feet, claws, fangs, bat's wings, devil's horns, bulging eyes and, perhaps, two heads!

Tips on monsters

1 Scales, eyes, gaping jaws or bones can be painted onto a dark background in luminous paint that will show up in an ultra-violet light effect (see page 55).

2 A shaggy, hairy body can be simply made from fur fabric, long-pile carpet or an old shag rug!

3 Scales can be created by cutting out scallops of shiny or self-adhesive fabric attached to a plain base fabric, so as to overlap each other. Smaller ones might be made from overlapping sequins.

4 Random spraying of a base fabric with different metallic fabric colours can be very effective.

5 Use poster paint or fabric dyes to create interesting fabric designs, but not on fur fabric.

Meanwhile, do not ignore the stereotypes of sheets for ghosts and cloaks and fangs for vampires. However hackneyed they might seem, these costumes really are the most simple and effective ways to get across the right message.

Gruesome details

Snakes, tentacles, tails and other gruesome bits can be made from cord, rope, string, cable, suction pads off children's toys, plastic corrugated vent pipe, fabric-covered flex, 'bungee' elastic, wide ric-rac braid or stuffed stockings or toes of tights, foil or paper garlands, reels of old photographic film or sound tape, and crepe paper slashed and rolled.

Blocks of foam can be used to make misshapen bodies, enormous shoulders or lumps. Make swellings and hunchbacks by stuffing sacks or pads of fabric with kapok or small pieces of foam or chopped-up tights, and then tying into place beneath the costume.

Cheesecloth soaked in sizing, shellac or various kinds of white flexible glue (such as PVA) can be squeezed into wrinkles and folds of flesh (see also page 105).

Aliens and robots

Aliens and robots which need a mechanized appearance can be concocted with all sorts of 'junk': pieces of old telephones, electrical tools and materials, egg boxes, dials, nuts, bolts and washers, plastic bottles and containers, toilet-roll tubes, corrugated cardboard, ping-pong balls and bed

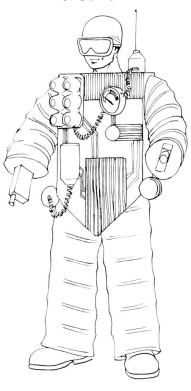

Jumble, sprayed with metallic paint, creates a good robotic or sci-fi effect

springs. Sprayed with metallic paint, this jumble can look like very effective sci-fi paraphernalia.

Tricks of the trade

Velcro additions

Costumes can assume all sorts of different styles by adding extra elements that are secured in place by Velcro. So an actress might begin in a simple sleeveless short dress and then have a section added at the hem to make it full-length (or vice versa). In the same way, sleeves of varying lengths can be added, as well as collars and cuffs. This is one way of creating a very versatile wardrobe.

Lengthen or shorten costumes with Velcro additions

Secret pockets and the pseudo striptease

In a farce such as *Not Now, Darling*, it may be necessary for an actress to pretend to do a striptease. The audience have to believe she is naked at the end of her 'routine'. She needs to be seen first in her underwear so the audience know what these underclothes look like. Then, once covered up with a coat that has been flung around her shoulders by her embarrassed fellow male actor, she continues to undress, shedding her sexy underclothes onto the stage.

The trick is to conceal identical pieces of underwear to those already seen by the audience in pockets inside the

Tricks of the trade

coat. These are tossed out until she is apparently stark naked!

Secret pockets can provide all sorts of useful ways to change clothes or appearance surreptitiously. If the actor is wearing an extra layer of clothing under the coat or cloak, this layer might be divested to reveal a new outfit below; the top layer is meanwhile hidden in the internal pockets of the cloak. Cloaks are better than coats because they leave the hands free but, in any event, it is obviously much easier to throw clothes out than to slip anything on! Certainly, it will be necessary to divert attention away from any wriggling under the coat or cloak if this is to be attempted.

However, if there is a distracting explosion, a puff of green smoke and the genie jumping out of the bottle on stage right, then Aladdin might well be able to slip on some fine jewels and be discovered holding a crown on stage left without too much attention being paid to his activities. None the less, it will need to be well rehearsed just in case anyone is looking his way.

Hat tricks

The bobbing hat

> **You will need**
>
> **1**
> A hat with a brim
>
> **2**
> 2 safety pins
>
> **3**
> A large strong elastic band

1 Fasten safety pins to the sweat band of the hat, one fixed above each ear position.

2 Place the elastic band so that it stretches around the inside of the hat but is looped over the safety pins to hold it securely in place.

3 The hat needs to be pulled down tightly over the actor's head.

4 Now, whenever appropriate – perhaps when the actor is introduced to somebody and shakes hands – he should raise his eyebrows so as to wrinkle his forehead.

5 This will make the hat rise up from the crown of his head and tip back and forth in greeting!

An elongated neck

> **You will need**
>
> **1**
> A hat with a brim
>
> **2**
> A coat with a collar

1 Place the hat on the actor's head.

2 Drape the overcoat over the actor's shoulders.

3 Tuck the back of the coat collar into the back of the hat brim. For extra security the collar and hat might be stitched together.

4 The actor needs to bend his (or her) elbows so as to hold the side of the hat brim with the hands. Make sure the audience cannot see the hands from the back or side view of the actor.

5 The actor stands with his back or side to the audience, looking at various items on the back or side of the stage – say, pictures in an art gallery hung at different heights or Jack's beanstalk growing ever taller.

6 As he looks at the higher items, the actor slowly and carefully raises his hands so that the hat and coat collar rise up.

7 His neck appears to stretch and elongate as he looks at the highest objects, and to then drop down again.

Pyrotechnics and related effects  Safety first

Pyrotechnics are probably what spring to mind first when the term 'special effects' is used. Certainly these comprise some of the most exciting effects. Pyrotechnics include transformation powder, flash powder, flash paper, sparklers, all the flashes and bangs a dedicated team of experts can pitch into the production and a host of detonator devices used only by professionals. Fog, smoke, and haze can be produced by a variety of fog machines and oil crackers. Used wisely by trained personnel, there are few effects as stunning and dramatic as a noisy explosion or filling the stage with swirls of coloured smoke or fog.

However, pyrotechnics can be dangerous and should never be handled by the untrained amateur. The equipment can be expensive, fireworks must be stored very carefully indeed and special licenses – or the services of a licensed professional – will need to be secured to implement many effects. Also, remember that it is better to use a few effects well than to pepper a production with too many 'specials'! There can be a temptation, especially if the company has invested heavily in the purchase or rental of a special machine to introduce effects more often than necessary. Stick to the script and the director's guidelines and be as disciplined in your choices of what to do as in your handling of the equipment.

Planning the pyrotechnics

It cannot be overemphasized that pyrotechnics must be used with safety as the first rule and with strict obedience to all laws. Never try to concoct or invent your own pyrotechnic device!

Pyrotechnics may come under the supervision of several departments, or one dedicated 'special' team, be the stage manager's responsibility or be handled by a professional. Whoever is ultimately in charge needs to be especially well organized for the handling of potentially dangerous material.

1 Read the play, highlighting the special effects. Make a list of these.

2 Discuss ideas for creating the effects with the director/producer, and the technical aspects with the rest of the team. Discuss whether professional help needs to be brought into the production to deal with any dangerous pyrotechnics.

3 Do any necessary further research on the exact effect needed and the best means to achieve this.

4 Highlight the special effects in your own cue sheet and then ensure that the stage manager highlights them in his or her cue book too.

5 Make a timetable. Show clearly who must do what, when, where.

6 Check over any pyrotechnics equipment owned by the group to ensure it is in good working order.

7 Organize the purchase, rental or manufacture of any further equipment needed. For obvious reasons, pyrotechnics cannot be sent through the mail so ensure you can get them at the appropriate time. There are some new substances that remain inactive until one is combined with another, and occasionally these may be available through the mail.

8 Check all aspects of the proposed site of any pyrotechnics used on stage. You should confer with lighting, props and set personnel to ensure that the effect is in a safe suitable position and that the site will be in good view when the effect is triggered.

9 Prepare the special effect equipment ahead of time. Try to allow plenty of time to practice with it in rehearsals and to continue to check the maintenance and safety of all the equipment. The cost of pyrotechnics may inhibit the amount of practice that can be afforded, so decide beforehand exactly how many 'spares' the budget will allow. You need to ensure, for example, that fog effects are placed where they will not trigger the smoke or fire alarms or where a build-up of fog might obscure stairs or exits.

10 Supervise special effects at dress and technical rehearsals.

11 Make any adjustments that are deemed necessary.

12 Oversee the effects throughout performances.

13 Afterwards, remove, return or store effects. Dispose of spent effects safely and as legally required.

14 Keep records to comply with all the required paperwork and 'red tape'. Also keep notes on how well the pyrotechnics worked, the suppliers used, and any lessons learned. This will save valuable time in later productions.

Safety first

It is not possible to cover all the complex national and local regulations that apply to pyrotechnics, fog machines, and so on in this short treatment. County (State in the USA), and municipal regulations, vary greatly. So it is of primary importance to call upon the experience of an

expert such as your supplier or to hire a pyrotechnic technician who will guide the production through the maze of regulations.

In the United States, the best safety guidelines can be found in the code developed by the National Fire Protection Association: the Code for the Use of Pyrotechnics in the Entertainment Industry (NFPA 1126).

Here are some of the most vital things to be done if you plan to use pyrotechnics and fog-producing techniques in a production. Some specific details apply to the USA only but, of course, safety factors are applicable, wherever you perform.

1 Consult your local fire or police department to see if pyrotechnics are allowed in your presentation space and, if so, what steps to take to comply with regulations. Pyrotechnics may not be permitted in certain circumstances and buildings, so it is best to know from the start just what is permissible.

Follow all laws and advice carefully.

In the UK, explosives cannot be kept or stored without a license so ensure that this is obtained. Your supplier may be able to advise on this. Sale of pyrotechnics to minors is almost universally prohibited by law.

2 Take expert advice. If required, organise the hire of pyrotechnic technicians whose qualifications and/or licenses are accepted by local authorities.

3 Be sure your theatre has insurance that will cover the use of pyrotechnics. In some cases local laws require certificates of insurance.

4 Transport pyrotechnic materials as required by national and local regulations (in the USA, check state regulations as well as those of the Department of Transportation).

5 Store and transport pyrotechnics in the proper containers, called 'magazines'. In the USA, different classes of pyrotechnics must be kept in different types of magazines. If the pyrotechnics for one day's work is taken to the theatre in a 'daybox' (type 3 portable magazine), an attendant must be with the daybox at all times.

6 Smoking, matches, open flames and spark-producing devices are not allowed within 50 feet of an outdoor magazine, or inside any room containing an indoor magazine. *Smoking must not be allowed in the vicinity of any pyrotechnics.*

7 When pyrotechnics or flame are generated on stage, all drops, curtains, costumes, and combustible props must be fire-retarded. Check that that this has been done and that everything is fireproofed up to the necessary standards. You may use aluminium foil to give extra protection to the immediate area of an effect. Ensure that any electrical wires in the vicinity of the effect are fully insulated and fireproof.

8 Carry out a test run without spectators or performers. In some cases, local fire officials require a test run at which they are present.

9 Plan to have at least one trained person standing by with a fire extinguisher to 'firewatch' during and after any pyrotechnic effect is fired.

10 Use the theatre's ventilation system or special fans to remove smoke from the stage and adjacent areas quickly and to keep smoke from the audience. Prevailing winds will work as ventilation during outdoor effects.

11 Design and practice blocking to ensure that performers and personnel are far away from pyrotechnics when these are ignited, and out of direct outflow from fog machines.

12 Never allow children around pyrotechnics or expose them to chemical fogs or loud blasts.

13 Post warnings on pyrotechnic storage areas and magazines and alert all personnel when effects will be used.

14 Use respirators, protective eyewear, hearing protection and other safety equipment if needed.

15 Fog machines or pyrotechnics must not be used if exit signs and routes will be obscured or smoke detectors or sprinkler systems set off.

16 Prepare for medical emergencies. Pyrotechnic fog is known to cause respiratory irritation: many fog fluid labels carry warnings for asthmatics. Make provisions for medical evaluation and treatment of any cast or crew member who needs it. It is unreasonable to expose large numbers of people to pyrotechnic smoke and fog chemicals night after night without your being prepared for respiratory problems. If illness or accident may be attributed to your special effects, keep accurate records of their use and people's exposure to them.

Store safely

When not in use, the pyrotechnics must be stored in a special magazine (essential in the USA) or metal container. Ideally, this should be kept in a separate locked room or at the very least somewhere isolated from all the main comings and goings. The room should be clearly designated to this end and a sign placed on the door warning everyone of the fact that there are explosives inside and of the inherent danger.

The more official the appearance the better

You can purchase standard signs (see page 154)

Don't smoke!
Never ever smoke in the vicinity of any pyrotechnics.

Mark plugs and switches
Always label clearly any plugs or switches used so that everyone can see at a glance which are involved.

Work safely
Always unplug equipment not in use. Make sure that no-one else has an opportunity to interfere!

Set up safely
Effects should not be set up earlier than necessary and or switched on until immediately prior to use. Only the professional experts loading the effects should hold any vital 'detonator' keys.

Warn others
As well as the notice on the store room, warn everyone of the dangers when the device is in use and point out the labelled plugs so that no mistakes can be made. Just as with stroboscopic lights, a note in the programme or in the venue may be needed to warn the audience that such an effect will be used.

Lock up
Always lock up safely and make sure keys are in safe keeping.

Keep a safe distance
Always ensure that any properties, flats, drops, trailing costumes – and stage hands and actors – are well clear of any pyrotechnic effect. Cables connected to any device should also be at least 2 metres (2 yards) long.

Handle dry ice with caution
Always wear gloves when handling dry ice. It can burn the skin. When breaking it up, cover it to prevent flying splinters causing any injury.

Follow instructions
As well as any advice from the police or fire departments and from your suppliers or professional technicians, always double check that you follow all the manufacturer's instructions to the letter.

Commercially prepared devices that create special effects are available and will be far safer than trying to create your own. So, despite our 'Create Your Own' theme to these books, this is one instance where we warn you to use only a ready-made device!

A mechanical explosion

Since pyrotechnics are so complicated and dangerous, and professional help so expensive, it is often better to opt for a 'mechanical' effect – one that simulates an explosion without involving true pyrotechnics. This may be a good option if you do not have the available skills and experience to use

pyrotechnics, if you cannot afford them, or if the authorities have refused permission for any fireworks or similar devices to be used in your venue.

Sound effects discs provide a good choice of noisy explosions and the debris may be projected by an air cannon. This is a metal tube with a compressed air tank at its base. It can shoot material up to 8 metres (26 feet) into the air. Use cornstarch, expanded polystyrene, crumbled cork or any suitable fabric that cannot hurt the cast or audience.

Alternatively, use an elastic or spring powered catapult or some means of dropping the debris from above. See pages 83 and 95 for further suggestions on the kinds of debris that add to the realism of a mechanical explosion effect and how to make objects fall from above. Combine these effects in the right order with good coordinated

Professional only effects

timing and the resulting explosion can be very convincing.

Generally, it is recommended that you use a professional technician whenever the effects you desire require the use of professional equipment or if you wish to use pyrotechnic chemicals which can detonate with explosive force, especially when these are used in a box, mortar or other such confining device.

Anything that flashes, burns, ignites, or explodes in a container should be considered dangerous. Almost all fuses, including squibs, 'quick matches' and other detonators contain unstable lead compounds and create lead fumes. These devices are not for novices. Hiring professional help may be beyond the budget – in which case it is best to concentrate on lighting, sound and mechanical effects, to achieve an explosion.

Transformation powder

Transformation powder burns very slowly, and comes in a range of colours such as green and amber. It therefore seems ideal for a prolonged effect and especially useful for a scene involving magic. Coloured effects, however, are usually more toxic as they use complex dyes or compounds which contain metals such as barium and copper. Whenever you consider

---

Professional effects

The following professional effects should be used only by a licensed pyrotechnics expert

Maroons

A maroon is somewhat similar to a 'banger' firework. This is the vital component that actually detonates and creates all the noise in a full-scale stage explosion. There are various sizes, each of which contains a different amount of pyrotechnic material. The maroon is detonated electrically by a special pyrotechnics detonator. To contain the explosion, the maroon is placed in a purpose-built bomb tank. This must never be completely closed or it will become highly dangerous. The technician will use only one maroon in a bomb tank at any one time.

1 Tell everyone where the bomb tanks are situated and when the explosion will be detonated.

2 Put notices up immediately before their use (not left about all the time or they will be ignored!).

3 Keep the area clear at the time of the explosion.

4 The pyrotechnics expert will be aware that an explosion should never be triggered if the view of the site is blocked for any reason. It is better to miss the special effect than to risk injury or fire.

Flash powder and paper

Flash powders and flash paper are made of nitrocellulose, which burns with a flash on ignition and then produces toxic and irritating oxides of nitrogen. Flash powder is highly inflammable and must be kept away from any open flame or heat source. This very fast-burning powder will create magical flashes and is excellent for a witch's cauldron, battle scenes and so on. If large amounts of flash powders are used in big flash-boxes, fountains, waterfalls, and flamepots, there can be significant amounts of toxic emissions.

These effects should be controlled by a pyrotechnic professional only because they require a source of ignition such as a fuse, an electric match, or a detonator.

When used in small amounts in the open, flash powders and paper are not so hazardous. For example, magicians use small pieces of flashpaper to give the illusion that they can create a flame with their hands.

The flash box

Just like maroons, flash powder must be safely contained in a strong metal box. In a sophisticated professional flash box system, a pre-made flash cartridge plugs into the flash box and is detonated from a low-voltage power supply situated in a switch box with a clearly marked 'fire' button. The flash is generally triggered off-stage by remote control – hence the warnings about clear visibility of the action on stage at the time.

Angled boxes

With an angled box, the angle of the cartridge platform is able to be altered. A confetti or streamer cartridge can be used in this and will make a stunning finale spectacle, provided no-one objects to the clearing up afterwards! To detonate the flash powder in the box, a pyrotechnic fuse may be used.

using transformation powders, obtain manufacturers' safety data sheets (MSDS) so that you can choose those without toxic metals or dyes. And then use only very small amounts. Alway store the transformation powder in its own metal container.

Ordinary firework sparklers are similar to transformation powder. These burn slowly and send out sparks. Generally they are safer used in outdoor productions only. A firewatcher should stand by – maintain vigilant common sense about safety.

Smoke and fog effects

Swirling fog can be used on stage and is created by dry ice, fired smoke puffs or by a special smoke machine. The effect is superb for ghostly scenes, misty moors or seas, battle zones, mysterious dance sequences, fire effects and for using in conjunction with many lighting special effects (see also pages 54 and 57).

Technically, real smoke or fog is composed of tiny particles and droplets suspended in the air. Haze can be either fog or smoke, but the droplets or particles are so small that they appear invisible until a beam of light hits them. Dozens of different chemicals are used to create fog or haze. Cryogenic gases, such as dry ice and liquid nitrogen are so cold that they will cause water vapour in the air to

---

Always wear gloves

Do not overdo the effect

Practice first to establish what you need to do

Make sure there is good ventilation

---

condense into tiny liquid droplets. The result is a fog that is accompanied by the gas that produced it.

Fog machines

Glycol foggers create a fine mist of water mixed with chemicals called glycols (including butylene glycol, propylene glycol, polyethylene glycol, and triethylene glycol).

Various types of oils are used in machines such as 'oil crackers' to produce a fine mist. These include glycerine, mineral, and vegetable oils. The oils to be used are specific to the machines – do not try to experiment.

Simulating smoke

Lighting fires in a theatre is taboo, for obvious reasons. However, you may hear of flammable devices such as 'smoke cookies', which are smoke-producing chunks or wafers. These emit fumes that look like smoke or haze, created when sal ammoniac (ammonium chloride) and other chlorides such as zinc and titanium chloride are heated. These are not healthy fumes, however, and the use of these devices is not recommended. Fog or smoke can also be created by burning materials such as frankincense and other such combustibles. This is a very risky and it is better to rely on dry ice and fog machines, including oil crackers, for creating fog or smoke effects.

Dry ice

Dry Ice Precautions

Always wear gloves when handling dry ice or placing it in water. Dry ice is frozen carbon dioxide gas (-110 F) and it can stick to the skin and cause freezer burns.

Do not store dry ice in a domestic freezer. It will deteriorate and the nearby food will be ruined.

Dry ice is a very effective way of filling the stage with smoke but should always be used with caution. You need to control the generation of the fog. The rate at which dry ice will produce fog depends on the size of the pieces of ice and the temperature of the water. It is very easy to overdo the effect because it is such a volatile material. The higher the temperature of the water and the smaller the pieces, the greater the amount of fog produced. If the temperature is too high and the pieces too small, the gas-releasing action will be violent.

Practice working with dry ice to avoid overdoing the effect. Otherwise, during the show, you may suddenly find that the cast and the front rows of the audience are gasping and choking. An opera singer directed to 'play dead' on stage next to a pool full of dry ice had a seizure due to lack of oxygen and had to be rushed to hospital!

In addition to the dramatic health risks, dry ice can cause subtle problems. Research on poorly ventilated buildings has shown that even a percentage or two of additional carbon dioxide in the air will affect people's ability to function. High carbon dioxide levels can impair a performer's mental acuity and reaction time, and make the audience feel fatigued.

Dry ice fog is cold, dense, and heavier than air. It may provide just the effect you want in a scene, as it will drop to the stage, fall into the orchestra pit, and flow out into the audience. The fog and the carbon dioxide gas that accompanies it should be controlled by good ventilation and by using as little fog as is necessary.

Smoke and fog effects

Pieces of dry ice can be melted in hot water in a small bath tub or similar container in the wings. To produce a good steady flow of vapour, it is better broken up into small pieces. First wrap the dry ice inside a sack or cloth so that stray splinters do not fly about and hit anyone in the eye. Then use a hammer to break up the block. Generally, however, it is easier, and much more controllable, to use a professional dry-ice machine.

Using a dry-ice machine

It is easier to control dry ice fog by purchasing or renting a dry-ice machine. The machine consists of a container in which water is heated by an electric element. A cage holds the dry ice, and it can be raised or lowered to control the amount of fog created. An opening or hose will direct the flow of fog from the machine.

The supplier of dry ice may not necessarily be the place that rents out the dry ice machine. Check this first.

Liquid nitrogen

Liquid nitrogen can be used in ways similar to dry ice, but it is more difficult to obtain, and the potential for spills and serious burns in increased. It is best handled by professionals.

Storage

Dry ice is not easy to store and generally it is best to get it from a supplier just a few hours prior to each performance. However, timing and distance may make this impractical. In these cases, seal the dry ice in an airtight plastic bag. Then bury this bag in an insulated box and surround it with expanded polystyrene. The dry ice may then remain stable for a day or so. Also, never store pyrotechnics, fog, or

smoke chemicals in domestic refrigerators or freezers. Keep food and chemicals away from near each other to eliminate the possibility of contaminating the food with tiny amounts of either the chemicals or their emissions. Dry ice stored in a domestic freezer will ruin the food.

Chemical fog machines

There are many different types of fog machines to choose from. In addition to pressurized water foggers, intended primarily for outdoor venues, the five basic types of units are:

> Pump-propelled foggers for glycol-water mixtures
>
> Gas-propelled foggers for mineral oil or glycol-water mixed
>
> Crackers for high grade mineral oil
>
> Crackers for glycol-water mixture
>
> Ultrasonic hazers for glycol-water mixture

Several different manufacturers make these various types of machines, and they all are designed for a specific brand of fluid. In fact, some machines use glycerine instead of glycols. Each machine makes a fog with its own unique look and behaviour. Consult an expert lighting designer to help you make the best choice.

Smoke guns

Smoke guns produce vaporized glycerine which looks like conventional smoke. The glycerine is forced through a heated pipe by compressed gas (usually carbon dioxide in an aerosol can) or a gas compressor. The smoke it produces smells strangely sweet, and it will coat things in its vicinity with a fine layer of glycerine. The smoke gun is not a gun at all. It may be a canister with a screw-in aerosol or a pump-operated machine where liquid is pumped up from a tank into a heat exchanger.

Some smoke guns offer a variety of effects. A range of spare cans, which can be simply screwed into place, allow the guns to be refilled easily and

A portable fog or smoke box

create a range of smoke effects, largely achieved through the various ways the smoke stays in the air and how slowly or quickly it disperses. The following can be simulated:

> A steaming kettle – a gush of steam that disperses quickly
>
> A misty morning – lingering smoke that swirls over the stage
>
> Dusty 'haze' smoke – this will 'seed' the air so that light beams can be seen more clearly

The smoke may contain small amounts of hazardous decomposition chemicals which will vary with the temperature of the heat exchanger through which it travels. Even simple gun smoke contains sulphur oxides that are strong irritants and can trigger asthma attacks.

LSX convertors

This pump-operated smoke gun is filled with LSX fluid. It sends out a heavy smoke but one that disperses more quickly than the usual standard smoke. The smoke will flow across the stage just like dry ice and its density is controlled by temperature. (Cold smoke is denser than warm smoke.) It is a narrow unit fitted on wheels and can fill the stage floor with mist just a few inches (or centimetres) high or billow smoke up to about 2 feet (600 mm) high.

Safety guidelines for fog and smoke effects

There are few laws that apply to use of fog machines and similar devices but occasionally regulations restrict fog use in certain public places. In the US, the Occupational Safety and Health Administration (OSHA) and similar state agencies require employers to protect personnel from hazards. For example, there are OSHA regulations limiting the amounts of certain fog chemicals to which workers can be exposed. If you use union workers, be aware that some union contracts require additional safety measures when fog and pyrotechnics are used.

There have been a number of incidents and several scientific studies which show that the use of certain effects can cause adverse health effects. Lawsuits and union actions have also been initiated by performers, musicians, and other personnel claiming injury.

Never use any type of fog machine unless you have a copy of the operator's manual or the manufacturer's directions for use. Follow all directions precisely. Deviating from these can damage equipment and compromise warranties – and may leave you personally liable for any harm to people or property which results. Never alter a machine or change the composition of the chemicals!

In order to protect your theatre's liability, it is wise to adopt the guidelines of professional organizations that set safety standards for use of these

left *A light curtain works brilliantly if made denser with smoke*

below *Back light a smoke screen to create a stunning silhouette*

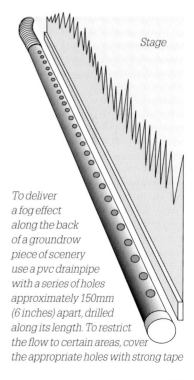

Stage

To deliver a fog effect along the back of a groundrow piece of scenery use a pvc drainpipe with a series of holes approximately 150mm (6 inches) apart, drilled along its length. To restrict the flow to certain areas, cover the appropriate holes with strong tape

effects, such as the Alliance of Motion Picture and Television Producers (AMPTP) and the Entertainment Services & Technology Association (ESTA) in the USA. The following is a compilation of the advice of both.

1 Always choose the safest product that will achieve the desired effect. The AMPTP guidelines restrict indoor effects to products containing propylene glycol, butylene glycol, polyethylene glycol, glycerine (if not heated above 700° F) and the cryogenic gases.

2 Use only the minimum concentration necessary to achieve the desired effect, and deliver it only to areas where it is needed.

3 Keep people away from the direct outflow of fog or haze generating machines.

4 Post warnings about when you will use effects and the potential hazards. Exclude all non-essential personnel when effects are used.

5 Periodically ventilate or exhaust the stage, or else give all personnel a break away from the stage at appropriate intervals. Use ventilation to keep audiences from being exposed.

6 Provide emergency access to fog or haze machines so they can be immediately turned off or serviced if they malfunction.

7 Never use any fog or smoke effect in amounts that will make the stage slippery or leave a residue on lights or electrical equipment.

You should obtain the manufacturer's material safety data sheets on the special effects products you consider for use. Evaluate these MSDSs in order to select the safest effects. Inform and train all potentially exposed personnel about the hazards of the effects and provide them with access to the MSDSs. Inform performers at audition about the effects that will be used.

Warn the audience with clear notices at the box office – and in the programme – about fog and smoke uses on the stage.

Fire!

There has been some discussion of how to create realistic fires in the properties section (see page 88) but it is worth mentioning again here since a smoke effect may well need to be used in conjunction with a fire simulation. This can be created with a powerful uplight, ideally a bright pulsing light under upward coiling smoke. Avoid using lights which have sharply defined beams.

You can blow air through silk flames to make them dance. Do ensure the silk is very, very fine indeed so that it can float easily. You may need to use fans to make the smoke move upwards but make sure these are not too noisy. Small ones work best. Or it may be possible to use a cooperative stage hand in a strategic position fanning the air with a large piece of card! Blow smoke in front of the silk and not directly onto the fabric or smoke particles will be soaked up by the material and eventually weigh this down.

A film projection of fire can also be combined with a smoke effect. Whether using fabric or a lighting effect, use yellows and oranges rather than red for the most realistic flames.

Fun pyrotechnics

Theatrical suppliers stock all kinds of preparations that will create exciting special effects. It is worth investigating some of these ideas, but do remember that none of these items are cheap and some of them are hugely expensive. Decide which will be the most useful and check that you are not overstretching the budget. Renting the more expensive equipment, like a confetti cannon or a bubble machine, may well be the better option unless this equipment is something you plan to use regularly.

Check out local party shops, joke stores, specialist magic shops and mail-order theatrical suppliers. They often stock interesting fun pyrotechnics or related special effects. Read the instructions carefully and make sure the effect is safe to use indoors.

Always give due consideration to health and safety factors and to legality and liability. Use professionals if necessary. But remember that a little imagination can go a long way to overcome budget restrictions and create fun pyrotechnic effects safely.

Speciality fun effects from stores or catalogues

Confetti cannons

Confetti balloons

Bubble machines or simple bubble blowers

Silver stars to sprinkle

Streamer cartridges

Spray cans of silly string

Snow sprays

Cobweb sprays

Conjuror's streaming ribbons

History

A dip into the past

Whatever the context of the production, players today generally perform in a contemporary theatre – using twentieth-century technology – to a twentieth-century audience with twentieth-century attitudes. The audience expectations are relatively high. They are used to cinema and television productions with all the pace and effects that film and photography can generate. Also, there are rules and regulations that demand high standards of safety to protect both audience, technicians and performers. So one cannot simply turn the clock back. Nor would one wish to. Many hundreds of theatres burned to the ground in the 1700s and 1800s when the flames from candles or oil lamps set light to fabrics or scenery. In 1845, some 1,600 people died in a blazing theatre in China.

However, we have much to learn from the history of theatre, and now and then it can be inspiring to dip into the past to see how certain production areas were tackled. Moreover, if one is staging a play set in a particular period,

Earliest theatres used natural hill-sides to create raked seating with excellent viewing and acoustics

it may help to create the right atmosphere if some of the techniques used at that time are reintroduced.

Typically, a Victorian music-hall or melodrama will work best in a fairly intimate theatre with no modern microphones visible to spoil the authentic flavour. A Greek play will seem most natural performed in an open arena. And while Shakespeare's plays can be translated to any period of time and work very well, if the director's intent is to capture the 'how-it-was-then' feeling, then Elizabethan costumes are a must.

So who did what when? What special effects were used? How did sound, lighting, scenery, costumes and so

on work together in the past to excite the audiences of long ago? And what are we likely to be able to achieve in the future?

Greek and Roman theatre

Theatres

Greek and Roman theatres were centres of spectacle and combat, as well as drama. Religious ritual and gladiator fights took place in vast arenas with multiple entrances.

In Greece these arenas were generally set into the hillside, using the natural contours, but later on and in Roman times the theatres were usually com-

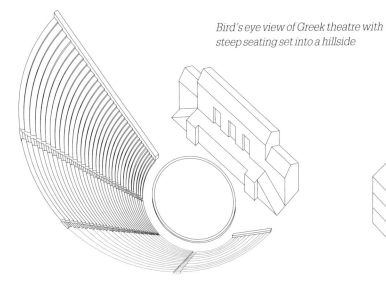

Bird's eye view of Greek theatre with steep seating set into a hillside

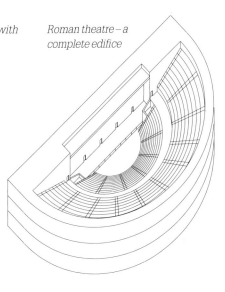

Roman theatre – a complete edifice

Greek and Roman theatre

plete, vast man-made edifices with tiered or raked seating for as many as 20,000 spectators.

Originally the central acting area was just flattened earth but in due course raised stages were built.

The shape of Greek and Roman arenas meant that both acoustics and visibility were excellent.

The first permanent stone theatre was built by Pompeius in 55-52 BC.

Sound and lighting

Sound

The bowl of the natural hillside or stone amphitheatre combined with the high structure behind the orchestra area created brilliant acoustics. The human voice was able to bounce up off the rear stage area which acted as a sounding board. The actors could be heard even by those in the highest, most distant seats.

Sound effects in Greek theatre were often generated by the chorus who would also dance, sing, and chant. One or two would play a musical instrument such as a lyre or pipe.

Member of an Ancient Greek chorus declaiming

Three Ancient Greek masks: these denoted sex, emotion and character

Lighting

The Ancient Greeks performed in daylight and merely held up an oil lantern to denote that, in the plot, night had fallen.

Other effects

Sets and scenic effects

Scenery was minimal but there is evidence that the Greeks and Romans sometimes used stage machinery. Revolving panels (periaktoi) with three sides denoting different places were used; cranes were implemented to fly in gods and goddesses.

Painting was being used to depict settings in the 4th century BC. Some 2,000 years ago the scenery was described as tragic (palatial columns), as comic (more homely dwellings), or as satyric (landscape), aided by the natural landscape all around.

As well as the actors performing in these formal theatres, there were strolling players too, whose theatres were simple timber platforms raised on posts. This stage was sometimes protected by an awning and backed by a curtained background scene.

Make-up

Masks were worn to denote sex (as only men performed), character or emotion – so make-up was not much in evidence!

Actors and costumes

Actors changed in dressing rooms set into the buildings that formed the backdrop façade.

Outrageous humour and slapstick arrived in the Roman period.

Special effects

In Roman times, battles were staged, sometimes against wild animals like lions and tigers.

Amphitheatres could be flooded to stage mock battles at sea or to show victims being fed to hungry crocodiles instead of lions: spectacle was everything!

The Middle Ages

In about AD 500 the Christian Church dominated much of the Western world, and since the Church considered drama, plays and players to be corrupt, there was little theatre in evidence in Europe.

In time, however, religious plays were allowed to be performed in churches. These led to miracle plays in the market place, and eventually to a much wider spread of theatre – although religious themes still dominated for a very long time. Travelling players and minstrels, masked bands and mummers plays developed legitimacy out of these beginnings.

Mummers plays, although still depicting Christian ideals, often involved legends such as St George killing the dragon, a rather frightening 'Wild Man' character and a masked band. They would generally perform at times of festival.

Theatres

In the first Church enactment of biblical stories, a stage might be set where the altar stood with one or two temporary platforms for the more distant scenes. This developed into the use of many different stages or platforms for different scenes – called 'mansions'.

In time, the performances moved from inside the church to just outside and thence, in due course, to the marketplace where mystery plays depicting Bible stories became a most popular form of entertainment. Audiences were generally standing.

Stage hands making sound effects

The various mansions depicting different scenes or stories were often housed on carts which could be wheeled around to various venues or groups of spectators.

By the 1200s travelling entertainers wandered all around Europe. A simple scaffold arrangement would be used as a mobile theatre. They might be performing in a market square one night and at a rich landowner's banquet the next. They had to travel light, carrying everything with them on loaded wagons; and they had to be able to set up for performances quickly. The stage might just be planks on barrels with cloth screens.

Special effects

Sound

During a miracle play, stage hands behind the scenes would shout, bang drums, clatter pots and pans, blow trumpets and fire the odd cannon.

Sets and scenic effects

With the first performances of religious plays, the popular use of different raised platforms for different scenes meant that there was little scene shifting involved. The audience moved instead, by turning to face the appropriate stage.

Make-up

Masks were worn, particularly for miracle plays.

Actors and costumes

Actors were generally itinerant travelling players, often regarded as vagabonds, moving from town to town but might also be members of the local guilds who would put on plays at a time of celebration or festival. Bright extravagant costumes were vital to 'professional' travelling players to ensure that they would attract sufficient attention when they arrived to guarantee an audience.

There were also wandering minstrels who could be singers, comedians, or acrobats or be solitary masters of many talents. Some would perform with puppets or mime while others might recite poetry.

Pyrotechnics and other effects

Heaven and Hell were common themes in mystery and morality plays, so smoke was made to belch out to represent the Devil's domain, often from Hell's mouth itself!

Devils and angels were flown by special machinery – at an astronomical cost borne by the Church.

16th century and Elizabethan theatre

**16th century and
Elizabethan theatre**

Theatre eventually became a separate entity from religious teachings, and this rebirth and fresh versatility gave rise to great writing. As any student of his plays is aware, Shakespeare relied a great deal on his brilliant descriptive dialogue. While the available techniques were limited, his text made up the deficit by giving his characters speeches that included evocative descriptions of what was happening, where and how.

Meanwhile, in Italy, the commedia dell'arte comedies were hugely popular with lots of knockabout humour and ribald jokes.

In 1597 the emphasis on song in Italian theatre gave rise to the first real opera when Peri's *Dafne* was performed. Similarly, the emphasis on dance in French theatre would eventually develop into the ballet.

*Arlecchino (or
Harlequin), a
character from
commedia dell'arte*

Theatres

The Elizabethans used a thrust stage with the audience arranged on three sides of the projecting stage, very close to the performers so there was lots of interaction. The Globe Theatre in London had a circular auditorium with the audience in galleries but still set around a thrust stage.

Commedia dell'arte was performed by travelling groups who initially used just a simple platform and a painted backcloth. As their popularity spread, the artists were invited to perform before the royal courts of Europe. Productions became much more lavish and complicated and in due course were largely performed in permanent theatres.

Raked stages rose at the back to increase the perspective effects of the scenery and led to the terms 'upstage' and 'downstage' – still used today for the rear and front sections of a stage, whether sloping or flat.

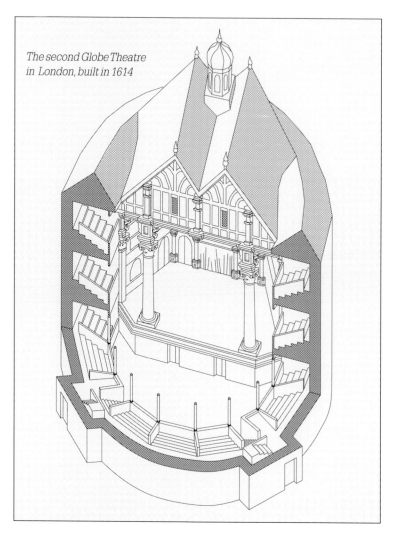

*The second Globe Theatre
in London, built in 1614*

Sound and lighting

Sound

Music was obviously important in Shakespeare's plays and many of the comedies include songs, while for the tragedies and historical plays, battle and storm noises were created by musical percussion instruments or special sound effect tools.

Lighting

The Italians had enormous influence during this period and experimented with lenses and colour filters made of silk. They also used coloured liquids or wine in glass vessels set in front of candles to create various light tints on the stage.

Angelo Ingegneri suggested that a darkened auditorium made the lit stage appear much brighter – something that we now take for granted.

In 1539 San Gallo of Florence made suns and moons by filling crystal spheres with water, lighting them from behind with candles and then moving them across the 'sky'.

In 1585 Scamozzi introduced lighting placed at the side of scenery and Inigo Jones replicated this to great effect in the English theatre.

Sets, scenic effects and props

Sets

Commedia dell'arte spread from Italy throughout Europe now. This was performed on a simple platform with a painted backcloth that might depict, for example, a stormy sea or a gloomy forest. This backcloth could be rolled up and down. Perspective vistas began to be employed in Italy but were aimed at the most important person in the audience and really worked only from that angle!

Trap doors were used in the stages.

Special Props

Lightning was made of jagged wood covered in shiny fabric and then flown across the stage on wires. Many other such heavenly bodies flew through the air on wire and thread.

Actors, make-up and costumes

Actors and make-up

At last the actor was released from wearing a physical mask, so powder and paint were used instead to create a kind of 'mobile' mask.

Paints were crude and made from vegetable dyes or crushed earth colours mixed with perfumed oils or animal fats.

Sometimes actors would smear their faces with a foundation of ham rind before applying a colour such as brick dust – hence the term 'ham actor'.

Performances were mostly in the natural daylight so the make-up did not need to be heavy.

Actors and Costumes

The roles portrayed by the commedia dell'arte were very colourful and vivid, so the costumes reflected this. They were also very predictable so that audiences became familiar with the characters and would recognize them instantly – such as the multi-coloured diamonds always associated with Harlequin's costume.

Pyrotechnics with a vengeance!

Real cannons were sometimes used and, in 1613, ignited debris from these set light to the thatch of the Globe Theatre in London and burnt it down to the ground!

17th century theatre

Racine and Molière were writing for the French theatre, and Molière founded the Comédie Française which is still active in Paris today.

Under James I of England, the first theatre licensing laws were issued. Actors, theatres and plays all became subject to the granting of a royal license.

This was the Jacobean period, with much pomp and ceremony, and elaborate masques to entertain the court. Often these culminated in fireworks

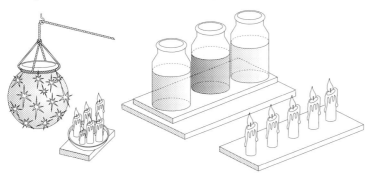

Crystal spheres and coloured liquids in glass vessels were set in front of candles

17th century theatre

and a grand ball. Aristocratic patrons sought the spectacular, and productions were lavish and expensive.

As the century progressed, often the effects were considered as important as the shows themselves and included storms, waterfalls and avalanches on the stage.

At street level, by contrast, theatrical productions were generally performed by travelling actors and were of a fairly low level, not far removed from fairground side shows.

Pageants were enormously popular, often depicting religious spectacles such as the building of Solomon's temple, Noah's Ark, or Jonah being swallowed by the Whale. Sometimes the actors were professionals; but most often they were the local craftsmen. A group of carpenters might be responsible for one scene and a group of painters for another.

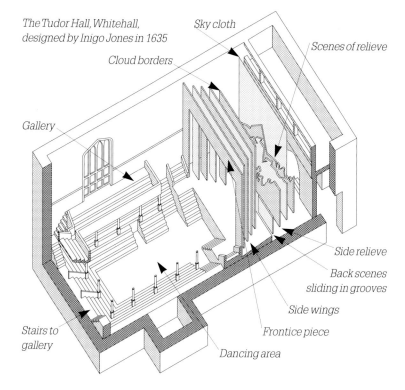

The Tudor Hall, Whitehall, designed by Inigo Jones in 1635

Sky cloth

Scenes of relieve

Cloud borders

Gallery

Side relieve

Back scenes sliding in grooves

Side wings

Stairs to gallery

Frontice piece

Dancing area

Travelling players performed on a simply erected scaffold stage

Theatres

Wheeled carts were still the most common for street theatre and pageants. Many of these carts became quite elaborate and cumbersome three-tiered affairs.

Commedia dell'arte was still very popular and the stages on which it was performed grew much larger and grander. The productions became far more elaborate and were eventually housed in permanent theatres by the end of the 17th century.

Inigo Jones designed Whitehall as a new royal palace specifically to be the finest possible backdrop for the ornate masques of the time. Everywhere, the restoration theatres were rich, splendid places, elaborately decorated and lit by chandeliers and a huge number of candles.

Lighting

Performances still took place mainly in daylight, but stage lighting was beginning to achieve lavish and dramatic effects with candle power and oil lamps.

Often a huge chandelier lit the forestage. This was supplemented by candles in the auditorium, and footlights and oil lamps on vertical poles behind the proscenium and in the wings. This was the first time that footlights were sunk below the level of

Candle power, often in the form of chandeliers, lit the stage

the stage. In due course oil wicks were floated on water to reduce the fire risk – hence the term 'floats'.

Lights could be swivelled: now they could shine into the wings or the back and not just on the scene of action. Sunrise, sunset and moon effects could be effected more realistically.

Sabbattini developed the effective use of lighting from one side.

In 1674 lights were dimmed for the first time in a production of *The Tempest* at the Dorset Garden Theatre. As the ship sank on stage, the chandelier was raised, the footlights lowered and shields were dropped over the wing lights.

Sets and scenic effects

Sets were lavish, with backcloths, flats and the illusion of space and distance created by perspective.

Louis XIV of France in his role of the sun god, Apollo

Italian stage machinery created spectacular effects

Backcloths and overhead skies were often made of silk.

In the 1650s, the young Louis, soon to rule as King Louis the XIV of France, was appearing in lavish ballets and masques at his own court, where performers dressed as gods and the Muses sat on platforms suspended by pulleys from the ceiling. The pulleys were hidden by flats and gauze painted as clouds. Louis, as Apollo, was flown up to the ceiling and disappeared – a grand finale!

It was during this century that wings painted with scenery were invented. Although we take them for granted now, this was the first time wings were ever used.

The Italians then went on to develop a synchronized wing system. This drum drive system with pulleys allowed entire sets to be changed in unison by a relatively small crew.

Italian architect Bernardo Buontalenti designed many very sophisticated machines that would move scenery and performers speedily.

17th century theatre

Sabbatini's machinery for rolling ocean waves

Niccolo Sabbattini

Italian stage technician Niccolo Sabbattini (*circa* 1574-1654) devised a wide variety of scenic effects and wrote a handbook on theatre machinery and magical effects. One of the best-known of these effects was a very clever system of depicting rolling ocean waves. These comprised a series of twisted shapes to represent rows of waves at sea. They were painted blue with the topmost edges white to simulate the crests of the waves. Arranged across the stage, one behind another, and set at increasingly higher positions towards the back of the stage, these rows of waves could be rotated in the wings by stage hands turning handles. The waves then appeared to undulate. Moving between the rows, actors or singers could simulate swimming through the sea, diving into it, bobbing on the waves, or drowning.

Other effects

Make-up

In England, when the Restoration arrived in 1660, women were allowed to act on the stage for the first time and sought more flattering make-up.

Cosmetics were still very crude. A whitening paste was made from fat and white lead while white chalk was

Lavish perspective scenery created a feeling of depth and distance

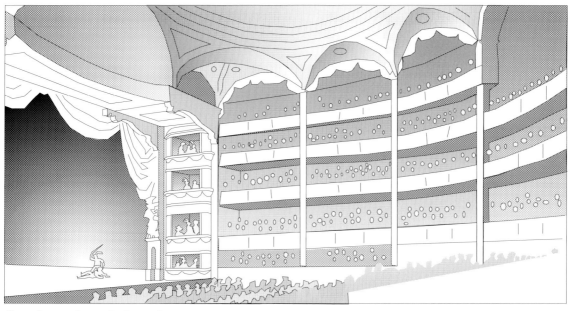

Boxes became increasingly popular through the 17th and 18th centuries, with the audience here overlapping the stage

used for powder. Burnt cork was applied as an eyeliner and for darkening the eyebrows. Carmine was put on the lips and cheeks.

French comedy actors used flour to whiten their faces.

Costumes

Baroque costumes were rich and exotic. No expense was spared in a masque that might involve many fabulous creatures – from gods to mermaids and monsters.

18th century theatre

Theatre-going became an increasingly popular form of entertainment, with more and more theatres being built as the century progressed. In 1700 there were a mere three theatres in Paris. By 1750 the number had grown to twenty and every large French town had its own theatre.

Circuses became more as we think of them today, expanding to include animal acts and clowns, as well as acrobats. Originally performed in huge circus rings in front of conventional theatre stages, the circus changed to become travelling theatre in the 19th century, spreading in line with the growth of the railways – an easier means to move from one place to another.

Theatres

New, fashionable playhouses sprang up everywhere, offering much more comfort; they were well lit and had permanent roofs.

English architect Inigo Jones (1573-1672) used *machina versatilis* to bewitch his audience with the illusion of perspective, framed within an ornamental arch – the proscenium arch had arrived! It became Europe's standard, and was to dominate theatre design from that point on, separating audience from cast.

Seats in boxes were especially popular for the élite, offering a degree of privacy for their private parties, while tiers of balconied seats and galleries housed the majority of the audience.

Effects

Lighting

Silk screens in rich colours like scarlet and blue were used to reflect light onto the stage. Coloured glass chimneys over oil lamps simplified lighting effects and colour changes.

Sets and scenic effects

Growing up in a family with a tradition of being architects and designers, Ferdinando Bibiena claimed to have invented the precise painting of buildings viewed at an angle and the

Early 19th century & Victorian & Edwardian

proper scientific use of perspective. His son, Guiseppe Bibiena successfully translated this more exact use of perspective to the theatre. Moving perspective sets developed, with vastly detailed scenic backdrops and with wings that changed on each side to create different scenes. In time, the detailed use of perspective became even more pronounced, with rows of cut-outs, one behind the other, lit by candlelight.

Henry Angelo introduced transparent backcloths so that visionary figures could be glimpsed behind while ballet companies also explored the use of gauze (scrim). Panoramas and dioramas appeared, used especially in pantomime.

In the 1760s, at the Court theatre in Drottningholm, Sweden, wings and shutters were mounted on frames attached to carriages that could run on rails below the level of the stage.

Later, in England, a similar system was introduced, but grooves above and below the wings replaced the rails and the stage itself opened in several places to allow scenery to slide in and out and actors to be transported into position on bridges. Intricate stage machinery was needed to manipulate all these effects. Backcloths and borders on rollers could be flown above the stage.

Pyrotechnics

Dramatic fog and fire effects became enormously popular.

The combination of spectacular effects like real waterfalls, beautiful heroines and melodramatic plots delighted Victorian audiences

Many of the stage devices that we take for granted today were invented and developed during the Victorian period, to be later improved by electronic controls. This was an evocative period, and a familiar one – as old time music halls and melodramas are often re-enacted to entertain modern audiences. This was also a time of great change, in and out of the theatre. Inventions such as electricity and photography spearheaded changes in all forms of art. This was a time of extravagant Grand Opera, Gilbert and Sullivan light operettas, melodrama and music hall. A great variety of drama, from the serious to the most popular light entertainment – from plays by Chekhov to Christmas pantomimes.

By 1890 Henrik Ibsen in Norway was promoting more naturalistic acting in his realistic dramas, such as *Hedda Gabler*. Melodramas vanished as quickly as they had arrived when cinema suddenly proved able to deliver even more life-like sensational material. In fact, many theatres that had once housed melodramatic productions were converted into cinemas.

Sets and scenic effects

The Magic Lantern – which could not only project slides but also cross-fade them, dissolving one scene into another – became a very popular form of entertainment. It was used early on as a theatre device in Drury lane in 1820 during a production of *King Lear*, creating patterns and colours on the stage and projecting them onto Edmund Kean himself in the title role.

Spectacular disaster or large-scale effects were much acclaimed – such

In 1902, in a production of Ben Hur, moving background scenery was combined with a treadmill in front so that live horses ran on the spot but appeared to be galloping furiously forwards in the chariot race.

whatever scene is outside. Working on this principle, huge dioramas were often created to circle round and create the effect of a vast landscape passing by. Actors, or any scenic device, could be static in front or move in the opposite direction to the background so as to create the impression of an even faster passage. Mirror flats were invented to reflect all the available light back onto the stage.

Sound and lighting

Sound

Mechanical sound effect machines could simulate all kinds of sound, including weather, transport noises and disasters (which were a very popular theme then). The properties department was generally in charge of the more conventional sounds such as bells ringing or a door slamming.

Lighting

In 1816 gas light was first used on stage in Philadelphia in the USA. It reached Covent Garden and Drury Lane in London one year later. For the first time all areas of the stage could be lit and seen with equal clarity. Now even the star of the show could move to the back of the stage and be seen in all his or her glory! He or she no longer had to lay dominant claim to the downstage area.

During the early nineteenth century, the arrival of the gasplate also meant

as sinking ships, submarines, or airships taking off.

In 1822 the new Opera in Paris used a water system to create real waterfalls and fountains on stage.

In 1854 the hydraulic lift was first used in the National Opera House in Budapest, Hungary.

In the 1860s Charles Fechter, manager of the Lyceum in London, introduced a prototype cyclorama. The cyclorama, with all its sky and scenic effects, was soon to become a professional theatre 'standard'.

Moving scenery creates the impression of movement in whatever is in front of it – just as a projected image of moving scenery out of a train or car window will give the impression that the train or car is moving along past

20th century theatre (from 1910)

that for the first time a central control could raise and dim the lights, giving much more control and allowing the fading and cross-fading of lights.

Gauze transformations were able to be exploited properly for the first time.

Gas also meant more controllable fire effects, setting suns and starlit skies.

Also in 1816, limelight arrived. Its first use was as a follow spot operated from the wings but soon its great intensity meant that it was being implemented for sun and moon beams. By the end of the century a large theatre might be using as many as thirty limelights in a single production.

In 1860 the combination of a hood and lens with a carbon arc created the first proper spotlight.

In 1878 Sir Henry Irving took over management of the Lyceum and developed many lighting innovations and controls, including masking to prevent light spill and the maintaining of a consistent darkness in the auditorium for the first time.

In 1879 the California Theatre in San Francisco was the first ever theatre to install electric lighting.

In 1881 a production of Gilbert and Sullivan's *Patience* at the Savoy in London was the first time electricity was used throughout a theatre performance in Europe.

In 1883, also in a Gilbert and Sullivan's production – this time *Iolanthe* – the fairies in the finale wore illuminated stars in their hair. The light was produced by means of a cell storing electricity which the fairies carried with them. So now the term 'fairy lights' was born!

Other effects

Make-up

In 1843 actresses at the Comédie Française in Paris complained that the new gaslight was too harsh. In order to counteract this effect, actors and actresses needed better make-up. Supply met the demand and, for the first time, stage make-up was produced commercially.

Pyrotechnics

Lycopodium and magnesium powder was used to create flashes. There were several serious fires in theatres as a result. Richard Wagner promoted the use of steam rather than these more dangerous substances.

20th century theatre (from 1910)

Up until the 1920s, most stage effects were still mechanical but, obviously, there has been a huge surge forward in electronics since then, and, particularly in recent years, this has had an immense effect on theatrical production at all levels.

The development of cinema, and in due course that of television, too, led to an equivalent growth in expertise in all the technical aspects of a dramatic production and, in particular, the field of special effects.

It also led to higher expectations in theatre audiences who quickly became used to the sophistication of camera effects.

This also saw a shift in responsibilities as special knowledge was needed by the operators. Today as computers become more and more involved, so the expertise necessary becomes more and more specialized – certainly in the professional theatre. That is to say, the technical know-how is more involved but computer memory is able to store and replicate complicated arrangements and can make some aspects simpler, once the operators have been trained in their use.

On the other hand, as well as being specialized, an expert in one field needs to be able to adapt to help or work with another, because the computer systems in many cases must be coordinated or even linked – as sound, light and pyrotechnics have to work together and time their effects to coincide perfectly. Often the boundaries in expertise become blurred.

However, all this technical brilliance does not come cheaply; the new systems are expensive and many an amateur production still relies on the mechanical means to achieve an end, and succeeds very well by doing so!

While the most popular plays and musicals will be performed every night in areas of dense population, such as London or New York (Agatha Christie's *The Mousetrap* has run continuously in London since 1952!), many theatres play host to repertory companies who perform a great variety of plays in a short period, which is stimulating for actors and audiences alike. Obviously, because of costs, the most lavish sets and special effects are reserved for the more permanent shows, but every play still requires special effects of one kind or another.

Theatres

In the twentieth century, theatres take many shapes and forms. The classic proscenium arch theatre is still most common, while several beautiful 18th century theatres have been restored in English cities like Bath and Bristol. However, experimental theatre has spread far and wide and stimulated much new theatre architecture.

Drama may often be performed in modern structures with high raked seating or thrust stages, or in the round, in real Roman arenas, or in its modern equivalent – purpose-built open air theatres. Some theatres have

world-wide. Meanwhile amateur theatre flourishes in English village halls, in school assembly halls, in converted spaces everywhere, on stage blocks, risers or rostra at the end of a college gym – or in semi-professional little theatres or college stages. Churches, once again, play host to plays or musicals, especially those with a religious flavour. But whatever the venue, the quality of the special effects has undergone continual improvements.

The development of cinema had a huge impact, especially in the facility to record and reproduce sounds, which cinema developed for its own purposes but which was quickly adapted by live theatre productions.

The magnetic tape recorder became freely available in the late 1940s, but it was the emergence of the compact magnetic tape in the 1950s which made theatrical sound systems much more versatile and easier to use.

The late 1950s and the 1960s saw a revolution in the quality of reproduced sound that still continues today, while the emergence of rock-'n'roll music spearheaded the growth of electronic sound and of sophisticated mixing consoles.

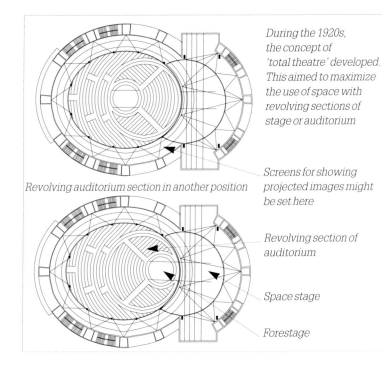

During the 1920s, the concept of 'total theatre' developed. This aimed to maximize the use of space with revolving sections of stage or auditorium

Revolving auditorium section in another position

Screens for showing projected images might be set here

Revolving section of auditorium

Space stage

Forestage

Sound and lighting

Sound

Mechanical effects were still the order of the day for a very long time although phonograph and gramophone records supplemented these. The development of loudspeakers and microphones meant the delivery of sound to specific sites on the stage and within the auditorium.

Lighting

The arrival of electric lighting had taken theatre into the new technical age and was exploited by theatres all over the world. By 1913 one-thousand watt lamps were available in Europe: spotlights began to replace footlights.

In 1916 Adolph Linnebach developed a system of shadow projection by means of which an image is created on a large-scale slide and then projected onto the stage.

In 1924 Adrian Samoiloff used the effect of different lighting colours on scenery and costume colours to create some quite spectacular effects. Conventional suits changed into pyjamas, dancing girls appeared to dress or undress, trees went from spring blossom to autumn leaves and back to bare winter branches.

The magic lantern had already been used to project ghosts, demons, skeletons and other apparitions onto the

been designed to convert from one form to another to suit the production and may, for example, mutate from a conventional seating structure in front of a 'picture' stage to become theatre in the round – by revolving sections of seating.

Outdoor performances flourish in parks and historic sites in summer, while street theatre and festivals have reinstated the travelling player's role

20th century theatre (from 1910 onwards)

stage, but in 1927 a magic lantern was used to project scenery for a production of Wagner's *The Flying Dutchman*.

The profile spot arrived in the USA in the 1930s, but it was another thirty years before British lamp manufacturers were able to produce one. (Importation was impossible because of the difference in voltages.)

By the 1950s modern dimmers and lighting equipment accelerated the improvements in lighting technology which culminated in computerized control systems by the 1980s.

Now there is a vast choice of lights, laser beams and holograms, fibre optics, sophisticated projection and batteries of lamps capable of supplying a once-unbelievable intensity of light. From candlelight to oil lamps, then gas, and now electricity, the stage has grown ever brighter.

Sets and scenic effects

Painted silks were no longer the order of the day as the more sophisticated lighting systems were able to create magic effects on inexpensive fabrics.

Hydraulic lowering and lifting devices were introduced in Holland in 1913 to lower entire stage sections to a basement area.

In the 1950s, projected slides and moving film were used to set the scene. Today, multimedia, which can mimic many forms of visual effect, has become part of the scenic 'fabric'.

While far greater realism in sets became possible and was used most convincingly, other ways to create atmosphere were being explored. Light and projection, symbolic pools of colour and optical illusion reflected

the abstract art movement in the middle of the century.

Finally, computer technology arrived and revolutionized the control systems in all special effects, especially lighting and sound, but also in the synchronized changing of scenery in professional productions.

Other effects

Make-up

Whereas the silent movie actors and actresses had used very heavy make-up to counteract the powerful glare of the carbon arcs, the arrival of the 'talkies' changed all this. The carbon lamps were too noisy and their sizzling sound was picked up by the microphones while filming. So silent incandescent bulbs were used instead and these, combined with the new panchromatic film, made the crudeness of the old style make-up look far too harsh and heavy.

Max Factor developed a whole new range of more subtle make-up. This in turn lead to a more natural approach to make-up in the theatre – a trend which was accelerated by the arrival of colour film in the cinema – until at last the refined cosmetics of today emerged to face the lights.

Pyrotechnics

Today pyrotechnics are highly sophisticated. Safety regulations have become more and more stringent to keep pace with the advances in what is virtually the ability to make controlled explosions, fire and flame!

Special effects computers can control this pyrotechnic wizardry and today the cannons are as likely to fire confetti as cannon balls!

So what does the future hold? We are well into the space age now with all the technology to leave our world behind or explore other planets.

How will this affect theatre? What discoveries will open up new vistas on our stage?

It is certainly a fast-changing world and multimedia and computer technology are giving ever greater control to the backstage team. However, if a computer system creates glitches, it can be far more disastrous than when the mechanical systems or even 'people' systems went wrong. The highly complicated nature of these techniques – which can give us such super-smooth operations – also leaves us at their mercy when they do 'go down', with few alternatives available. Generally, however, they are remarkably reliable and likely to become even more so.

Computer-generated images and special effects promise much. Film creators believe they will soon be able to generate new movies starring famous past stars (such as Marilyn Monroe) by 'cloning' their images and using computer-generated movements, motion picture photography and digital trickery to recast them in fresh roles in brand new films among their present day star equivalents!

Meanwhile, is 360-degree cinema perhaps a modern-day equivalent of the 'mansions' used in the miracle plays of the Middle Ages when the audience turned to face different scenes on different platforms? As cinema effects become ever more exciting and realistic, and computerized animation is able to create the most dynamic monsters we have ever known, the theatre will undoubtedly soon be incorporating some of these film techniques too, just as it has done in the past. It will also need to be ever more vigorous and exhilarating in order to compete with the home computer, the Internet and interactive media – as well as cinema and television – which, as ever, have the potential to steal audiences or keep them at home.

But every theatre-goer knows that there is still nothing like a live performance to stimulate the human mind. And there is still nothing more exciting than being a part of this, to be involved in a production – whether back stage or on stage. Perhaps as the electronic age, stunning communica-

tion systems, and the global village hurtle us all into a shared future, there will be an even greater need to create our own individual make-believe in live theatre, rather than accepting the mass media entertainment of film and television.

Moreover, the theatre has always drawn on its past as well as its current and future trends. Just as the theatre swoops into the technical age of wizardry, many present-day theatre buildings choose to replicate the arena theatres of Ancient Greece, the proscenium arch is still the first choice for many a local amateur production, and there will always be an audience for street theatre which, fundamentally, is much as it was in the Middle Ages.

The world of theatre is vast. Lavish futuristic productions can enthral us without posing any real threat to the effectiveness of simple human drama enacted on a bare stage. Highly technical productions will continue to amaze us with their innovation and spectacle – and no doubt real actors, dancers and singers will soon be performing on stage with their computer-generated fellows.

Ultimately, however, drama is about people and what happens to them – or might. So there will still be a place for a small group of people on a low budget in an unsophisticated theatre. An enthusiastic and well-rehearsed live performance will continue to impress its audience – with or without the space-age technology.

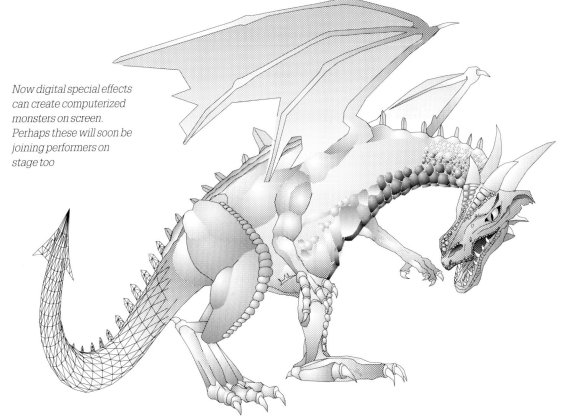

Now digital special effects can create computerized monsters on screen. Perhaps these will soon be joining performers on stage too

Special projects

The play has been chosen and a production is underway. Fired with enthusiasm, the several departments discuss presentation and plan for their particular areas of responsibility. In many cases, the special effects will bring all these techniques together to create the right atmosphere and dramatic impact.

Here follows a review of some specific projects to illustrate the different ways there might be to achieve an effect. There is a detailed analysis of one solution, and hopefully lots of inspirational ideas to help every group to approach problems imaginatively and so create the most exciting special effects in their future productions.

Ghosts

Ghosts and apparitions are enormous fun to create. Because a ghost is an illusion, considered – by most of us, at any rate – to be a figment of the imagination, this is a grand opportunity to experiment with effects and to let the special effects team's imagination run wild! An apparition is any fantasy – an unreal being in the unreal world of theatre. Make the most of this chance to amaze your audience and delight the cast too, who revel in these special moments of theatre, when we return to the dreams of childhood and magic can really seem true.

Sound accompaniment

Creating a ghost or apparition is in essence a visual effect and therefore falls mainly into the lighting effects domain. None the less, suitable eerie music or sound effects will of course help to create the right atmosphere and make the audience more receptive to whatever optical tricks you are about to play on them.

Moreover, if a mechanical device or scenic change is being used, this may make noises which can be conveniently covered by an apt sound effect. Some eerie music might be sufficient, of course. Depending on the particular setting, consider other suitable sound effects which can add to the ghostly effect.

> ### Ghostly sounds
>
> A moaning, whistling or howling wind
>
> Rattling chains
>
> Creaking boards and doors
>
> Thunder
>
> A resonant thumping heart-beat
>
> Whispers and/or sighs
>
> Distant sobbing or wailing
>
> Ghostly groans

Ghost options

The ghost is generally of distinct human shape but might of course be a headless horseman, an amorphous shape (the classic 'sheet-style' ghost), a ghost train, a ghost ship (*The Flying Dutchman*) or an animal (*The Hound of the Baskervilles*).

There are various options to choose from in order to create a ghostly effect that will best suit the demands of the play and the resources of the theatre.

Consider the following:	Projection of moving images	Swirling smoke
Using mirrors or glass	Fluorescent paint and ultra-violet light	Transformation powder
Gauze transformation		Projection of slides
Shadows	Smoke screens	Lighting shafts or curtains

Pepper's Ghost

If you are lucky enough to have a theatre with raised seating, an orchestra pit, or with sufficient room in the wings to accommodate plate glass, a plastic sheet, or mirrors – and room to achieve the right angles – then a truly magical effect can be achieved.

A ghost can be made to appear on stage apparently from nowhere, perhaps appearing seated on a previously empty chair or walking across the stage. This effect is called 'Pepper's Ghost' because it was first used in 1862 by Professor John Henry Pepper who impressed Queen Victoria in the royal performances of his illusionist's effects.

One advantage is that, because the phantom figure is only a reflection, it can walk through obstacles and the other actors are able to pass through it or thrust swords right through the figure – which adds enormously to the magical effect. This needs to be well rehearsed, however, and the stage floor marked for guidance because the actors on stage, unlike the audience, cannot actually see the ghost.

So long as the hidden actor is brightly illuminated the ghost will be visible to the audience but instantly fades away once the level of light directed towards him decreases.

Nowadays, although plastic can be used instead of plate glass, gauze

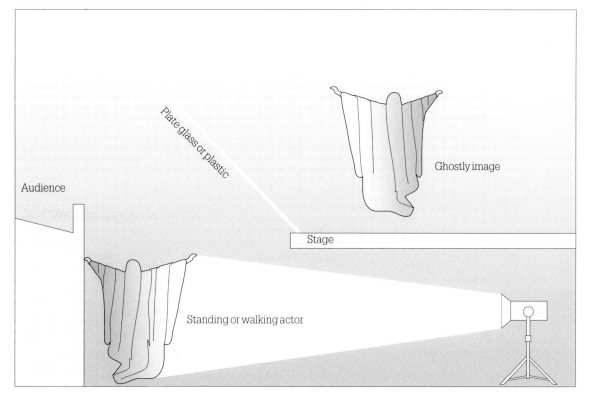

Plate glass or plastic

Ghostly image

Audience

Stage

Standing or walking actor

Pepper's Ghost appears to drift across the stage

If the stage is dimly lit, when the light below the stage is switched on, the image of the ghost actor will be reflected onto the stage above.

If there is sufficient space in the orchestra pit for the actor to walk, the ghost can appear to float right across the stage.

screens and projection require less space, and so Pepper's Ghost is rarely used. But that is all the more reason why it will amaze an audience if you can find a way to cope with the practicalities. This is in contrast to its contemporary Victorian audiences who in time became familiar with the technique – so much so that small boys threw paper balls onto the stage to see if they could bounce them off the invisible pane of glass!

Pepper's Ghost appears on an empty chair

With light A on and light B switched off, the audience sees only an empty chair.

However, when both lights A and B are switched on, the glass acts as a mirror and the reflection of the actor sitting in chair 2 off stage will suddenly appear on stage in chair 1.

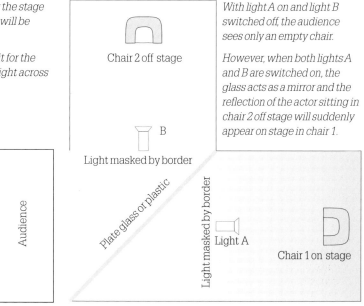

Chair 2 off stage

B

Light masked by border

Audience

Plate glass or plastic

Light masked by border

Light A

Chair 1 on stage

Ghosts

Framing a ghostly face

A very effective ghost can be brought 'into focus' and magically replace another image by using a gauze or scrim transformation. (For further details on the technicalities of achieving this see page 44.)

The advantage of a gauze transformation is that it is relatively simple and cheap to set up while still creating a superb magical effect. It does need careful planning to get the right lighting angles, very careful timing and a disciplined actor who stands in exactly the right place.

If space is limited, you will have to be particularly well organized and some final adjustments will probably need to be made when you have the actual actor and the set in position. Make sure you establish the height of the actor and exact location of his or her head before deciding where to place the picture frame or whether any kind of platform needs to be built to raise the actor up to a specific height.

By gradually reducing front light on a gauze (or scrim) and simultaneously bringing up back light on the person behind, a solid wall – or, in this case, a painting – seems to melt away and the ghost face appears in its place.

It may be helpful to hang black fabric immediately behind the gauze. This can be drawn away just prior to the effect occurring, so that no upstage areas are lit ahead of the effect. Then the actor or actress can move into position without risk of being detected by the audience.

In the case described here, a curtained booth has been erected to isolate the lighting effect. The ghost behind the gauze picture will need to be lit by

lights rigged on the upstage side of the gauze.

1 Paint gauze with a suitable scene. Close-woven sharkstooth gauze is easier to paint and to make look opaque – but it is less transparent and harder to 'dissolve' away. The thinner the gauze or its surface painting, the steeper the angle of light required to make it opaque.

2 View of structure as seen from above. Curtains prevent light spill and lamps are set above to give sharply angled overhead light.

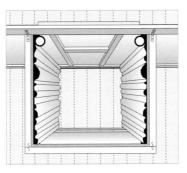

3 The actor – dressed as a ghost, skeleton, witch or whatever – slips quietly into position.

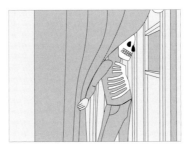

4 The lights are brought up on the actor playing the ghost or skeleton at exactly the same time as the lights on the gauze shining from out front are dimmed.

5 The scene in the picture magically fades away and the ghost's face appears in the picture frame instead. He can, of course, talk, leer, laugh and act in the normal way for the character – and move within the limitations dictated by the lighting area. His face will slip into shadow and be less visible if he moves it out of the light beams.

Magic appearances and disappearances

Since the first devil burst through a trap door or gods and angels flew in on clouds, from miracle play to masque to pantomime and children's theatre, exciting entrances and exits have been part of the theatrical experience.

The Demon King

So how do you begin if the play demands that the Demon King has to appear suddenly on the stage in a way that will startle the audience?

Magic appearances and disappearances

There are various possibilities that might be used in isolation or in conjunction with one or another. Some involve specialized equipment; others just a black out and good timing.

Sound effects

These sudden appearances will all need some kind of sound effect to underline the 'shock' element, such as:

A loud clap of thunder

A clash of cymbals

A drum roll followed by a loud bang and/or crashing cymbal

A discordant chord on the piano

A rising and descending whistle or siren.

(Prettier noises would be needed for a fairy's appearance, such as tinkling bells or sweet music.)

Lifts and lift-off

A lift is really one of the quickest ways to make a dramatic entrance and if shot up far and fast enough, can actually project the Demon up into the air, too. Presumably if one has sufficient under-stage space to accommodate a lift, there is also sufficient head height to achieve this propulsion without risk. But do check head heights first! ◆

The mechanics of lifts are described on page 78.

The Demon will need to stand on the platform of the lift which will rise by means of pulleys and ropes or chains or a motorized system until the platform is level with the stage floor.

Add some green smoke, give the Demon lurid, evil make up and suggest he make a vicious laugh or snarl on arrival and you should successfully terrify all the youngest children in the audience! In fact, you may be surprised how little it takes to make small children nervous and might need to 'tone down' the Demon's appearance to suit your audience – especially if you plan to have a matinee performance specifically aimed at the youngest members.

As well as projecting demons into the air, the lift might be used more slowly for a genie to grow out of the bottle or for a ghost or wizard to gradually materialize from smoke or shadows.

As the lift rises, the actor appears on the stage as if by magic

Consider the following visual effects:

A gauze transformation

A lift or trap door in the stage

A sliding or rotating panel at the back or side of the set

A rotating piece of scenery – suspended or on a turntable

A black-out in conjunction with a fast entrance

The Demon simply leaps into position from the wings

A trampoline in the wings to propel him up and on

A trucked conveyance to wheel him on

A dramatic puff of coloured smoke

Swirling smoke from dry ice or a smoke gun*

Sparks or stars – projected images or pyrotechnics*

A brilliant flash – can be coloured*

A 'photographic' flash

Thunder and lightning

Flying a drape or piece of scenery away to reveal the Demon

Stroboscopic lighting

The Demon might be flown in (see page 150)

He might arrive on roller blades for an updated entrance, but this will work only on a rational sized stage and he must never go too near the edge of the stage, of course! ◆

* See also pages 125-129 in the Pyrotechnics chapter for a description of the kind of bangs and flashes available.

Magic appearances and disappearances

The melting snowman

A stage lift might also be used effectively to make someone disappear. It could descend quickly amid sparks and flashes as the Demon King vanishes. It might also creep down very slowly and this can be particularly effective for, say, the Wicked Witch dying in *The Wizard of Oz,* or for a melting snowman.

The effect of a melting snowman will work most smoothly if a lift is used, as described below, but can be equally effective without one – provided there is sufficient space below the stage for someone to stand with his or her head through a trap door in the stage floor. The top of the snowman might need to be supported with a pole or broom held below. The actor gradually stoops lower, bending his knees ever more, dropping down and and lowering the pole as the snowman melts.

1 Snowman stands proud and tall. Apart from the head – which will need some kind of very light structure – the costume fabric is supported only by the actor beneath. The bottom edge of the snowman's costume is fixed in place to the main stage so that it is retained outside the lift edges.

2 The lift moves very slowly down. The bottom of the snowman starts to crumple.

3 The lift drops yet further. The actor might tilt his head slightly so that the snowman's head sags a little to one side. This will add to the pathos of the situation.

4 By now the body has virtually sunk to the ground and the audience will be feeling very sorry for the poor snowman!

5 The melting is complete. Make sure the head is sufficiently lightweight to remain at the stage level, supported by the heap of fabric. You do not want it to be so heavy that it sinks into the lift shaft.

Flying people

Flying across the stage is always one of those effects that looks like fun to do, and, as most of us harbour a secret desire to fly like Peter Pan, seems an exciting proposition. In actual practice, however, it involves being strapped up into a harness that then has to be hidden below the costume – and being rigged up in this way can prove to be a fairly uncomfortable operation!

The actor should be encouraged to complain of any discomfort or fears in the early stages. It is much easier to adjust a harness and work out a proper fitting at the beginning than to have to make later alterations because the actor has maintained a 'grin and bear it' stance earlier.

The harness is connected via a hook that is generally situated centrally on the back, between the shoulder blades and up towards the neck. This is fine for flying almost vertically and makes for an easier landing, but if a more horizontal plane is required, then the hook will need to be fixed in a lower position.

Magic appearances and disappearances

Make sure that:

1

The harness is safely strapped.

2

The harness and rigging are capable of taking the weight of the actor.

3

The actor can move – and breathe – while flying.

4

The harness does not rub against the skin.

5

The flying device is a sound one from a recommended specialist. *Never try to create a home-made flying device; this could be extremely dangerous.*

◆

Make sure the costumer is aware of the need for a back opening in the costume at the correct position.

The actor will need to help create sufficient momentum by starting as far back from the suspension apparatus as possible and then helping to create a swing forwards in the right direction as the harness lifts him (or her) up and off. A good deal of practice is needed to ensure a smooth takeoff and precise landing – and both the actor and the off-stage operator need to coordinate the movements and timing before the flying will begin to look anywhere near natural.

Sophisticated flying systems are available which can move actors laterally and also rotate them, if necessary. In any case, a special off-stage operator will be needed who is experienced in handling the equipment and guiding the beginner.

Flying Peter Pan

1 Fit the harness onto the actress. Make sure that the fit is secure but comfortable, that nothing chafes the skin and that the actress can move her limbs and breathe freely.

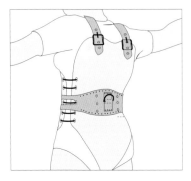

2 Make sure the harness hook is in the right position. It needs to be central and fairly high. Peter Pan will then fly virtually vertical but with a slight lean forwards. The costume will be worn over the harness to disguise both this and the hook fixings. Practice as much as possible to attain exactly the flying effects required and perfect coordination between Peter Pan and the off-stage operator.

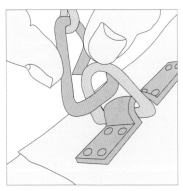

3 Before Peter Pan springs into action always make a final check to ensure that the harness is fixed very firmly and securely to the flying apparatus.

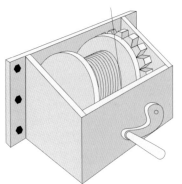

4 The flying operator will be in charge of the winding and flying mechanism. He or she must work in perfect synchronization with the flying Peter Pan to ensure that the flight has the right lift.

5 Peter Pan will need to propel herself towards the landing spot (in this case, the chimney) on 'take-off'.

6 The flying operator must ensure that the actor drops downward at precisely the right moment so that Peter Pan is able to land perfectly in the prescribed spot.

Hanging

A similar harness may be implemented for a hanging scene. If the victim is simply found swinging from a beam, this is not too difficult to contrive. However, if a sudden dramatic drop is required, then the suspending apparatus will be under much greater strain than for conventional flying or hanging and must be able to deal with the force of a violent jerk as well as the actor's weight. A pseudo hanging rope will be needed around the neck of the actor – and it goes without saying that this must remain slack throughout the operation! ◆

Trains and transport

Vehicles create dramatic impact. One of the most spectacular moments in the musical *Miss Saigon* is when an apparently full-scale helicopter lands on the stage. And what danger would the heroine tied to a railway track in a melodrama face – or the passengers in *The Ghost Train* fear – without a steam locomotive? Creating one is easier said than done, but do not be cowed by the enormity of the challenge. There are ways to give the impression of vehicles that can excite an audience and convey the power and momentum of the particular means of transport concerned that are well within the scope of even the smallest company on a tiny stage. Analyze the vehicle first and consider these aspects:

Movement

The kind of movement is important. With any vehicle, it is generally rhythmic and this can be helped by actors moving in the right way, too, balancing on the bus, lurching from side to side on a ship, swaying on a train, as in *The Music Man*, and so on. Movement can also be replicated in light and sound, with pulsating lights and an appropriate rhythmic drumming or humming of wheels to underscore the particular vehicle.

Sound

The sound is a vital element. A distant whistle to prepare the audience, an approaching train sound and then a really thunderous roar as the locomotive rushes by will do as much to say 'train' as any visual effect – and may even suffice alone.

In the same way, the drone of an airplane, the slap and dip of a boat's oars or the explosive roar of a rocket taking off will stimulate the senses and make the audience receptive to any other effects that can be thrown into the melting pot!

Light

Lighting effects can be used to show ripples moving through water or the fire of ignition when a rocket is launched, but these effects are especially dramatic in a night scene. Car headlight beams might sweep the stage, for example, or a Parisian *bateau mouche*, merry with lights that define its outline, could be seen to float past on the River Seine, its distant music playing.

Night-time light effects will work well for fairground scenes, too (as in *Carousel*) when the lights will need to make patterns or 'chase' each other to suggest the moving rides.

The visual effect

If you have a sufficient stage area, good access to this from the back of the building, and ample wing space, the vehicle might be the real thing – a carriage, vintage car or a motorcycle. It might be a full-size or nearly full-size construction of a mock-up vehicle. This might pass across the stage on tracks or by being trucked. Carefully constructed scale models of the real thing might go by in the distance. Excellent lighting, good realistic movement and a regard for the perspective of the scene in its entirety are vital, or the model will at best seem stilted and, at worst, appear ridiculous.

Alternatively, the vehicle could be a static piece of scenery in which the actors play their roles: such a scenic device could be two-dimensional or a full three-dimensional vehicle.

The view behind the vehicle – or through the windows – might be created by projection of a moving background image (see page 54).

Whatever the effect, the audience will have a mental image of what is happening, even if the vehicle itself is not entirely visible. This can be greatly helped by good dialogue and the actors' reactions to the vehicle, such as pointing up at a plane or following the progress of a runaway car or a taxi they are desperately trying to hail by turning their heads and bodies in the appropriate way.

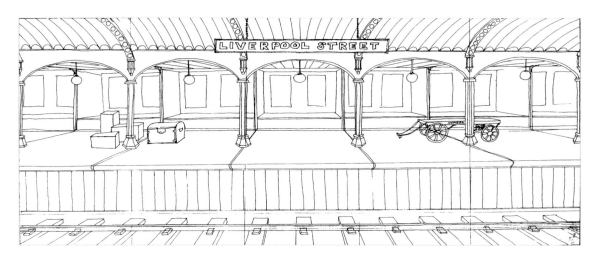

A train passing by

A train hurtling through a station can be simulated with no real train imagery at all.

1 First create good well-researched scenery to suggest a convincing railway station as a backdrop to the other effects.

2 Record the right progression of good-quality sound effects. If stereo sound can be used and played out through carefully positioned speakers, this will add enormously to the realism. Record the sounds of the distant train, the actual passage of the train through the station, and then its fading away into the distance as a coherent whole.

3 Play train noises loudly so that they are convincing, especially the close-up roar which needs to rattle the audience's bones a little!

4 Use dry ice or a smoke gun to create a sudden gushing of steam that fills the stage.

5 Create a rhythmic flashing of lights across the back of the stage.

This flashing of lights can be achieved by placing several mirror faces on a record-player turntable. The mirrors should be linked, standing upright, to make a kind of crown shape with each mirror facet facing out. Direct a light to bounce off these mirrors onto the back of the stage. As the turntable revolves, the flashing oblongs of light seem to chase each other across the back – just like the windows of a moving train lit up at night. Experiment with the relative positions of the lights, mirrors, and steam – and with the speed of the turntable – until the right effect is achieved.

Do not attempt to maintain any effect like this for too long. It is the sudden, instant combining of noise, lights and smoke that 'wows' the audience, and it needs to happen fast and furiously before they have time to think too hard about what they are experiencing. The credibility of the stage effect – without actually showing a real train image at all – can be quite amazing.

One of the vital elements in creating a good stage effect is to be positive that it can be achieved by one means or another and to 'brainstorm' the idea to all the technical experts and enthusiasts who will pour their expertise into the pool of know-how. From this will emerge the best teamwork – and your best effects.

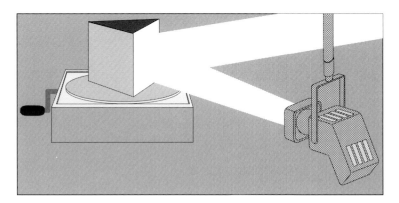

Useful addresses

UK

Colour changers

Camelont
Unit 2
Cameron House
12 Castlehaven Road
London NW1 8QW
☎ 0171-284-2502
Fax 0171-284-2503

Fibre optics

Par Opti Projects
Unit 9
The Bell Ind Est
Cunnington St
Chiswick Park
London W4 5EP
☎ 0181-995-5179
Fax 0181-994-1102

Gauzes

JD Macdougall
4 McGrath Road
London E15 4JP

Gobos

DHA Lighting
3 Jonathan St
London SE11 5NH
☎ 0171-582-3600
Fax 0171-582-4779

Blanchard Works
Kangley Bridge Road
Sydenham
London SE26 5AQ
☎ 0181-59-2300
Fax 0181-659-3153

Lasers

Laser Magic
LM House
2 Church Street
Seaford
East Sussex BN25 1HD
☎ 01323-890752
Fax 01323-898311

**Laser Point
Communications**
44/45 Clifton Rd
Middlesex HA7 1DA
☎ 0181-206-2733
Fax 0181-206-1432

Lighting

Strand Lighting Ltd
North Hyde House
North Hyde Wharf
Hayes Road Heston
Middlesex UB2 5NL
☎ 0181-560-3171
Fax 0181-568-2103

Lighting, sound & special effects

Gradav Emporium
613 - 615 Green Lanes
Palmers Green
London N13 4EP
☎ 0181-886-1300

Gradav Hire
Units C6 & C9
Hastingwood Trading
Estate
Harbet Road
Edmonton
London N18 3HR
☎ 0181-803-7400
Fax 0181-803-5060

Kave Theatre Services
15 Western Road
Hurstpierpoint
West Sussex BN6 9SU
☎ 01273-835880
Fax 01273-834141

Lighting, sound, special effects make-up and staging equipment

Stage Services
Stage House
Prince William Road
Loughborough
Leicestershire
LE11 0GN
☎ 015509-218857
Fax 01509-265730

Machinery

Hall Stage
The Gate Studios
Station Road
Borehamwood
Hertfordshire WD2 1DQ

Triple E Engineering
B3 Tower Bridge
Business Pk
Clements Rd
London SE16 4EF

Unusual Rigging
4 Dalston Gardens
Stanmore
Middlesex HA7 1DA
☎ 0181-206-2733
Fax 0181-206-1432

Paint

**Brodie and Middleton
Ltd**
68 Drury Lane
London WC2B 5SB
☎ 0171 836 3289/3280
Fax 0171 497 8425

Party things

BGS
152c Finchly Road
London NW11 7TH
☎ 0181 201 9222
Fax 0181 201 9111

Projection

AC Lighting
Unit 3
Spearmast Ind Est
Lane End Road
Sands
High Wycombe
Buckinghamshire
HP12 4JG

Howard Eaton
Winterlands Resting
Oak Hill
Cooksbridge
Lewes
East Sussex BN8 4PR
☎ 01273-400670
Fax 01273-401052

Optikinetics
38 Cromwell Road
Luton
Bedfordshire LU3 1DN
☎ 01582-411413
Fax 01582-400013

White Light
57 Filmer Road
London SW6 7JF
☎ 0171-731-3291
Fax 0171-371-0806

Pyrotechnics

**Jem Pyrotechnics and
Special Effects
Company**
Vale Road Industrial
Estates
Boston Road
Spilsby
Lincolnshire PE23 5HE
☎ 01790-754052
Fax 01790-754051

**Jem Smoke Machine
Company**
Vale Road Industrial
Estates
Boston Road
Spilsby
Lincolnshire PE23 5HE
☎ 01790-754050
Fax 01790-754051

Le Maitre
312 Purley Way
Croydon
Surrey CRO 4XJ
☎ 0181-686-9258
Fax 0181-680-3743

Scenery & Fittings

Streeter & Jessel
3 Gasholder Place
The Oval
London SE11 5QR
☎ 0171-793-7070
Fax 0171-793-7373

Signs

Seaton Limited
Department AQ
PO Box 77
Banbury
Oxon OX16 7LS
☎ 0800 585501
Fax 0800 526861

Sound Effects Libraries

ASC Ltd
1 Comet House
Caleva Park
Aldermaston RG7 4QW

**Digiffects Sound
Effects**
Music House (Intl) Ltd
5 Newburgh Street
Soho
London W1V 1LH

Stage Make-Up

Charles Fox
22 Tavistock St
London WC2

L. Leicher
202 Terminus Road
Eastbourne
East Sussex BN21 3DF

**National Operatic
& Dramatic
Association**
NODA House
1 Crestfield Street
London WC1H 8AU
☎ 0171-837-5655
Fax 0171-833-0609

Theatre Zoo
28 New Row
London WC2

Tattoos temporary

Tattoo FX
Chapel House
Trefin
Haverfordwest
Pembrokeshire
SA62 5AU
☎ 01348 837073
Fax 01348 837063

Textiles, paint & make-up

Brodie & Middleton
68 Drury Lane
London WC2B 5SP
☎ 0171-836-3289/80
Fax 0171-497-8425

Useful addresses

USA

Blacklights

Wildfire Inc.
11250 Playa Court
Culver City
CA 90230-6150
☎ 310-398-3831
Fax 310-398-1871

China Silk

Horikoshi NY, Inc.
55 West 39th Street
New York NY 10018
☎ 212-354-0133

Fibre Optics

Fiber Optic Systems
2 Railroad Ave
Whitehouse Station
NJ 08889
☎ 201-534-5500
Fax 201-534-2272

Mainlight
PO Box 1352
Boxwood Ind Park
402 Meco Drive
Wilmington DE 19899
☎ 303-998-8017
Fax 302-998-8019

Gobos

Great American Market
826 N Cole Ave
Hollywood CA 90038
☎ 213-461-0200
Fax 213-461-4308

Rosco
36 Bush Ave
Port Chester NY 10573
☎ 914-937-5984
Fax 0181-937-1300

Lasers

Image Engineering
10 Beacon Street
Somerville
MA 02111143
☎ 617-661-7938
Fax 617-661-9753

Make-up

Theatrical Supply
256 Sutter Street
San Francisco
California 94102

M Stein Cosmetic Company
430 Broome Street
New York City 110018

Plazma Globes, Crackling Neon

Larry Albright & As.
419 Sunset
Venice CA 90291
☎ 310-399-0865
Fax 310-392-9222

Lighting

Strand Lighting Inc
Second Floor
151 West 25th Street
New York NY 10001
☎ 212-242-1042
Fax 212-242-1837

Projection

Optikinetics
Rt 1 Box 355B
Doswell VA 23047
☎ 804-227-3550
Fax 804-227-3585

Pyrotechnics

Group One
USA distributors for Jem
Pyrotechnics and Jem
Smoke Machines
80 Sea Lane
Farmingdale
NY 11735
☎ 516-249-3662
Fax 516-753-1020

Pyrotex Inc
3335 Keller Springs Rd
104 Carrolton TX 7500
☎ 214-248-6564
Fax 214-380-1770

Sound Effects Libraries

Gefen Systems
6261 Variel Avenue
- Suite C
Woodland Hills
CA 91367

Dimension Sound Effects
27th Dimension Inc
PO Box 1561
Jupiter
Florida 33468

Valentino Inc
151 West 46th Street
New York NY 110036

Strobes, Lighting Effects

Diversitronics
231 Wrightwood
Elemhurst IL 60126
☎ 708-833-4495
Fax 708-833-6355

Jauchem & Meeh
43 Bridge Street
New York NY 11201
☎ 718-875-0140
Fax 718-596-8329

Bibliography

Judith Cook
Back Stage
Harrap Limited, 1987

Davies, Gill
Staging a Pantomime
A & C Black, 1995

Govier, Jacquie
Create Your Own Stage Props
A & C Black, 1980

Govier, Jacquie and Davies, Gill
Create Your Own Stage Costumes
A & C Black, 1996

Encyclopaedia Brittanica

Hoggett, Chris
Stage Crafts
A & C Black, 1975

Jackson, Sheila
Costumes for the Stage
The Herbert Press, 1978

Pilbrow, Richard
Stage Lighting
Studio Vista, 1979

Streader, Tim & Williams, John A
Create Your Own Stage Lighting
Bell & Hyman
Prentice Hall Inc. 1985

Thomas, Terry
Create Your Own Stage Sets
A & C Black
Prentice Hall Inc. 1985

Walne, Graham
Effects for the Theatre
A & C Black, 1995

Young, Douglas
Create Your Own Stage Faces
Bell & Hyman 1985
Prentice Hall Inc. 1985

Further Reading:

For the latest books on drama and theatre contact A & C Black (UK) and Watson Guptill (Backstage Books) USA who publish a wide range of relevant books and will be happy to supply brochures and listings.

Glossary and UK/USA terms

3D
Three dimensional or creating this effect

A dead
Predetermined position for a flown item

Acting area
The area of the stage in which the actors perform; area separation

Adapter or splitter
A means by which two or more electrical devices can be made to share the same power point

Aluminium
Aluminum

Ampere
A measurement of the rate of flow, or current, of an electrical circuit

Apron
Part of the stage projecting into the auditorium in front of the house curtains

Area separation
Dividing the acting area of the stage into suitable units that can be lit independently or together

Auditorium
The audience area beyond the stage

Backcloth
A scenic canvas or 'drop' used across the back of the stage, often serving as a sky-cloth

Backstage
The non-acting area behind the proscenium arch

Bar
Pipe or barrel above the stage for the suspension of lighting and scenery; may be called a batten

Barn doors
Four separately hinged doors on a pivoted frame at the front of Fresnels or PC's. These can be used to shape the beam and prevent spill light Not suitable for profile spots

Batten
Bar from which lighting equipment can hang: also applied to compartment-type lighting or border-lights

Batten
Scenic wood lengths for tautening cloth at top or bottom or timber used to join flats

Boom or light tree
A vertical pipe which can support several luinaires on a number of boom arms.

Border
A horizonatally placed flat or cloth hung from bar or ceiling grid to mask lights and flown scenery from the audience

Box set
A room setting with only three walls

Brace cleat
Attachment on the back of a flat to which the stage brace is hooked

Braces
Supports, usually adjustable, that are fixed to flats. May be screwed to the floor but are mostly secured by weights

Castor
Caster

Centre
Center

Centre line
A line running through the exact centre of the proscenium arch

Chasing lights
Lights that flash on and off quickly in succession

Cinemoid
Cellulose acetate which is used to make colour filters in the UK

Cleat
Fitting on flats to which throw lines are secured

Cloth
Area of scenic canvas hanging vertically

Colour
Color

Composite gel
Difference coloured pieces of colour gel cut to fit together into one colour frame

Control cable
Cable to connect desk to dimmer racks

Costumier
Costumer

Cotton
Cotton wool or cotton balls or a cotton fabric

Cross plugging
A system whereby several luminaires can be made to share the same circuit or dimmer alternately or at different times

Cross-fade
To fade or change from one lighting stage to another

Cue
The moment at which a set, sound or lighting change will be initiated. The cue may be a line in the play, a change of tempo in a song, or a particular piece of action of stage - whatever has been entered on the cue sheet

Cue sheet
A chart on which all the special effects, lighting or sound cues of a production are recorded and which the board operator or electrician will use. The stage manager may also use one

Cut cloth
Parts cut away for foliage effect etc.

Cut-out flat
A shaped flat in plywood or hardboard

Cyclorama or sky-cloth
Either a smooth plastered wall or a stretched, curved or straight backcloth hung at the rear of the stage. It is sometimes painted white and then lit as required

Desk (lighting)
Board or console

Desk or board
Controller for lighting racks. May also be used when referring to a sound mixer

Dimmer
A device which regulates the power in the circuit feeding a lamp, so as to alter the intensity of the light

Diorama
A scenic view or representation made with a partly translucent painting. If the light shining through it is varied, then the effects change

Down stage
Front half of stage

Dry ice
Frozen carbon dioxide which can be used to produce mist or steam effects

Earthing
Means by which, for safety reasons, metal parts of electrical equipment may be wired to the ground

Elevation
Scale drawing of a side view of stage or stage unit

Feedback
The sound of the speakers is picked up in the mics and re-amplified. Early signs are a 'colouring' and then that only too familiar whistle! Do not confuse with foldback

Fill light
Light which fills the shadows the key light creates

Fish skin
Fulle setting

Flare
Usually refers to lighting spill, or can be spectral-flare rainbow effects

Flat
Standard unit of scenery with a wooden frame and canvas, plywood or hardboard covering

Flies
The area above the stage where scenery and lighting equipment can be suspended out of sight or 'flown'

Float mics
Microphones arranged across the front of stage

Floats
Area across the front of stage or lanterns used there, often floods

Floats or footlights
A batten of lights set at the front of the stage, which in historical times consisted of floating oil-wicks

Floodlights/floods
Fixed wide angle general spread lighting units, used for illuminating large areas of the stage or cyclorama

Floods
Floodlights giving a wide beam of light, sometimes ellipsoidal reflectors

Floor cloth
Canvas floor covering

Flown
Housed in flies

Fly mics
Microphones suspended - usually above the stage

Flies
The area over the stage itself

Glossary

Focusing
In theatrical terminology, this does not necessarily mean achieving a sharp focus. Instead it describes organization of the direction, positions, shape, and cover of the beam - as directed on the lighting plan by the lighting designer

FOH
Front of House

Foldback
A signal through speakers or headphones to enable members of the cast, crew, band, etc. to hear whatever sounds that are necessary to enable them to complete their task

Gate
Aperture between the light source and the lens on a profile shutter; may have built-in shutters with which the beam can be shaped, as well as runners which allow for the insertion of an iris or gobo

Gauze or scrim
Large-weave cloth used for scenic effects which can be rendered either transparent or opaque according to the direction and intensity of the lighting

Gauze
Scrim

Gelatine/gel
A colour filter medium for lighting, which is made of animal gelatin; it is rarely used nowadays

Gobo (or cookie)
Template of thin metal with cutout design or pattern which can be projected; normally used with profile spotlights

Grid
Wood or metal flats bearing pulley blocks

Ground plan
Scale drawing of a set as seen from above

Ground row
Shaped pieces of standing scenery 60-90cm (2-3 feet) high

Ground-row lighting
Strip light lighting scenery from below; lengths of shallow lighting equipment or battens, for low-level lighting effects

Hire company
A rental company

House bar
A permanent flying line

House curtain
The main curtain in a proscenium theatre

House
Everything beyond the stage

House lights
Auditorium lighting

Hum
A sinusoidal signal at a low frequency. Generally associated with mains frequency - 50Hz. An unscreened signal lead near to a mains cable or transformer is frequently the cause

Key light
A light of high intensity, or the most dominant direction of light; the most imortant light on a set which focuses attention, such as moonlight through a window

Lamps
The high-power electric light bulbs used in theatrical lighting equipment

Left stage or stage left
The area on the left of an actor facing the audience

Leg
Long narrow strip of fabric. Black for masking

Legs
Unframed scenery, canvas wings, or curtains which are hung vertically to mask the sides of the stage

Levels
Rostra, ramps and steps above the main stage

Lighting bar
Lighting or electrics batten, or pipe

Lighting plan or plot
A scale drawing detailing the exact location of each luminaire used in a production and any other pertinent information

Lines
Hemp ropes for raising and lowering scenery

Luminaires
The instruments, lanterns, or units used to light the stage; lighting fixtures

Magazine battens
Border lights or battens which are 'flown' above the stage (UK)

Mains operated
British term meaning electrically powered, using the 'mains' voltage at local or domestic level

Marking
Laying out coloured tape to mark the position of scenery

Masking
To hide certain parts of the stage or equipment from the audience, using scenic devices

Masque
A popular court entertainment in 16th and 17th century Europe, performed by masked players and usually based on a mythological theme. It often included music, dance, and poetry, as well as spectacular effects

Master
A dimmer control (a fader) which controls other submasters, which in turn control the dimmers

Mic
Mike or microphone

Mix
A setting of the controls in sound or lighting

Mock-up
A structural model of the stage and set, often a forerunner to the final detailed model, made to scale

Monitors
Speakers, frequently wedge shaped, used to replay the foldback mixes

Mould
Mold

Neighbour
Neighbor

O.P.
Opposite prompt or 'stage right'

Off stage
Space outside the performance area

On stage
Inside the performace area

P.S.
Prompt side - stage left

Pairing lamps
Joining more than one luminaire to one circuit

Panoramas
A painted cloth which can be wound across the stage to reveal a constantly changing view

Pantomime
English children's fairy tale production put on annually at Chrismas and the New Year

Patching
Using a cross-connect panel which allows any of the stage circuits to use any of the dimmers

Pin hinge
A backflap hinge with a removable pin to act as a pivot. 2 pieces of scenery may be held together using pin hinges. Each half of the hinge is attached to a piece of scenery. A loose pin is inserted through them both. The pivot action of the hinge remains unimpaired

Plot
General list required by all departments noting exact requirements and cues for the entire show

Practical
A lighting fixture or property which is apparently used on the set by the actors during the production, and so is visible to the audience and must be operational. Can also mean any fixture or prop which is illuminated

Preset
A group of faders. Can also mean a pre-arranged lighting state being held in readiness for future use

Profile flat
Alternative to the cut-out flat

Profile spot
Ellipsoidal reflector spotlight; provides a soft or hard-edged beam of light focused by a lens system

Programme
Program

Props Properties
Anything used on stage (not scenery, wardrobe, light or sound)

Proscenium arch
The stage opening which, in a traditional theatre, separates the actors from the audience: sometimes called the 'fourth wall'

Glossary

Pyrotechnics

May mean fireworks, but in lighting circles generally refers to any bangs, flashes or smoke that might be required!

Rake

Sloped auditorium or stage to facilitate viewing

Raked stage

A sloping area of stage which is raised at the back (up stage) end

Returns

The number of ways from mixer to stage/amplifiers

Rig

The lighting construction or arrangement of equipment for a particular production

Risers

The vertical part of a step

Roller

Mechanism for hanging canvas cloth

Rostrum

A platform

Roundel

Can mean a coloured glass filter used on striplights. In the historical circumstances, it refers to a small circular window or niche

Run-through or run

Seeing a performance of a play (or one aspect of it, such as lighting) all the way through, from beginning to end

SCR

Abbreviation for a silicon-controlled rectifier; a solid state semi-conductor device which operates as a high-speed switch and is used in dimmers

Scrim

See gauze

Set

To prepare the stage for all the scenery and furniture used

Shutters

Part of a luminaire which determines the profile of the beam and can be used to prevent lighting spill on the edges of the stage or set

Sightlines

Imaginary lines drawn from the eyes of the audience to the stage, to determine the limits of stage which will be visible from the auditorium

Sky-cloth

See Cyclorama

Specials

Any light which is used for a special purpose or isolated moment in a production rather than being used for general area lighting

Spill light

Unwanted light which spills over its required margins or shows through a gap

Spot bar

Batten or pipe on which spotlights are hung

Stage cloth or drop

A vertical area of painted canvas which can be a backcloth, front cloth, or drop cloth, depending on its position on the stage

Stage left

Left to the actor when facing the audience

Stage right

Right to the actor when facing the audience

Strike the set

Dismantling scenery

Strike

To remove. The opposite of set

Tab

Curtain - front tabs are the main house curtains

Tabs

Stage curtains across proscenium arch

Throw distance

Distance between a luminaire and the area on the stage that it will light

Thrust stage

A stage which is surrounded by the audience on three sides

To fly

To suspend in the air

To focus

To 'set' the lantern directions, beam spread, beam shaping and, with profile spots, the sharpness of the beam edge

To mix

To operate the mixer desk

To plot

To make notes of level setting, cue points, cue times, etc. Applies equally to lighting and sound notes

Tormentors

Masking flats angled up stage and set at the edge of the proscenium

Trap

A door in the stage floor of large theatres, used for special effects and entrances

Traverse

Tabs set on a track across the stage

Trim

Scenery or masking hanging parallel to the stage

Truck or wagon

A mobile platform for scenery

Up stage

Rear half of stage. The area of the stage furthest from the audience

UV

Ultra Violet. Available in flood and strip versions. Must not be dimmed! At is most effective when used with care and UV paint

Vapour

Vapor

Volt

A unit measurement of electrical pressure between two points in a single circuit

Wagon

See Truck

Wing curtains

The soft masking of the wing space

Wings

The area to either side of the acting area

Wipe track

A single tab track, usually full stage width

Index

Index